# PRACTICAL MEDITATION

A Way of Life for the Individual and the Family

**You can AWAKEN your Life with MEDITATION!**

Alateme Sonari, Ph.D.

# Practical Meditation
## For the Individual & the Family

First Edition
Practical Meditation: A Way of life for the Individual and the Family
Copyright © 2018, UNISM All Rights Reserved
1390 SE 122nd Avenue, Portland, Oregon 97233, U.S.A.
Printed in the United States of America
ISBN 978-0-9819251-4-1

## Table of Contents

Introduction --- 6
How to Prepare for Meditation --- 11
    Place of Meditation --- 11
    Time for Meditation --- 14
    Meditation Sounds --- 16
    Meditation Position --- 18
    Meditation Practice & Lifestyle --- 21
    Meditation Goals --- 27
Meditation in the Sacred Texts --- 29
    Meditation in the Upanishads --- 29
    Meditation in the Buddhist Sutras --- 30
    Meditation in the Bhagavad Gita --- 32
    Meditation in the Tanakh --- 35
    Meditation in the New Testament --- 35
Individual Meditation Program --- 36
    Introduction --- 36
    Individual Meditation: First Month --- 40
    Individual Meditation: Second Month --- 64
    Individual Meditation: Third Month --- 90
    Individual Meditation: Fourth Month --- 115
    Individual Meditation: Fifth Month --- 140
    Individual Meditation: Sixth Month --- 166
Family Meditation Program --- 192
    Introduction --- 192
    Family Meditation: First Month --- 197
    Family Meditation: Second Month --- 228
    Family Meditation: Third Month --- 262
    Family Meditation: Fourth Month --- 296
    Family Meditation: Fifth Month --- 328
    Family Meditation: Sixth Month --- 361
Appendices --- 394
    Appendix A: Meditation and Living Practices --- 395
Sources --- 400

## Introduction

Meditation is being silent in order to get an insight. Meditation is focusing your attention on a thing in order to figure it out. Meditation is reflecting on an experience in order to understand it. Meditation is contemplating on an idea in order to make sense of it. Meditation is concentrating the mind on one central subject. Meditation is thinking about something to such an extent that it totally fills your mind. Meditation is just being quiet in order to enjoy the silence.

Definitions and explanations for meditation are many but practical meditation is based on the idea that life is a meditation. Most if not all of us have been absorbed in thoughts at one time or another. Sometimes we have been so absorbed that we loose awareness of ourselves; we become one with our thoughts. Becoming one with our thoughts is the height of creativity and we become what we think about. The problem with untrained thinking is that we could easily drift into negative modes of thought. Generally negative thoughts are unhealthy if they are not balanced with their corresponding positive ones. Our attempt is to help you to meditate on the things that bring peace to your life rather than worries. Thus our purpose is to give you the tools to enable you to manage your thoughts. Our belief is that once you are able to take control of your thoughts you could realize almost anything in your life! Peace of mind, purity of thought, self-control, mental alertness, emotional balance, physical strength, connectedness, and self-awareness, a sense of purpose, self-confidence, and good health are some of the many benefits to the person who manages his or her thoughts.

It is true that meditation has many benefits but not many people are practicing it. Meditation is still regarded as the domain of the spiritual seeker but there are four main reasons why meditation is still not widely practiced. The first and probably the most cited reason is that meditation is not easy. Well, it is not easy because no one taught us how to meditate when we were growing up. Most things that are new to us take time and practice before we could be used to them. According to Swami Sivananda 'Meditation is painful in the beginning but it bestows immortal bliss and supreme joy in the end.' Meditation seems painful because it is new to us. Like most things in life the moment we begin to practice it with a purpose it would become second nature.

Another often cited reason is that 'meditation is a foreign intrusion into our culture'. Meditation is often regarded as an Eastern discipline. "They have their ways and we have our ways", someone might say. This attitude actually limits the flow of knowledge and in the end it is the individual who suffers. We become stuck to our traditional ways of thinking with no room for new thoughts and therefore no room for growth. However if you are loyal to your beliefs you may still find out more about meditation without adopting foreign practices. For instance if you are a Christian you could find out about what Christians do when they meditate or if you are a Muslim you could find out about what Muslims do when they meditate. In this way you could remain loyal to your beliefs and benefit from a foreign idea.

If life is a meditation, as some people believe we are all meditating in one form or other. The practice of meditation will help you to master your thoughts. The third reason is that 'meditation arouses mystical states' and neophytes do not know how to deal with their experiences. Yes, meditation could heighten your sense of awareness but there is really nothing to worry about those states of mind. If you are concerned there are many qualified meditation practitioners all over the world. If you are not sure where to begin the best place to start is with a recognized Temple or Church. The last reason is ignorance. Many people do not know the importance of meditation in life. Now you know and we hope this guide will help you to get started.

This program is put together mostly for the beginner and for those who find it difficult to meditate or to control their minds. We are unable to control our minds because our thoughts are everywhere. We think about unholy things, money problems, missed opportunities and our failures the moment we are alone. If we are not thinking about these things we are feeling jealous, resentful, envious and sometimes even angry. No one could concentrate with all these intruders. But the good news is that through the practice of meditation you could train your mind to be free of all the undesirables and to have mastery over your thoughts. Pictures of saints, saviors and angels as well as inspirational passages are great objects of meditation. In training to achieve control over your mind concentrate on a picture, when your mind wonders bring it back to the picture. Continue this exercise until you become good at keeping the picture in your mind for as long as possible. You could do the same with your breath, inspirational passages, your favorite pet, a snow covered meadow, a flower or a past uplifting or joyful experience.

I specially recommend using meaningful experiences of the past when your mind dwells on negative or unfulfilling thoughts. Most negative thoughts catch us off guard and before we know it we are seriously dwelling on the thought to the extent that it literally consumes us. The first positive step in dealing with a negative thought is to follow it to its cause. Is the negative thought resentment, anger, or a loss? Who is the person at the other end of the thought? What happened? If the thought is a recurring one it is important that you address it immediately and stop it on its track. There are exercises to do this in the book. If the thought is just a distraction and has no internal value you may replace it with a positive past experience as soon as you realize it.

In order to make meditation enjoyable for the beginner it is important that you first determine what you intend to get out of it. In other words I want you to set a goal for your meditation program. It could be peace of mind, quitting a bad habit, purity of thought or developing self-confidence. The goal should be such that it motivates you to action at all times. Second we want you to decide to complete the program the moment you begin. This means that you will decide to do all the exercises in any of the two programs you choose.

The Book is divided into four sections: Preparing for Meditation, Meditation in the Sacred Texts, Individual Meditation Program and the Family Meditation Program. Preparing for Meditation covers most of the things you need to begin a meditation program including the place of meditation, time for meditation, meditation sounds, meditation position, etc. Meditation in the scared Texts includes references to meditation in religious books like the Bhagavad Gita, the Upanishads, the Tanakh, the New Testament and the Buddhist Sutras. The individual meditation program is a practical goal-oriented meditation program for the beginner. It runs for six months with meditation practices for seven days every week. And the family Meditation Program is for the family. Like the Individual meditation program it also runs for six months with meditation practices for seven days every week.

You will notice that some of the meditation exercises have been repeated over the course of the program. This is intentional to emphasize the importance of those exercises. We expect you to do these exercises on a daily basis. The first one is a Breathing Exercise to help to calm you down and prepare you for meditation. In this exercise it is recommended for you to inhale for four seconds. Hold the breath for four seconds. Exhale for four seconds. Hold the exhalation for four seconds. Repeat the process for as many times as possible. The second is a Counting Exercise also intended to calm you down and prepare your mind for meditation. In this exercise it is recommended that you count from 50 backwards, that is 50, 49, 48, etc, until you reach 1. Now count the normal way from 1 to 50. Next try counting from 1 to 100 and from 100 to 1. Concentrate on your counting and see the figures in your mind's eye as you count. The third exercise is the Past Mindfulness Exercise. In this exercise it is recommended that you take inventory of your activities during the day. Where did you go? What did you do? Who did you meet? What did you contribute? How did you affect your environment? How did the environment affect you? The main purpose of this exercise is to reflect on the immediate past for improvement in the future. The Fourth exercise is the Future Mindfulness Exercise. In this exercise it is recommended that you visualize the next day of your life in the family and at work, at school or wherever you plan to be. What do you want to see happen? For the family you might want harmony, understanding and unity. For work you might want to see that you are doing your work well. For school you might want to get along with your teachers, classmates and getting good grades. You know what you want to realize, give, contribute or share the next day. Make it happen! The purpose of this exercise is to give you some control on your day and influence it in a positive way. Obviously the demand of the environment on your life is considerable and they range from family demands to the demands of your career or employment. In this exercise you decide in advance what you want your day to be.

We thank you for giving us a try and we wish you the best in your meditation practices. If we knew an easier way we would share it with you because your success is our success. However one way that has worked for some people is to meditate in groups. You could also practice meditation with a teacher. UNISM offers group meditation as well as individual meditation sessions. Please give us a call for more information.

UNISM
One LOVE, One PLANET, One PEOPLE
UNISM is dedicated to the dissemination of the message of Universal Love. We live in a friendly, loving, healing, guiding and giving Universe! You are loved without conditions and you are blessed without requirements!

# How to Prepare for Meditation

*A sacred place is a necessity for everybody. You must have a room or a certain hour a day or so where you do not know what was in the newspapers that morning, you don't know who your friends are, you don't know what you owe to anybody, you don't know what anybody owes you; but a place where you can simply experience and bring forth what you are---what you might be. This is the place of creative incubation. And first you might find that nothing is happening there, but if you have a sacred place and use it and take advantage of it something will happen.* Joseph Campbell.

### Place for Meditation
Meditation is best accomplished in a secluded and quiet place but you could meditate in any place and at any time given a proper frame of mind. Any comfortable place will do. Some meditate on their beds, others in the fields, a corner of their home or a combination of them.

### The Sleeping Bed
The sleeping bed is very comfortable for meditation but also an easy place to fall asleep. Try to stay awake if you are using your bed for meditation. However we encourage you to be active in your pursuit of meditation. Thus we do not recommend the sleeping bed as a place for meditation.

*A Natural Environment*

Secluded natural environments like a river, wood, forest, field or the desert add value to meditation. In most cases they are quiet and the feel of the environment can enhance your meditation practice. Have you ever gone fishing in a boat by yourself along a river? If you were the only person at the time you probably enjoyed the quietness and the spiritual quality of the environment. You can experience the same silence in a wood or forest or any other natural environment that your love.

*A Corner of your Home*

Do you have a sanctuary or sacred place in your home as explained by Joseph Campbell? Your sanctuary can be at a corner of your bedroom, living room or a room in your office. You could also use the corner of your child's room. This corner wherever it may be should be set aside exclusively for meditation and prayer. You need a table or a desk and a chair. Cover the surface with a tablecloth and decorate it with materials that evoke a spiritual presence. You may use the picture of a savior, a saint, an angel or a favorite picture of yourself. You may also use a natural scene that captures your imagination like a sun rise, a sun set, a river, flowers, trees, a snow capped mountain or any other natural scene that you prefer. If you believe in a particular religion you could have the symbol of the religion. In UNISM we use the Universal Love and the Unconditional Love banners. You may also have a diary, writing pad, a pen, a dictionary, and your favorite religious books. You may use soft inspirational music if you care. Have some candles and incense. When all is ready you may dedicate the corner or room for the psychological benefit that a ritual provides for those who partake in it. It does not have to be elaborate. You could play a spiritual music, read a spiritual book or light some candles, incense and pray or affirm according to your preference and inclination. Your sanctuary will now become a place you associate with mystery, freedom, inspiration, goodness, patience, compassion, hope faith, beauty, power, miracles and all the spiritual things you can think about. You can now use your sanctuary for prayer and meditation as well as for resolving challenges and conflicts in your life.

### House of Prayer

Meditating in a house of prayer such as a church or temple has the advantage of holiness. Saints, angels, stain glass windows and religious symbols have the effect of evoking a meditative state of mind. If the place of worship is available to you during the time of your meditation, it could be an encouraging place to meditate.

### The Temple within Your Soul

The Temple within your soul is the perfect place for meditation in the sense that you could meditate at any time and at any place. The challenge however is how to get into the inner recesses of your soul; how to gain access to the holy of holies! This, itself is a practice of meditation and by the time you are done with setting up the temple within your soul you would have advanced in your meditation practices. Begin by first decorating your place of meditation within your soul. Have a table, a tablecloth, a couple of candles, incense on an incense burner, a comfortable temple regalia, an inspirational music, a favorite picture of yourself, a chair and any other material that you care to use. Now go within and set up the table. Unfold the table if it is a folding table and place it at a corner facing the East. The sun rises in the East and signifies the beginning of day. In the same way when you go into your sanctuary you will be facing the East in order to begin your day. Treat yourself to a new day after problems, conflicts, uncertainties or when having a difficult day. Now place the tablecloth on the table followed by the candles. Place one candle to the North and the other to the south at the East end of the table. Now place your favorite picture between the candles. Next place the incense burner between your picture and one of the candles. Finally get the chair and place it by the table. Like the sacred place at the corner of your room you need to dedicate your inner temple. Have a shower, clean up and put on your temple clothes. Walk into your sacred place, light the two candles and the incense and sit on the chair. Next listen to a celestial music or begin a short breathing exercise and when you are calm read a psalm and offer your dedication prayer or affirmation. Stay there for about 15 minutes or so and close the session by first putting off the candles and the incense. You may use your thumb and index finger to extinguish the candlelight or a candle extinguisher. As you put off the candlelight you repeat the following: As the light of the candle is extinguished so the UNIVERSAL LIGHT is born in my soul! Amen. You can now leave your inner temple, remove your temple regalia and go about your normal business. The next time you go into your inner temple is to meditate or to pray. Dedication is done only once.

### *Time for Meditation*

Certain times are good for meditation; good in the sense that one is more likely to have positive results at those times as compared to other times. But in fact it all depends on the state of mind of the individual. Thus one could meditate at any time provided one is physically ready and mentally present during the meditation.

*Morning Meditation*

Morning meditation starting around 5:00 AM is considered to be one of the best periods for meditation. If you follow a traditional work schedule you go to bed around 9:00 PM and wake up around 5:00 AM, you may begin your morning meditation around 5:30 AM. At this time the body is well rested and the mind is alert. Most people can meditate with ease. If you do not have a normal work schedule like those who work at night, an afternoon or evening might be good for you. In this case it is advisable for you to begin your meditation after you are well rested. If you have a traditional work schedule you are encouraged to have a shower and clean up as soon as you wake up in the morning. Cleaning up include brushing your teeth, using the toilet, etc. Put on your meditation clothes if you have one and immediately go to your scared place to meditate. It is important that you meditate before you eat or do anything outside preparing you for meditation.

*Afternoon Meditation*

Afternoon meditation begins around 12:00 Noon. For the one who has a 9 to 5 job this is a convenient time to meditate because you are usually on break. The disadvantage is that you are away from your sacred place and the question is 'where do you meditate'? This is the time to take advantage of your inner temple as discussed in the last section. You could also retire to a nearby park, wood or river to begin your meditation. Seize every opportunity to be silent; because silence is the food of the soul.

*Evening Meditation*

Evening meditation could begin around 8:00 PM. By this time you must have rested from work and the food you ate around 6:00 PM must have been digested. In effect you are ready for a good night sleep but watch out not to fall asleep during your meditation.

This is a good period for those who work the graveyard shift. Help yourself with meditation before you go to work. It could be the antidote for all the irritating things you are going to face at work.

## Random Meditation

Random means you have no fixed time. You could meditate at any time if you feel like it. But it is a good practice to have a schedule for meditation in addition to random meditation. A fixed time that you look forward to could enhance your life from the happiness you derive from it. When you have a fixed time for meditation you look forward to this moment with joy. Each meditation brings you closer to your goal thus it is a good practice to meditate as often as you want even if it is just for 15 minutes, 10 minutes, 5 minutes or 1 minute. Even the shortest duration of time you spend on meditation adds to your spiritual growth.

## Meditation Sounds

Sound is an important part of meditation in the sense that it calms us down, elevates our consciousness and attunes our minds to the inner reaches of our being or the soul if you like. The proper sound takes us out of this world into a mythological place of joy, love, health and peace. In other words sound has the tendency to take us within. While there we could heal our selves and experience peace. Meditation sounds are many and it is up to you to choose the ones that compliment your being.

## The Mantra

A mantra is a spiritual formula repeated by a person for the realization of an objective. Allah, Brahman, Jehovah, Christ, Krishna, Buddha or God could be used as mantra. A popular mantra is "Om Mani Padme Hum". Some believe that saying the mantra **Om Mani Padme Hum**, out loud or silently to oneself, invokes the powerful benevolent attention and blessings of Avalokiteshvara (Tibetan Chenrezig, Chinese Guanyin), the embodiment of compassion. Generally mantras are used to gain control and peace in times of anxiety and uncertainty. We could reap this benefit when we use mantra at the beginning of our meditation practice. Mantras could also help us to deal with bad habits. When next you are inclined to repeat an addiction or an obsession, use your favorite mantra to stop your inclination. We could use mantras to dispel evil in our environment. Use your favorite mantra if you sense evil in your environment. Finally we could use mantra to improve our health or to save us from danger. Nevertheless some professionals believe that mantra should only be used as a means to an end and discarded completely otherwise they would become crutches. In this sense they recommend using meaningless mantras like Ha, Hu or Ho.

*Nature Sounds*

Nature sounds are waterfalls, cricket sounds, rain, waves, or similar sounds. We can use nature sounds to prepare us for meditation because of the relaxing, soothing or calming effect they have on us. They remind us of places we have been before and keep us in a meditative mood. We may also use them throughout the meditation period as long as they are not a distraction from our focus. One meditation exercise is to imagine a turbulent sea that gradually becomes quiet to the extent that you can even hear a pin drop. This exercise leads you from the outer chamber with noise and distractions to the silence of the inner chamber. There are many free nature sounds on the Internet but for a weekend project you may go to the coast or any natural environment and record your own nature sounds. We recommend audio sounds for your meditation.

*Meditation Music*

The type of meditation music to use in your practice will depend on your preference but it is important to choose the ones that touch your soul as opposed to your body. Music that touches your soul induces a meditative mood within you but the ones that touch your body makes you want to dance. With that said the music you choose doesn't really matter as long as it touches your soul. It could be classical, flute, oboe, instrumental, or any other type of music that you prefer.

**Meditation Position**

The position you assume during meditation is an important one. Your goal for a meditation position is comfort. You want to be comfortable in the position you assume and without any kind of irritation irrespective of the duration of your meditation. You can use any of the following positions as long as it is comfortable for you but not too comfortable as to fall asleep. It is also advisable to try some of the positions that are new to you because they may work best for you if you take the time to practice and get used to them.

*Standing or Walking Position*

The standing meditation position comes in handy when we are in line waiting for our turn or when we are doing house chores. Use the time to practice deep breathing or to concentrate your attention on an idea or a problem. Since most chores are repetitive they have a way of taking your mind away from the activity and helping you to meditate. Walking or jogging also has the effect of taking your mind away from the exercise to a meditative mood. Do not hesitate to take advantage of such moments to practice your meditation.

*Lying Position*

You could meditate lying on a meditation mat or on your sleeping bed. The bed has the advantage of sleeping immediately after meditation but make sure you do not fall asleep while meditating. Some may see meditating on the sleeping bed as being too comfortable and with no extra effort made in order to practice. The meditation mat solves this problem with the extra effort needed to locate your mat and spreading it at your meditation corner and putting away the mat after your practice.

*Sitting Position*

The sitting position is one of the most popular positions for beginners. You could sit on the floor, on a meditation mat or on a chair. Sit comfortably with the spine erect and legs relaxed. Place your hands lightly on your lap with palms turned up. Relax your shoulders. As a beginner you may rest your back against the chair you are sitting on but do not allow the body to sag. Beginners sitting on a meditation mat may place the mat by a wall and sit with their back against the wall. Supporting your body on the back of a chair or a wall is only a temporary measure to aid your initial meditation practice. You should be able to sit erect without any support as time progresses and more especially during normal breathing exercises.

*Prayer Position*

There are several prayer positions including but not limited to kneeling with clasped hands by your face, standing with clasped hands by your face, kneeling with raised hands toward heaven, and standing with raised hands toward heaven. The choice of which of these prayer positions for your meditation practices is up to you but some believe that raising the hands toward heaven has the effect of increasing your spiritual energy. Raise your two hands toward heaven and experience the spiritual upsurge! Try it!

*Tailor Position*

The Tailor position requires that you sit on the floor and bend your two knees so that the heel moves toward your buttocks. Next bend the other knee in the same fashion but place the leg over the other bent leg. This seems to be the most popular meditation position but not everybody can use it. You may try it but do not put too much strain on your back and body. It involves sitting with your feet

*Burmese Position*

The Burmese position is so named because it originated from Burma. In this position both feet rest on the floor. Place one foot in front, and the other behind it, so that neither leg crosses on top of the other. The knees should also rest on the floor for proper balance. This position might also need some practice more especially for beginners.

*Seiza Position*

The seiza position is commonly used in Japanese martial arts but it originated from China. It involves kneeling on the floor and folding the legs underneath the thighs, and resting the buttocks on the heels. You can sit seiza with a pillow or without a pillow. You can also use the seiza bench for proper support by keeping your weight off your feet and helping to keep your spine straight.

*The Lotus Position*

The Lotus potion originated from India as the proper posture for meditation. The Buddha and Shiva are often depicted sitting in the lotus position. In this position one sits down on the floor or a meditation cushion and places each foot on opposite thighs.

### Half Lotus Position

In the half lotus position only the left foot is placed on the right thigh and the right leg is tucked under.

*Meditation Practice & Lifestyle*

Meditation practice concerns the practice of meditation but specifically addresses the art of the practice including the frequency of meditation, duration of meditation, breathing during meditation, prayer for meditation, food, exercise and your body.

*Duration of Meditation*

It is not important to have a time limit for your meditation but as a beginner it is advisable to meditate for a comfortable time period like 5 minutes and gradually increase it to as long as your comfort demands. For instance you could meditate for 5 minutes during the first week, 10 minutes during the second week, 15 minutes during the third week, 20 minutes during the fourth week, 25 minutes during the fifth week, 30 minutes during the sixth week until you reach a time that suites your lifestyle and schedule. The next issue is how to determine the time in the midst of your meditation. Checking the time in order to know when to end your meditation could be a source of distraction. One way of determining the time is to choose a meditation exercise that included counting. I practice a version of Isha Kriya by Sadhguru. In order to determine the duration of each meditation practice I experimented with counting mentally. By counting I was able to determine how much time I spent on each meditation practice.

*Breathing during Meditation*

Breathe easily and rhythmically. Rhythmic breathing slows down the functions of the body. Train the breath mentally to become quiet and slow. As the body and heart beat become quiet, so does the mind respond until both mind, and body become stilled and silent. We recommend practicing deep breathing regularly. Inhale for four seconds. Retain the breath for four seconds. Exhale for four seconds. Hold the exhalation for four seconds. Inhale for four seconds.

*Prayer for Meditation*

It is advisable to begin your meditation with a prayer. Prayers have the effect of preparing the mind for meditation. When you pray you may lift your hands toward heaven, be in your favorite meditation position or place your right hand at the location of your heart. You may use the Universal Love Prayer or a favorite prayer. Try to pray from memory instead of reading. Here are a couple of meditation prayers.

Great Architect of the Universe may I be a channel through which thy Holy ones approach the world. May I be a center for the radiation of thy power? Teach me to travel light, as do all who travel on the path. Break the bonds that bind. Teach me to give myself entirely to thy service, to attune myself to thy will. Teach me to lay down the simple personal life for the great Cosmic Life, and to love with the love of GOD. Anonymous.

Oh LOVE who pervades the Universe. We thank you for your unconditional Love. Your Presence is our Guiding Light. And your Love is our ornament. Protect us from evil. And heal us of all infirmities. Lead us at the crossroads of life. And reassure us when we are in doubt. Be our guide when we are helpless. And impress upon us that you are near. Give us the courage to ignite the Light within us. And let IT glow wherever we go. To enable us to help others to see their own Lights. For our own Enlightenment and for the triumph of Universal Love. Amen. UNIVERSAL HOLY BOOK: Book of Love: 7:1-17

Food

Consider the following quotes and be wise. The first quote is by Adelle Davis and the second is by Samuel Johnson. Eat breakfast like a king, lunch like a prince, and dinner like a pauper. He who does not mind his belly will hardly mind anything else. Watch what you eat and eat the proper foods. Generally we should avoid red meat and stay clear of heavy, spicy, hot and fried food. Chicken, fish, eggs fruits, vegetables, nuts, whole wheat, brown rice and honey are recommended. Do not meditate with a full stomach. Give two hours after a heavy food before you meditate and one hour after a light meal.

**Exercise**

The following quotes regarding exercise are worthy of note. Physical activity is an excellent stress-buster and provides other health benefits as well. It also can improve your mood and self image (**Jon Wickham**). A lack of exercise robs the body of an essential ingredient (**Karen Sessions**). Movement is a medicine for creating change in a person's physical, emotional, and mental states (**Carol Welch**). Exercise is good for your mind, body, and soul (**Susie Michelle Cortright**). Lack of activity destroys the good condition of every human being, while movement and methodical physical exercise save it and preserve it (**Plato**). It is exercise alone that supports the spirits, and keeps the mind in vigor (**Cicero**).

There is no doubt that regular exercise is good for you. Walking, jogging, tennis and swimming are good forms of exercise. Exercising for at least thirty minutes a day is recommended. Enjoy fresh air and walk barefoot whenever you can.

### Cigarettes, Drugs & Alcohol

**This is a direct quote from the Universal Holy Book about cigarettes, Drugs and Alcohol:** Smoking cigarettes or tobacco is bad for you. Using drugs or anything that alters the peace within your body is bad for you. They are deadly, addictive and they usually have side effects. You don't need them to enhance your strength. You don't need them to improve your memory. You don't need them to lose weight. You don't need them to control your weight. You don't need them to appeal to your peers. You don't need them to fit in. You don't need them to develop muscles. You don't need them to feel good. You don't need them for anything. You don't need them at all. Your body is designed to give you a sense of peace at all times. **Universal Holy Book: The Book of Life 6:90-103**

**Your Body**

Your body is MY BODY. Keep it fit always. Keep it fit by exercising regularly. Keep it fit by eating the proper foods. Keep it fit by managing your thoughts. Keep fit by managing your emotions. And keep it clean always. Keep it clean by having a regular bath. Keep it clean by brushing your teeth regularly. Keep it clean by shaving if you have beards. Keep it clean by maintaining the peace within your body. Keep it clean by having a regular medical checkup. **Universal Holy Book: The Book of Life 1:63-74**

### Your Mind

Your mind is MY MIND. Rest your mind on noble thoughts. Use your mind to create your world. Use your mind to change your life. Use your mind for your own good. Use your mind for the good of all creatures. Use your mind for the good of the Earth. Use your mind for the good of the Universe. **Universal Holy Book: The Book of Life 1:75-82**

### Dress for Meditation

**You may acquire a special robe for meditation. Usually one that is free and non-constricting will do. A graduation gown or an angelic outfit is recommended. Both clothes give you the feeling that you are partaking in a ceremony**

### Meditation Subjects

Meditation involves entering the great world within, closing the outside doors and windows, shutting out all distractions and living yourself to the stillness within. Here you may examine the subject or problem under consideration. Once in the stillness within you let your thoughts to go as far as you are able on the subject, and open yourself to suggestions from the Divine Mind. Your choice of a subject for meditation could be divided into three categories: Attributes, Objects and Inspirational Sources. Attributes include Love, Faith, Compassion, Joy, Patience, Beauty, etc. Objects include a flower, a lighted candle, a crystal ball, a rough sea, etc and Inspirational sources include the Divine, a favorite savior, a favorite spiritual teacher, angels, a song, a poem, etc.

Meditation Process

You could mediate without any ceremonies but when meditating in your sanctuary you may consider the following process:

1. Determine in advance when to meditate in your sanctuary and stick to the time.

2. Clean up before meditation.

3. Retire to your sanctuary and play your favorite music or sound.

4 Light two candles and incense and put off the electric light.

5. Concentrate on your breathing. Learn to breathe deeply and rhythmically. Try the following exercises:

-Inhale for four seconds. Hold the breath for four seconds. Exhale for four seconds. Hold the exhalation for four seconds. Repeat the process for as many times as possible.

-Have your lips slightly open. Breathe in slowly and deeply. Hold the breath for a moment. Exhale slowly through your nose until your lungs are completely discharged. Repeat this process for as many times as possible.

-Breathe in slowly and deeply. Think of the breath as SPIRIT. Hold this breath and use it first to purify your head region including your brain, eyes, etc. Exhale slowly with all the impurities, pains, diseases, etc., leaving that area of the body and making it whole. Repeat the same technique with you chest region including the heart, liver, etc. Repeat with the remaining internal parts of your body. You may practice this exercise daily.

6. Reduce the volume of the music or put it off completely according to your preference.

7. Read a psalm, pray or repeat your favorite mantra.

8. Meditate on the assigned subject for the session. Let your mind examine the subject, reflect on the subject and be open to impressions from your soul.

9. You may end your meditation with an affirmation or a prayer.

10. Put off the candles and the incense at the end of your meditation.

Using candles and incense is optional. It all depends on you preferences. Most people use candles and incense to create a meditative state. It is like going to a temple or a church to pray. Stain glass windows, saints and angels create a meditative state for the individual and people who use candles and incense want to create an environment that is conducive to meditation and prayer.

*Meditation Goals*

I have reserved goal setting till the last in order to drive the point home that you need a goal even in your meditation practice if you want to succeed. Consider going to a bus station or an airport for a ticket to travel without a destination; you won't get the ticket. You must know where you are going in order to get a ticket to travel to your destination. In the same way if you want to succeed in your meditation you ought to know where you want to be or what you want from it.

For instance do you want to kick a bad habit? Maybe your goal is to control your temper. Perhaps you want to lower your blood pressure or to improve your self-confidence. You know what you want from your meditation but whatever it is it should have the following characteristics:

- it is conceivable so that you could see it in your mind's eye;

-it is believable meaning that you believe in it;
-it is achievable;
-it is measurable and it is controllable meaning that realizing the goal is within your control.

Goals are very important in the sense that they clarify our dreams and desires; they motivate us and give us a sense of purpose. Set your goals for meditation before you begin your practice to guide you in the direction you want to go!

# Meditation in Sacred Texts

If you really want to be a master of what you do it is very important for you to device your own methods because no one has the truth or all of us have the truth. I am including meditation from different sources to give you many options. Learn from all of them but in the end come up with your own method!

*Meditation in the Upanishads: Svetasvatara Upanishad 2.8-17*

With upright body, head, and neck lead the mind and its powers into thy heart; and the OM of Brahman will then be thy boat with which to cross the river of fear. And when the body is in silent steadiness, breathe rhythmically through the nostrils with a peaceful ebbing and flowing of breath. The chariot of the mind is drawn by wild horses, and those wild horses have to be tamed.

Find a quiet retreat for the practice of yoga, sheltered from the wind, level and clean, free from rubbish, smoldering fires, and ugliness, and where the sound of waters and the beauty of the place help thought and contemplation.

These are the imaginary forms that appear before the final vision of Brahman: a mist, a smoke, and a sun; a wind, fire-flies, and a fire; lightning, a clear crystal, and a moon. When the Yogi has full power over his body composed of the elements of earth, water, fire, air, and ether, then he obtains a new body of spiritual fire which is beyond illness, old age and death.

*The first fruits of the practice of Yoga are: heath, little waste matter, and a clear complexion; lightness of the body, a pleasant scent, and a sweet voice; and an absence of greedy desires.*

*Even as a mirror of gold, covered by dust, when cleaned well shines again in full splendor, when a man has seen the Truth of the Spirit he is one with him, the aim of his life is fulfilled and he is ever beyond sorrow. Then the soul of man becomes a lamp by which he finds the Truth of Brahman. Then he sees God, pure, never born, everlasting; and when he sees God he is free from all bondage.*

*This is the God whose light illumines all creation, the Creator of all form from the beginning. He was, he is and forever he shall be. He is in all and he sees all. Glory be to that God who is in the fire, who is in the waters, who is in plants and in trees, who is in all things in this vast creation. Unto that Spirit be glory and glory.*

**Meditation in the Buddhist Sutras: Sutra on the Contemplation on Buddha Amitayus 9-11**
*Buddha then replied:*

*'You and all other beings besides ought to make it your only aim, with concentrated thought, to get a perception of the western quarter. You will ask how that perception is to be formed. I will explain it now. All beings, if not blind from birth, are uniformly possessed of sight, and they all see the setting sun. You should sit down properly, looking in the western direction, and prepare your thought for a close meditation on the sun; cause your mind to be firmly fixed on it so as to have an unwavering perception by the exclusive application of your mind, and gaze upon it in particular when it is about to set and looks like a suspended drum.*

*'After you have thus seen the sun, let that image remain clear and fixed, whether your eyes be shut or open;-such is the perception of the sun, which is the First Meditation.*

*'Next you should form the perception of water; gaze on the water clear and pure, and let (this image) also remain clear and fixed (afterwards); never allow your thought to be scattered and lost.*

'When you have thus seen the water you should form the perception of ice. As you see the ice shining and transparent, you should imagine the appearance of lapis lazuli.

'After that has been done, you will see the ground consisting of lapis lazuli, transparent and shining both within and without. Beneath this ground of lapis lazuli there will be seen a golden banner with the seven jewels, diamonds and the rest, supporting the ground. It extends to the eight points of the compass, and thus the eight corners (of the ground) are perfectly filled up. Every side of the eight quarters consists of a hundred jewels, every jewel has a thousand rays, and every ray has eighty-four thousand colors which, when reflected in the ground of lapis lazuli, look like a thousand million suns, and. it is difficult to see them all one by one. Over the surface of that ground of lapis lazuli there are stretched golden ropes intertwined crosswise; divisions are made by means of strings of seven jewels with every part clear and distinct.

'Each jewel has rays of five hundred colors which look like flowers or like the moon and stars. Lodged high up in the open sky these rays form a tower of rays, whose storeys and galleries are ten millions in number and built of a hundred jewels. Both sides of the tower have each a hundred million flowery banners furnished and decked with numberless musical instruments. Eight kinds of cool breezes proceed from the brilliant rays. When those musical instruments are played, they emit the sounds "suffering," "non-existence," "impermanence," and "non-self "; such is the perception of the water, which is the Second Meditation.

'When this perception has been formed, you should meditate on its (constituents) one by one and make (the images) as clear as possible, so that they may never be scattered and lost, whether your eyes be shut or open. Except only during the time of your sleep, you should always keep this in your mind. One who has reached this (stage of) perception is said to have dimly seen the Land of Highest Happiness (Sukhavati).'

'One who has obtained the Samadhi of supernatural calm is able to see the land of that Buddha country clearly and distinctly: this state is too much to be explained fully; such is the perception of the land, and it is the Third Meditation.

'You should remember, Ananda, the Buddha words of mine, and repeat this law for attaining to the perception of the land of the Buddha country for the sake of the great mass of the people hereafter who may wish to be delivered from their sufferings. If any one meditates on the land of that Buddha country, his sins which bind him to births and deaths during eighty million kalpas shall be expiated; after the abandonment of his present body, he will assuredly be born in the pure land in the following life. The practice of this kind of meditation is called the "right meditation." If it is of any other kind it is called "heretical meditation."'

### Meditation in the Bhagavad Gita: Self Control: Bhagavad Gita 6:10-28

Let the student of spirituality try unceasingly to concentrate his mind; let him live in seclusion, absolutely alone, with mind and personality controlled, free from desire and without possessions.

Having chosen a holy place, let him sit in a firm posture on a seat, neither too high nor too low, and covered with a grass mat, a deer skin and a cloth.

Seated thus, his mind concentrated, its functions controlled and his senses governed, let him practice meditation for the purification of his lower nature.

Let him hold body, head and neck erect, motionless and steady; let him look fixedly at the tip of his nose, turning neither to the right nor to the left.

With peace in his heart and no fear, observing the vow of celibacy, with mind controlled and fixed on Me, let the student lose himself in contemplation of Me.

Thus keeping his mind always in communion with Me, and with his thoughts subdued, he shall attain that Peace which is Mine and which will lead him to liberation at last.

Meditation is not for him who eats too much, nor for him who eats not at all; nor for him who is overmuch addicted to sleep, nor for him who is always awake.

But for him who regulates his food and recreation, who is balanced in action, in sleeping and in waking, it shall dispel all unhappiness.

When the mind, completely controlled, is centered in the Self, and free from all earthly desires, then is the man truly spiritual.

The wise man who has conquered his mind and is absorbed in the Self is as a lamp which does not flicker, since it stands sheltered from every wind.

There, where the whole nature is seen in the light of the Self, where the man abides within his Self and is satisfied, there, its functions restrained by its union with the Divine, the mind finds rest.

When he enjoys the Bliss which passes sense, and which only the Pure Intellect can grasp, when he comes to rest within his own highest Self, never again will he stray from reality.

Finding That, he will realize that there is no possession so precious. And when once established there, no calamity can disturb him.

This inner severance from the affliction of misery is spirituality. It should be practiced with determination and with a heart which refuses to be depressed.

Renouncing every desire which imagination can conceive, controlling the senses at every point by the power of the mind;

Little by little, by the help of his reason controlled by fortitude, let him attain peace; and, fixing his mind on the Self, let him not think of any other thing.

When the volatile and wavering mind would wander, let him restrain it and bring it again to its allegiance to the Self.

Supreme Bliss is the lot of the sage, whose mind attains Peace, whose passions subside, who is without sin and who becomes one with the Absolute.

Thus, free from sin, abiding always in the Eternal, the saint enjoys without effort the Bliss which flows from realization of the Infinite.

***Meditation in the Tanakh: The Call of Samuel: 1 Samuel 3:3***

Samuel, the son of Hannah and Elkanah, ministered before the Lord under Eli. One night Samuel was lying down in the temple when the Lord appeared to him. Samuel was meditating on the Ark of God before he heard the voice of the Lord. *The lamp of God had not yet gone out, and Samuel was lying down in the house of the LORD, where the ark of God was.*

*Meditation in the New Testament: Philippians 4:8*

Finally, brothers, whatever is true, whatever is noble, whatever is right, whatever is pure, whatever is lovely, whatever is admirable—if anything is excellent or praiseworthy—think about such things.

# Individual Meditation Program

*Meditation is not for him who eats too much, nor for him who eats not at all; nor for him who is overmuch addicted to sleep, nor for him who is always awake. But for him who regulates his food and recreation, who is balanced in action, in sleeping and in waking, it shall dispel all unhappiness.* **Bhagavad Gita 6:16-17**

*Introduction*

The individual meditation program is intended for all people. The topics of meditation are drawn from the Universe. The purpose is to help the aspirant to find peace, love, faith, understanding, success, self-confidence, joy and happiness. The fact is that all these spiritual qualities are within us but somehow we got disconnected at some point in our life. Individual meditation practice presents an opportunity for you to reconnect with yourself and in so doing reconnect with all creatures. We want to re-connect with all creatures because we were one from the beginning; we got disconnected because of too much emphasis on our differences. There is no doubt that we live in a world of many differences. If we look around us we see men and women, black and white, young and old, tall and short, rich and poor, humans and animals, insects and birds, trees and plants and the list goes on and on. We are all different because we have different faces and we live in different homes, we have different cultures, our skin colors are different, we believe in different religions and we come from different countries. We have been indoctrinated to believe that the differences are real or absolute and that we should live our lives with those differences in mind. Some cultures even teach their children to despise other people with a different skin color or religion because they are inferior. Further they are taught to regard animals as lower forms of living things and as such are only good for game.

Children with this kind of upbringing could grow up to become separated adults. They see nothing unifying in the universe and feel at home only within their ethnicity. Separating ourselves from others may have played a uniting role in the past more so when outsiders were a threat to our survival. We lived in different geographical regions and it was up to us to protect our locality for adequate supply of food and the safe upbringing of our offspring. But even then we were not always self sufficient because other geographical areas produced things that we needed for our existence. Thus we began to trade with people who were different from us but produced the things we needed. From trading came competitive games, intermarriage, interchange of ideas and other cultural values. This state of affairs continued till this day in attempts to bring us closer together and to realize our oneness. The United States of America stands as a good example where this oneness is being tested. With due respect to the first nation we have all come to this land from different parts of the world to be under one umbrella irrespective of our differences. No doubt there were problems at the beginning including slavery, lynching, segregation and discrimination but we have come a long way since Martin Luther King Jr. delivered his "I have a dream" speech in Washington in 1963.

We are still matching and the Universe is leading us. The Universe is leading us to a time when our actions will no longer be determined by our differences but by our compassion for each other. The Universe is also preparing us. The Universe is preparing us to learn the lessons of unity consciousness by bringing us to one place, the United States of America. By living under one umbrella we could discern the truth of our oneness. But the truth of our oneness has always been with us. We were all born through the union of a man and a woman. During pregnancy the fetus and the mother are intimately connected with the help of the umbilical cord. The connection between the mother and the newborn baby, though not physical, continued after birth. The parents and the baby form a family. The three people remain connected in a family. The mother or the parents care for the baby till adulthood. Later a chance for another connection happens when the adult finds a suitable life partner for another opportunity to have a family.

Most of us were brought up to love our families and parents make an extra effort to encourage us to care for our brothers and sisters. As our parents continue to remind us not to hit our siblings and relations but to love them we become used to the idea and grew up with it and family became important to us. Later in life some of the organizations we join also tell us that we are like family and that we should love each other. Since we are familiar with the word family from our childhood we could immediately make the connection and treat our church members for example, as brothers and sisters. Could we make the same connection with the global family? The global family does not just contain the human family but all families on the planet. Could we make the connection to include all families on our planet?

It is doubtful to think that we could ever become one family when we consider religious violence, racism and nationalism. Differences have always separated us but to consciously use them as a rallying ground against others is a challenge we must each try to address because in the end we have a common destiny and there are no exceptions. Thus let us rise above the limiting effects of religion, race and nationalism and as Dr. Martin Luther King said become: ------disciplined nonconformists who are dedicated to justice, peace and brotherhood and if we believe that "…….all of life is interrelated. We are caught in an inescapable network of mutuality; tied in a single garment of destiny. Whatever affects one directly, affects all indirectly. As long as there is poverty in the world, no one can be totally rich…Strangely enough, I can never be what I ought to be until you are what you ought to be. You can never be what you ought to be until I am what I ought to be. This is the way the world is made. I didn't make it that way, but this is the interrelated structure of reality."

Thus with the interrelated nature of life in your mind march forward and reconnect with yourself and with the rest of creation. Life is a meditation and we become what we think about. Learn a new way of thinking and become what you really want to be. Yes by the creative thoughts you hold you can change your life and that is the secret of life!

# Individual Meditation: First Month

*Goal*

The goal of the first month of meditation is to prepare your environment, mind and body for meditation. Your environment including your neighborhood, home, etc could be a source of distraction. Are you at peace with your neighbors? Does your home bring out the best in you? This is an opportunity to find out potential conflicts in your environment and resolve them. Next consider your state of mind. Do you have any mental issues like guilt feelings, resentment, and similar feelings that encroach on your thoughts? It is time to address them. Finally check out your physical body and make sure all is right with you.

Month 1, Week 1, Day 1

Survey your home and decide on a suitable place for meditation. You will do all your meditations in this place. You may choose a corner of your bedroom, living room or a room in your office. You may also use a corner in your child's room. Whichever room you choose let it be used exclusively for meditation and prayer. Furnish the corner you have chosen with a table or a desk and a chair. Cover the surface with a tablecloth and decorate it with materials that evoke a spiritual presence according to your preferences. You may use the picture of a savior, a saint, an angel or a favorite picture of yourself. You may also use a natural scene that captures your imagination like a sun rise, a sun set, a river, flowers, trees, a snow capped mountain or any other natural scene that you prefer. If you believe in a particular religion you could have the symbol of the religion. You may also have a diary, writing pad, a pen, a dictionary, and your favorite religious books. You may use soft inspirational music if you care. Have some candles and incense. When all is ready you may dedicate the corner or room for the psychological benefit that a ritual provides for those who partake in it. It does not have to be elaborate. You could play a spiritual music, read a spiritual book or light some candles, incense and pray or affirm according to your preference or inclination. Your sanctuary will now become a place you associate with mystery, freedom, inspiration, goodness, patience, compassion, hope, faith, beauty, power, miracles and all the spiritual things you can think about. You can now use your sanctuary for prayer and meditation as well as for resolving challenges and conflicts in your life.

## Month 1, Week 1, Day 2

Look around your immediate surrounding for things that might distract you and address them. Begin with your kitchen including the pantry, cupboards and refrigerator. Gather all the things that you do not use or are a source of distraction. Remove rotten foods and expired foods and throw them away. Gather canned food that you have not used for more than six months that are still good and put them in a box. Arrange and clean the refrigerator. Arrange and clean the pantry and other food storage places. Check out pots, pans, knives, spoons and forks that you do not use and put them in another box.

Retire to your sacred place and practice a relaxation exercise. Inhale for four seconds. Hold the breath for four seconds. Exhale for four seconds. Hold the exhalation for four seconds. Repeat the process for as many times as possible.

Next take inventory of your activities today. Where did you go? What did you do? Who did you meet? What did you contribute? How did you affect your environment? How did the environment affect you? Is there any thing you did that you could have done differently? How could you have done it next time?

Lastly visualize the next day of your life in the family and in the office or wherever you would be the next day. What do you want to see happen? For the family you might want harmony, understanding and unity. For work you might want to see that you are accomplishing your work goals and getting along with your boss and co-workers.

**Month 1, Week 1, Day 3**

Survey your family room today. Check out your fireplace, curtains, chairs, tables and other furnishings. Do you have enough room? Are there distractions? Could you use a new curtain? Arrange and clean your living room and remove all items that are a source of distraction or that you don't use. Place books, magazines, records, CDs, DVDs and whatever you think could be better used elsewhere in another box. Next retire to your sacred place when you are done.

Retire to your sacred place and practice a relaxation exercise. Inhale for four seconds. Hold the breath for four seconds. Exhale for four seconds. Hold the exhalation for four seconds. Repeat the process for as many times as possible.

Next take inventory of your activities today. Where did you go? What did you do? Who did you meet? What did you contribute? How did you affect your environment? How did the environment affect you? Is there any thing you did that you could have done differently? How could you have done it next time?

Lastly visualize the next day of your life in the family and in the office or wherever you would be the next day. What do you want to see happen? For the family you might want harmony, understanding and unity. For work you might want to see that you are accomplishing your work goals and getting along with your boss and co-workers.

**Month 1, Week 1, Day 4**

Step into your bedroom and sit down on the bed. Check out the room and notice your closets, chairs, tables, lamps, books, lamp stands, mirrors, drawers, pillows, sheets, curtains, comforters, blankets, etc. Could you use a new curtain? How about a new bed? Have you considered new clothes? Are there any distractions? What about things that you don't need? Gather all of them together and place them in a box. Now clean and arrange your bedroom.

Retire to your sacred place and practice a relaxation exercise. Inhale for four seconds. Hold the breath for four seconds. Exhale for four seconds. Hold the exhalation for four seconds. Repeat the process for as many times as possible.

Next take inventory of your activities today. Where did you go? What did you do? Who did you meet? What did you contribute? How did you affect your environment? How did the environment affect you? Is there any thing you did that you could have done differently? How could you have done it next time?

Lastly visualize the next day of your life in the family and in the office or wherever you would be the next day. What do you want to see happen? For the family you might want harmony, understanding and unity. For work you might want to see that you are accomplishing your work goals and getting along with your boss and co-workers.

**Month 1, Week 1, Day 5**

Check out your surrounding environment. If you live in a house make sure there are no irritating objects or conditions outside your home; in front and at the back. Mow your lawn, sweep the ground. If you live in an apartment you can also clean up the areas within your control like the front of your door and the back.

Retire to your sacred place and practice a relaxation exercise. Inhale for four seconds. Hold the breath for four seconds. Exhale for four seconds. Hold the exhalation for four seconds. Repeat the process for as many times as possible.

Next take inventory of your activities today. Where did you go? What did you do? Who did you meet? What did you contribute? How did you affect your environment? How did the environment affect you? Is there any thing you did that you could have done differently? How could you have done it next time?

Lastly visualize the next day of your life in the family and in the office or wherever you would be the next day. What do you want to see happen? For the family you might want harmony, understanding and unity. For work you might want to see that you are accomplishing your work goals and getting along with your boss and co-workers.

**Month 1, Week 1, Day 6**

Clean any remaining areas of your home and gather all the items that are either distractions or you do not use them. Recycle or discard the unusable items and donate the rest to those who could use them. Do not sell them. Instead give them away with love in your heart.

Retire to your sacred place and practice a relaxation exercise. Inhale for four seconds. Hold the breath for four seconds. Exhale for four seconds. Hold the exhalation for four seconds. Repeat the process for as many times as possible.

Next take inventory of your activities today. Where did you go? What did you do? Who did you meet? What did you contribute? How did you affect your environment? How did the

environment affect you? Is there any thing you did that you could have done differently? How could you have done it next time?

Lastly visualize the next day of your life in the family and in the office or wherever you would be the next day. What do you want to see happen? For the family you might want harmony, understanding and unity. For work you might want to see that you are accomplishing your work goals and getting along with your boss and co-workers.

**Month 1, Week 1, Day 7**

Attend a church, a temple, or any other meeting that brings you together with people for a common goal. If you do not have one you may begin today and find one that meets your interest and inclination. If you want you could also organize a group of your own. For instance you could start an Awakened Living Study Program. You may contact UNISM for more information.

Retire to your sacred place and practice a relaxation exercise. Inhale for four seconds. Hold the breath for four seconds. Exhale for four seconds. Hold the exhalation for four seconds. Repeat the process for as many times as possible.

Choose your favorite meditation posture and practice using the posture. For instance, if you use supports for your back during meditation start practicing your favorite posture without any support.

Next take inventory of your activities today. Where did you go? What did you do? Who did you meet? What did you contribute? How did you affect your environment? How did the environment affect you? Is there any thing you did that you could have done differently? How could you have done it next time?

Lastly visualize the next day of your life in the family and in the office or wherever you would be the next day. What do you

want to see happen? For the family you might want harmony, understanding and unity. For work you might want to see that you are accomplishing your work goals and getting along with your boss and co-workers.

**Month 1, Week 2, Day 1**

Look at yourself all over. Take a good look. What do you see? Are your nails done? Have you had a haircut lately? Are your beards trimmed? Are your clothes clean? If not begin to work on yourself. Give your body a special treatment for a change. If you have been growing a beard this is the time to have a shave. Next do not put off seeing the dentist anymore. Go ahead and set up the appointment. How about health issues like weight, high cholesterol, high blood pressure, etc? It is no longer safe to keep ignoring them. See your physician and give life another chance! Do you have any eyesight problems that require surgery? Go ahead and make the appointment because another day might be too late. After you have done with all the things you need to do regarding your body have a cleansing shower. Let the water run from your head to your feet. As it does so, let it wash all the impurities of your mind and body down into the drain. Feel the cleansing of your mind and body as the impurities enter the drain.

Retire to your sacred place and practice a relaxation exercise. Inhale for four seconds. Hold the breath for four seconds. Exhale for four seconds. Hold the exhalation for four seconds. Repeat the process for as many times as possible.

Next take inventory of your activities today. Where did you go? What did you do? Who did you meet? What did you contribute? How did you affect your environment? How did the environment affect you? Is there any thing you did that you could have done differently? How could you have done it next time?

Lastly visualize the next day of your life in the family and in the office or wherever you would be the next day. What do you want to see happen? For the family you might want harmony, understanding and unity. For work you might want to see that you are accomplishing your work goals and getting along with your boss and co-workers.

### Month 1, Week2, Day 2

Retire to your sacred place and practice a relaxation exercise. Inhale for four seconds. Hold the breath for four seconds. Exhale for four seconds. Hold the exhalation for four seconds. Repeat the process for as many times as possible.

Next reflect on Responsibility **by the Buddha**

Everything that happens to us is the result of what we ourselves have thought, said, or done. We alone are responsible for our lives.

Next take inventory of your activities today. Where did you go? What did you do? Who did you meet? What did you contribute? How did you affect your environment? How did the environment affect you? Is there any thing you did that you could have done differently? How could you have done it next time?

Lastly visualize the next day of your life in the family and in the office or wherever you would be the next day. What do you want to see happen? For the family you might want harmony, understanding and unity. For work you might want to see that you are accomplishing your work goals and getting along with your boss and co-workers.

### Month 1, Week 2, Day 3

Retire to your sacred place and practice a relaxation exercise. Inhale for four seconds. Hold the breath for four seconds.

Exhale for four seconds. Hold the exhalation for four seconds. Repeat the process for as many times as possible.

Next consider the following passage from the Universal Holy Book and reflect on it: *Your body is MY BODY. Keep it fit always. Keep it fit by exercising regularly. Keep it fit by eating the proper foods. Keep it fit by managing your thoughts. Keep fit by managing your emotions. And keep it clean always. Keep it clean by having a regular bath. Keep it clean by brushing your teeth regularly. Keep it clean by shaving if you have beards. Keep it clean by maintaining the peace within your body. Keep it clean by having a regular medical checkup.* The Book of Life1: 63-74

Next take inventory of your activities today. Where did you go? What did you do? Who did you meet? What did you contribute? How did you affect your environment? How did the environment affect you? Is there any thing you did that you could have done differently? How could you have done it next time?

Lastly visualize the next day of your life in the family and in the office or wherever you would be the next day. What do you want to see happen? For the family you might want harmony, understanding and unity. For work you might want to see that you are accomplishing your work goals and getting along with your boss and co-workers.

**Month 1, Week 2, Day 4**

Retire to your sacred place and practice a relaxation exercise. Inhale for four seconds. Hold the breath for four seconds. Exhale for four seconds. Hold the exhalation for four seconds. Repeat the process for as many times as possible.

Next consider the following passage from the Universal Holy Book and reflect on it: Your MIND is my MIND. Rest your mind on noble thoughts. Use your mind to create your world. Use your mind to change your life. Use your mind for your own good. Use your mind for the good of all creatures. Use your mind for the good of the Earth. Use your mind for the good of the Universe! The Book of Life 1: 75-82.

Next take inventory of your activities today. Where did you go? What did you do? Who did you meet? What did you contribute? How did you affect your environment? How did the environment affect you? Is there any thing you did that you could have done differently? How could you have done it next time?

Lastly visualize the next day of your life in the family and in the office or wherever you would be the next day. What do you want to see happen? For the family you might want harmony, understanding and unity. For work you might want to see that you are accomplishing your work goals and getting along with your boss and co-workers.

## Month 1, Week2, Day 5

Retire to your sacred place and practice a relaxation exercise. Inhale for four seconds. Hold the breath for four seconds. Exhale for four seconds. Hold the exhalation for four seconds. Repeat the process for as many times as possible.

Now reflect on **Man and Living by the Dalai Lama: Man----sacrifices his health in order to make money. Then he sacrifices money to recuperate his health. And then he is so anxious about the future that he does not enjoy the present; the result being that he does not live in the present or the future; he lives as if he is never going to die, and then dies having never really lived."**

Next take inventory of your activities today. Where did you go? What did you do? Who did you meet? What did you contribute? How did you affect your environment? How did the

environment affect you? Is there any thing you did that you could have done differently? How could you have done it next time?

Lastly visualize the next day of your life in the family and in the office or wherever you would be the next day. What do you want to see happen? For the family you might want harmony, understanding and unity. For work you might want to see that you are accomplishing your work goals and getting along with your boss and co-workers.

**Month 1, Week 2, Day 6**

Retire to your sacred place and practice a relaxation exercise. Inhale for four seconds. Hold the breath for four seconds. Exhale for four seconds. Hold the exhalation for four seconds. Repeat the process for as many times as possible.

Now reflect on "My Wage" by Jessie Belle Rittenhouse:

I worked for a menial's hire,
Only to learn, dismayed,
That any wage I had asked of Life,
Life would have paid.

Next take inventory of your activities today. Where did you go? What did you do? Who did you meet? What did you contribute? How did you affect your environment? How did the environment affect you? Is there any thing you did that you could have done differently? How could you have done it next time?

Lastly visualize the next day of your life in the family and in the office or wherever you would be the next day. What do you want to see happen? For the family you might want harmony, understanding and unity. For work you might want to see that you are accomplishing your work goals and getting along with your boss and co-workers.

### Month 1, Week 2, Day 7

Attend a church, a temple, or any other meeting that brings you together with people for a common goal. If you do not have one you may begin today and find one that meets your interest and inclination. If you want you could also organize a group of your own. For instance you could start an Awakened Living Study Program. You may contact UNISM for more information.

Retire to your sacred place and practice a relaxation exercise. Inhale for four seconds. Hold the breath for four seconds. Exhale for four seconds. Hold the exhalation for four seconds. Repeat the process for as many times as possible.

Choose your favorite meditation posture and practice using the posture. For instance, if you use supports for your back during meditation start practicing your favorite posture without any support.

Next take inventory of your activities today. Where did you go? What did you do? Who did you meet? What did you contribute? How did you affect your environment? How did the environment affect you? Is there any thing you did that you could have done differently? How could you have done it next time?

Lastly visualize the next day of your life in the family and in the office or wherever you would be the next day. What do you want to see happen? For the family you might want harmony, understanding and unity. For work you might want to see that you are accomplishing your work goals and getting along with your boss and co-workers.

### Month 1, Week 3, Day 1

Retire to your sacred place and practice a relaxation exercise. Inhale for four seconds. Hold the breath for four seconds.

Exhale for four seconds. Hold the exhalation for four seconds. Repeat the process for as many times as possible.

Now reflect on your relationships. Have you hurt anyone in the past that is still bothering you? Have you tried to apologize with the person or persons? If all efforts to reconcile have failed you may follow this program of reconciliation. Recall the person in your mind. Try to see the wrong in the situation and feel what it means to be in the victim's position. Accept what you have done with real regret and ask for reconciliation. Write a letter to the person you have hurt if you are unable to apologize directly to the person. Write the complete account including all the unhappy details. State what you did that hurt the person and admit to the person that you were wrong and ask for forgiveness and reconciliation. Put the letter in an envelope, seal it and address it to the person. With the letter in your right hand apologize to the person and visualize having a friendly conversation with the person and experience the reconciliation. Shake hands with the person and say "thank you for this reconciliation, it is time for us to move forward with our lives!" Burn the letter and feel all the hurt, guilt and resentment burning away for the good of all concerned. Repeat a favorite prayer or affirmation and go about your normal business. If you have more than one person you have hurt in the past do a separate treatment for each person.

Next take inventory of your activities today. Where did you go? What did you do? Who did you meet? What did you contribute? How did you affect your environment? How did the environment affect you? Is there any thing you did that you could have done differently? How could you have done it next time?

Lastly visualize the next day of your life in the family and in the office or wherever you would be the next day. What do you want to see happen? For the family you might want harmony,

understanding and unity. For work you might want to see that you are accomplishing your work goals and getting along with your boss and co-workers.

**Month 1, Week 3, Day 2**

Retire to your sacred place and practice a relaxation exercise. Inhale for four seconds. Hold the breath for four seconds. Exhale for four seconds. Hold the exhalation for four seconds. Repeat the process for as many times as possible.

Next reflect on Peace **by the Buddha**

Peace comes from within

Do not seek it without

Next take inventory of your activities today. Where did you go? What did you do? Who did you meet? What did you contribute? How did you affect your environment? How did the environment affect you? Is there any thing you did that you could have done differently? How could you have done it next time?

Lastly visualize the next day of your life in the family and in the office or wherever you would be the next day. What do you want to see happen? For the family you might want harmony, understanding and unity. For work you might want to see that you are accomplishing your work goals and getting along with your boss and co-workers.

**Month 1, Week 3, Day 3**

Retire to your sacred place and practice a relaxation exercise. Inhale for four seconds. Hold the breath for four seconds. Exhale for four seconds. Hold the exhalation for four seconds. Repeat the process for as many times as possible.

Next reflect on Compassion **by the Buddha**

Pity arises when we are sorry for someone.
Compassion is when we understand and help wisely.

Next take inventory of your activities today. Where did you go? What did you do? Who did you meet? What did you contribute? How did you affect your environment? How did the environment affect you? Is there any thing you did that you could have done differently? How could you have done it next time?

Lastly visualize the next day of your life in the family and in the office or wherever you would be the next day. What do you want to see happen? For the family you might want harmony, understanding and unity. For work you might want to see that you are accomplishing your work goals and getting along with your boss and co-workers.

### Month 1, Week 3, Day 4

Retire to your sacred place and practice a relaxation exercise. Inhale for four seconds. Hold the breath for four seconds. Exhale for four seconds. Hold the exhalation for four seconds. Repeat the process for as many times as possible.

Reflect on the following passage: Let hope lead your way. Be persistent in your quest. Go with patience wherever the journey takes you. Stick to courage to keep you on the path. And include love in your heart for all creatures. Develop your talent for your own good along the way. Use your talents for the good of all creatures. Learn the lesson and move on when you make a mistake. Do not cry over your losses and failures. There is no loss in the Universe! **Universal Holy Book: The Book of Life 1: 89-98.**

Next take inventory of your activities today. Where did you go? What did you do? Who did you meet? What did you contribute? How did you affect your environment? How did the

environment affect you? Is there any thing you did that you could have done differently? How could you have done it next time?

Lastly visualize the next day of your life in the family and in the office or wherever you would be the next day. What do you want to see happen? For the family you might want harmony, understanding and unity. For work you might want to see that you are accomplishing your work goals and getting along with your boss and co-workers.

**Month 1, Week 3, Day 5**

Retire to your sacred place and practice a relaxation exercise. Inhale for four seconds. Hold the breath for four seconds. Exhale for four seconds. Hold the exhalation for four seconds. Repeat the process for as many times as possible.

Now reflect on **Compassion by MarleyA**: Compassion is empathy, caring, love, and morality. Compassion is feeding the hungry, sheltering the homeless, caring for the poor. Compassion is all the little tasks you do for ones you love like picking up the toys that Little One leaves in a trail, or comforting Sister after an argument, encouraging Friend in an endeavor, or just making sure that all your loved ones know how much you care. Compassion is reaching out to those you know, and strangers. It is imagining your feelings in someone else's situation and acting to make them feel better. I see compassion in the tent city that the church across the street has established. I see compassion in the canned food drives that our school supports and watching as the days go by and the boxes of goods overflow. I see compassion in how my sister treats all the little critters she finds around the house and yard, the way she nurtures her plants and watches over the pets. And the most compassionate thing I think one can offer, is to give up something you want knowing that others will appreciate it more or hoping it will give them joy when that is scarce in their lives.

Next take inventory of your activities today. Where did you go? What did you do? Who did you meet? What did you contribute? How did you affect your environment? How did the environment affect you? Is there any thing you did that you could have done differently? How could you have done it next time?

Lastly visualize the next day of your life in the family and in the office or wherever you would be the next day. What do you want to see happen? For the family you might want harmony, understanding and unity. For work you might want to see that you are accomplishing your work goals and getting along with your boss and co-workers.

**Month 1, Week 3, Day 6**

Retire to your sacred place and practice a relaxation exercise. Inhale for four seconds. Hold the breath for four seconds. Exhale for four seconds. Hold the exhalation for four seconds. Repeat the process for as many times as possible.

Now reflect on the following: Through meditation and by giving full attention to one thing at a time, we can learn to direct attention where we choose. **Eknath Easwaran**

Next take inventory of your activities today. Where did you go? What did you do? Who did you meet? What did you contribute? How did you affect your environment? How did the environment affect you? Is there any thing you did that you could have done differently? How could you have done it next time?

Lastly visualize the next day of your life in the family and in the office or wherever you would be the next day. What do you want to see happen? For the family you might want harmony, understanding and unity. For work you might want to see that you

are accomplishing your work goals and getting along with your boss and co-workers.

**Month 1, Week 3, Day 7**

Attend a church, a temple, or any other meeting that brings you together with people for a common goal. If you do not have one you may begin today and find one that meets your interest and inclination. If you want you could also organize a group of your own. For instance you could start an Awakened Living Study Program. You may contact UNISM for more information.

Retire to your sacred place and practice a relaxation exercise. Inhale for four seconds. Hold the breath for four seconds. Exhale for four seconds. Hold the exhalation for four seconds. Repeat the process for as many times as possible.

Choose your favorite meditation posture and practice using the posture. For instance, if you use supports for your back during meditation start practicing your favorite posture without any support.

Next take inventory of your activities today. Where did you go? What did you do? Who did you meet? What did you contribute? How did you affect your environment? How did the environment affect you? Is there any thing you did that you could have done differently? How could you have done it next time?

Lastly visualize the next day of your life in the family and in the office or wherever you would be the next day. What do you want to see happen? For the family you might want harmony, understanding and unity. For work you might want to see that you are accomplishing your work goals and getting along with your boss and co-workers.

*Month 1, Week 4, Day 1*

Retire to your sacred place and practice a relaxation exercise. Inhale for four seconds. Hold the breath for four seconds. Exhale for four seconds. Hold the exhalation for four seconds. Repeat the process for as many times as possible.

Has anyone hurt you in the past that you have not forgiven? It is harmful to go through life with hate or resentment because as we think so we are! This is a program to forgive all the people who have hurt you in the past. First recall the person. Reflect on the details of the event. Feel the pain and the hurt for the last time. Now write a letter to the person that mistreated, harmed, hurt or did you some injustice. In your letter describe the event in detail including what they did and how you felt. Feel the hurt and conclude the letter with a note of complete forgiveness. "I forgive and release you John Doe so that we both may begin a new chapter in our lives." Put the letter in an envelope and address it to the person. With the letter in your right hand have a verbal conversation with the person. Talk out what the person did and how you felt. Meditate on the conversation and completely release the person with your unconditional forgiveness. Burn the letter and see your hurt and resentment being burned away to ashes. Follow the same procedure for all those who have hurt you in the past.

Next take inventory of your activities today. Where did you go? What did you do? Who did you meet? What did you contribute? How did you affect your environment? How did the environment affect you? Is there any thing you did that you could have done differently? How could you have done it next time?

Lastly visualize the next day of your life in the family and in the office or wherever you would be the next day. What do you want to see happen? For the family you might want harmony, understanding and unity. For work you might want to see that you

are accomplishing your work goals and getting along with your boss and co-workers.

### Month 1, Week 4, Day 2

Retire to your sacred place and practice a relaxation exercise. Inhale for four seconds. Hold the breath for four seconds. Exhale for four seconds. Hold the exhalation for four seconds. Repeat the process for as many times as possible.

Now meditate on the following statement: Nowhere can man find a quieter or more untroubled retreat than in his own soul.
**~Marcus Aurelius**

Next take inventory of your activities today. Where did you go? What did you do? Who did you meet? What did you contribute? How did you affect your environment? How did the environment affect you? Is there any thing you did that you could have done differently? How could you have done it next time?

Lastly visualize the next day of your life in the family and in the office or wherever you would be the next day. What do you want to see happen? For the family you might want harmony, understanding and unity. For work you might want to see that you are accomplishing your work goals and getting along with your boss and co-workers.

### Month 1, Week 4, Day 3

Retire to your sacred place and practice a relaxation exercise. Inhale for four seconds. Hold the breath for four seconds. Exhale for four seconds. Hold the exhalation for four seconds. Repeat the process for as many times as possible.

Now reflect on Virtues **by the Buddha**

Serenity, respect, simplicity, self-control, purity of thought are virtues of the mind.

Generosity, stillness, gratitude, happiness, purity of feeling are virtues of the heart.

Next take inventory of your activities today. Where did you go? What did you do? Who did you meet? What did you contribute? How did you affect your environment? How did the environment affect you? Is there any thing you did that you could have done differently? How could you have done it next time?

Lastly visualize the next day of your life in the family and in the office or wherever you would be the next day. What do you want to see happen? For the family you might want harmony, understanding and unity. For work you might want to see that you are accomplishing your work goals and getting along with your boss and co-workers.

### Month 1, Week 4, Day 4

Retire to your sacred place and practice a relaxation exercise. Inhale for four seconds. Hold the breath for four seconds. Exhale for four seconds. Hold the exhalation for four seconds. Repeat the process for as many times as possible.

Reflect on the following passage: You were born to share your gifts and talents with the Earth. You were born to contribute to the good of the Earth. You were born to contribute to the good of the Universe. You were born to create. You were born to give. You were born to nurture your own divinity. You were born to realize Enlightenment. **Universal Holy Book: The Book of Life 1: 223-229.**

Next take inventory of your activities today. Where did you go? What did you do? Who did you meet? What did you contribute? How did you affect your environment? How did the environment affect you? Is there any thing you did that you could have done differently? How could you have done it next time?

Lastly visualize the next day of your life in the family and in the office or wherever you would be the next day. What do you want to see happen? For the family you might want harmony, understanding and unity. For work you might want to see that you are accomplishing your work goals and getting along with your boss and co-workers.

**Month 1, Week 4, Day 5**

Retire to your sacred place and practice a relaxation exercise. Inhale for four seconds. Hold the breath for four seconds. Exhale for four seconds. Hold the exhalation for four seconds. Repeat the process for as many times as possible.

Now reflect on Perception by **Thick Nhat Hanh:** A man was rowing his boat up stream on a very misty morning. Suddenly, he saw another boat coming down stream, not trying to avoid him. It was coming straight at him. He shouted, "Be careful! Be careful!" but the boat came right into him, and his boat was almost sunk. The man became very angry, and begun to shout at the other person, to give him a piece of his mind. But when he looked closely he saw that there was no one in the other boat. It turned out that the boat just got loose and went down stream. All his anger vanished, and he laughed and he laughed. If our perceptions are not correct, they may give us a lot of bad feelings.

Next take inventory of your activities today. Where did you go? What did you do? Who did you meet? What did you contribute? How did you affect your environment? How did the environment affect you? Is there any thing you did that you could have done differently? How could you have done it next time?

Lastly visualize the next day of your life in the family and in the office or wherever you would be the next day. What do you want to see happen? For the family you might want harmony,

understanding and unity. For work you might want to see that you are accomplishing your work goals and getting along with your boss and co-workers.

### Month 1, Week 4, Day 6

Retire to your sacred place and practice a relaxation exercise. Inhale for four seconds. Hold the breath for four seconds. Exhale for four seconds. Hold the exhalation for four seconds. Repeat the process for as many times as possible.

Now reflect on the following: Meditation is the dissolution of thoughts in Eternal awareness or Pure consciousness without objectification, knowing without thinking, merging finitude in infinity. Sivananda Saraswati

Next take inventory of your activities today. Where did you go? What did you do? Who did you meet? What did you contribute? How did you affect your environment? How did the environment affect you? Is there any thing you did that you could have done differently? How could you have done it next time?

Lastly visualize the next day of your life in the family and in the office or wherever you would be the next day. What do you want to see happen? For the family you might want harmony, understanding and unity. For work you might want to see that you are accomplishing your work goals and getting along with your boss and co-workers.

### Month 1, Week 4, Day 7

Attend a church, a temple, or any other meeting that brings you together with people for a common goal. If you do not have one you may begin today and find one that meets your interest and inclination. If you want you could also organize a group of your

own. For instance you could start an Awakened Living Study Program. You may contact UNISM for more information.

Retire to your sacred place and practice a relaxation exercise. Inhale for four seconds. Hold the breath for four seconds. Exhale for four seconds. Hold the exhalation for four seconds. Repeat the process for as many times as possible.

Choose your favorite meditation posture and practice using the posture. For instance, if you use supports for your back during meditation start practicing your favorite posture without any support.

Next take inventory of your activities today. Where did you go? What did you do? Who did you meet? What did you contribute? How did you affect your environment? How did the environment affect you? Is there any thing you did that you could have done differently? How could you have done it next time?

Lastly visualize the next day of your life in the family and in the office or wherever you would be the next day. What do you want to see happen? For the family you might want harmony, understanding and unity. For work you might want to see that you are accomplishing your work goals and getting along with your boss and co-workers.

# Individual Meditation: Second Month

Goal

The goal of the second month of meditation is to help you to decide what you want and work toward achievement and fulfillment. You will consider a group of questions put together to touch 9 areas of your life as represented by the Wheel of Life: Physical Environment, Career, Money, Health & Well Being, Family, Friends, Personal Development and Growth, Significant other and Romance, and Fun and Recreation. The Wheel of Life represents Fulfillment and Balance.

**Month 2, Week 1, Day 1**

Retire to your sacred place and practice a relaxation exercise. Inhale for four seconds. Hold the breath for four seconds. Exhale for four seconds. Hold the exhalation for four seconds. Repeat the process for as many times as possible.

Now reflect on the questions and note the ones that directly affect you.

Is your life a big lie?
Do you exercise regularly?
When was the last time you went on a vacation?
Do you have a spiritual home?
Do you consider yourself healthy?
Do you have a secret life?
When was the last time you played with a squirrel?
Are your beliefs inclusive?
Does your job or career give you joy and fulfillment?
When was the last time you read a favorite book?
Are you happy with your children?
Are you enjoying a happy family life?

Do you spend lots of time watching pornography?
Do you lose your temper often?
When was the last time you watched a favorite movie?
Are you happy with your spouse?
Are any areas of your life stressful?
Do you have a healthy relationship with your friends?
Do you have financial problems?
When was the last time you attended a seminar?
Do you give freely?
Does your home bring the best within you?
Are you at peace in your neighborhood?
Do you wake up at the same time daily?
Are you keeping your dreams on hold because of apparent lack of resources?
When was the last time you attended a concert?
Could you look in the mirror and say that you are a success?
When was the last time you surprised someone with joy and happiness?

Next take inventory of your activities today. Where did you go? What did you do? Who did you meet? What did you contribute? How did you affect your environment? How did the environment affect you? Is there any thing you did that you could have done differently? How could you have done it next time?

Lastly visualize the next day of your life in the family and in the office or wherever you would be the next day. What do you want to see happen? For the family you might want harmony, understanding and unity. For work you might want to see that you are accomplishing your work goals and getting along with your boss and co-workers.

### Month 2, Week 1, Day 2

Retire to your sacred place and practice a relaxation exercise. Inhale for four seconds. Hold the breath for four seconds. Exhale for four seconds. Hold the exhalation for four seconds. Repeat the process for as many times as possible.

Count from 100 backwards that is 100, 99, 88, etc, until you reach 1. Now count the normal way from 1 to 100. Next try counting from 1 to 200 and from 200 to 1. Concentrate on your counting and see the figures in your mind's eye as you count.

Now reflect on your career, hobby, work, occupation or employment. Are you happy with what you do for a living? Does what you do for a living contribute to the general good? Does what you do for a living have opportunities for growth? Are you stuck in your position? Are you doing your best at work? Meditate on these questions and open your mind to receive inspiration to address areas of conflict.

Next take inventory of your activities today. Where did you go? What did you do? Who did you meet? What did you contribute? How did you affect your environment? How did the environment affect you?

Lastly visualize the next day of your life in the family and in the office or wherever you would be the next day. What do you want to see happen? For the family you might want harmony, understanding and unity. For work you might want to see that you are accomplishing your work goals and getting along with your boss and co-workers.

### Month 2, Week 1, Day 3

Retire to your sacred place and practice a relaxation exercise. Inhale for four seconds. Hold the breath for four seconds.

Exhale for four seconds. Hold the exhalation for four seconds. Repeat the process for as many times as possible.

Count from 100 backwards that is 100, 99, 88, etc, until you reach 1. Now count the normal way from 1 to 100. Next try counting from 1 to 200 and from 200 to 1. Concentrate on your counting and see the figures in your mind's eye as you count.

Now consider your financial health. Are you comfortable with your income? Are you living within your means? Do you have any financial problems? What could you do to ease your financial problems? Meditate on these questions and try to achieve balance in your finances.

Next take inventory of your activities today. Where did you go? What did you do? Who did you meet? What did you contribute? How did you affect your environment? How did the environment affect you?

Lastly visualize the next day of your life in the family and in the office or wherever you would be the next day. What do you want to see happen? For the family you might want harmony, understanding and unity. For work you might want to see that you are accomplishing your work goals and getting along with your boss and co-workers.

**Month 2, Week 1, Day 4**

Retire to your sacred place and practice a relaxation exercise. Inhale for four seconds. Hold the breath for four seconds. Exhale for four seconds. Hold the exhalation for four seconds. Repeat the process for as many times as possible.

Count from 100 backwards that is 100, 99, 88, etc, until you reach 1. Now count the normal way from 1 to 100. Next try counting from 1 to 200 and from 200 to 1. Concentrate on your counting and see the figures in your mind's eye as you count.

Now consider your overall health. Would you say that you are healthy? Do you exercise regularly? Do you eat the proper food? What kind of thoughts do you hold? Are they healthy thoughts? Are they unhealthy thoughts? Reflect on ways to achieve balance.

Next take inventory of your activities today. Where did you go? What did you do? Who did you meet? What did you contribute? How did you affect your environment? How did the environment affect you?

Lastly visualize the next day of your life in the family and in the office or wherever you would be the next day. What do you want to see happen? For the family you might want harmony, understanding and unity. For work you might want to see that you are accomplishing your work goals and getting along with your boss and co-workers.

**Month 2, Week 1, Day 5**

Retire to your sacred place and practice a relaxation exercise. Inhale for four seconds. Hold the breath for four seconds. Exhale for four seconds. Hold the exhalation for four seconds. Repeat the process for as many times as possible.

Count from 100 backwards that is 100, 99, 88, etc, until you reach 1. Now count the normal way from 1 to 100. Next try counting from 1 to 200 and from 200 to 1. Concentrate on your counting and see the figures in your mind's eye as you count.

Now reflect on Responsibility by the Dalai Lama: Responsibility . . . lies with each of us individually. Peace, for example, starts within each one of us. When we have inner peace, we can be at peace with those around us. When our community is in a state of peace, it can share that peace with neighboring communities, and so on. When we feel love and kindness towards others, it not only makes others feel loved and cared for, but it helps us also to develop inner happiness and peace. And there are ways in which we can consciously work to develop feelings of love and kindness. For some of us, the most effective way to do so is through religious practice. For others it may be non-religious practices. What is important is that we each make a sincere effort to take our responsibility for each other and for the natural environment we live in seriously.

Next take inventory of your activities today. Where did you go? What did you do? Who did you meet? What did you contribute? How did you affect your environment? How did the environment affect you?

Lastly visualize the next day of your life in the family and in the office or wherever you would be the next day. What do you want to see happen? For the family you might want harmony, understanding and unity. For work you might want to see that you are accomplishing your work goals and getting along with your boss and co-workers.

**Month 2, Week 1, Day 6**

Retire to your sacred place and practice a relaxation exercise. Inhale for four seconds. Hold the breath for four seconds. Exhale for four seconds. Hold the exhalation for four seconds. Repeat the process for as many times as possible.

Now reflect on the following: You cannot see clearly, because you are so full of expectations, hopes, desires. Your eyes are covered with many layers of dust: you need a deep cleansing of your eyes. That's what meditation is. Let the thoughts disappear, the hopes disappear, the desires disappear. Then you have a clarity, then your eyes are perfect mirrors. Only then, in that silent state of your vision, will you know the secrets of the beyond. Bhagwan Shree Rajneesh

Next take inventory of your activities today. Where did you go? What did you do? Who did you meet? What did you contribute? How did you affect your environment? How did the environment affect you? Is there any thing you did that you could have done differently? How could you have done it next time?

Lastly visualize the next day of your life in the family and in the office or wherever you would be the next day. What do you want to see happen? For the family you might want harmony, understanding and unity. For work you might want to see that you are accomplishing your work goals and getting along with your boss and co-workers.

**Month 2, Week 1, Day 7**

Attend a church, a temple, or any other meeting that brings you together with people for a common goal. If you do not have one you may begin today and find one that meets your interest and inclination. If you want you could also organize a group of your own. For instance you could start an Awakened Living Study Program. You may contact UNISM for more information.

Retire to your sacred place and practice a relaxation exercise. Inhale for four seconds. Hold the breath for four seconds. Exhale for four seconds. Hold the exhalation for four seconds. Repeat the process for as many times as possible.

Choose your favorite meditation posture and practice using the posture. For instance, if you use supports for your back during meditation start practicing your favorite posture without any support.

Next take inventory of your activities today. Where did you go? What did you do? Who did you meet? What did you

contribute? How did you affect your environment? How did the environment affect you? Is there any thing you did that you could have done differently? How could you have done it next time?

Lastly visualize the next day of your life in the family and in the office or wherever you would be the next day. What do you want to see happen? For the family you might want harmony, understanding and unity. For work you might want to see that you are accomplishing your work goals and getting along with your boss and co-workers.

## Month 2, Week 2, Day 1

Retire to your sacred place and practice a relaxation exercise. Inhale for four seconds. Hold the breath for four seconds. Exhale for four seconds. Hold the exhalation for four seconds. Repeat the process for as many times as possible.

Count from 100 backwards that is 100, 99, 88, etc, until you reach 1. Now count the normal way from 1 to 100. Next try counting from 1 to 200 and from 200 to 1. Concentrate on your counting and see the figures in your mind's eye as you count.

Now consider your life goals. Deciding on a goal for your life could take some time if you have not thought about the issue before. However a goal doesn't have to be grand, like changing the world, which is actually vague, but it could be as simple as losing 10 pounds. Besides no one says you have to pursue all your goals at the same time; you could take one goal at a time. You may begin by setting a work goal. What is your work, career, employment or job goal? What do you want to give? What do you want people to know when they consider your work? Meditate on your work goals and write them down.

Next take inventory of your activities today. Where did you go? What did you do? Who did you meet? What did you

contribute? How did you affect your environment? How did the environment affect you?

Lastly visualize the next day of your life in the family and in the office or wherever you would be the next day. What do you want to see happen? For the family you might want harmony, understanding and unity. For work you might want to see that you are accomplishing your work goals and getting along with your boss and co-workers.

**Month 2, Week 2, Day 2**

Retire to your sacred place and practice a relaxation exercise. Inhale for four seconds. Hold the breath for four seconds. Exhale for four seconds. Hold the exhalation for four seconds. Repeat the process for as many times as possible.

Count from 100 backwards that is 100, 99, 88, etc, until you reach 1. Now count the normal way from 1 to 100. Next try counting from 1 to 200 and from 200 to 1. Concentrate on your counting and see the figures in your mind's eye as you count.

Now consider your health goals. What are your health goals? What will be your healthy weight? How are you going to achieve this weight? Meditate on your health goals and write them down.

Next take inventory of your activities today. Where did you go? What did you do? Who did you meet? What did you contribute? How did you affect your environment? How did the environment affect you?

Lastly visualize the next day of your life in the family and in the office or wherever you would be the next day. What do you want to see happen? For the family you might want harmony, understanding and unity. For work you might want to see that you

are accomplishing your work goals and getting along with your boss and co-workers.

**Month 2, Week 2, Day 3**

Retire to your sacred place and practice a relaxation exercise. Inhale for four seconds. Hold the breath for four seconds. Exhale for four seconds. Hold the exhalation for four seconds. Repeat the process for as many times as possible.

Count from 100 backwards that is 100, 99, 88, etc, until you reach 1. Now count the normal way from 1 to 100. Next try counting from 1 to 200 and from 200 to 1. Concentrate on your counting and see the figures in your mind's eye as you count.

Next consider your financial goals. What are your financial goals? How much do you want to save for your retirement? How much do you need for recreation, travels and entertainment? How are you going to make the income? Meditate on these questions and write down your financial goals.

Next take inventory of your activities today. Where did you go? What did you do? Who did you meet? What did you contribute? How did you affect your environment? How did the environment affect you?

Lastly visualize the next day of your life in the family and in the office or wherever you would be the next day. What do you want to see happen? For the family you might want harmony, understanding and unity. For work you might want to see that you are accomplishing your work goals and getting along with your boss and co-workers.

Month 2, Week 2, Day 4

Retire to your sacred place and practice a relaxation exercise. Inhale for four seconds. Hold the breath for four seconds.

Exhale for four seconds. Hold the exhalation for four seconds. Repeat the process for as many times as possible.

Count from 100 backwards that is 100, 99, 88, etc, until you reach 1. Now count the normal way from 1 to 100. Next try counting from 1 to 200 and from 200 to 1. Concentrate on your counting and see the figures in your mind's eye as you count.

Now consider your educational goals. What is the level of your education? Does it fit with your present career goals? Does lifelong learning mean anything to you? What are you doing to improve your level of education? Reflect on these questions and try to achieve balance.

Next take inventory of your activities today. Where did you go? What did you do? Who did you meet? What did you contribute? How did you affect your environment? How did the environment affect you?

Lastly visualize the next day of your life in the family and in the office or wherever you would be the next day. What do you want to see happen? For the family you might want harmony, understanding and unity. For work you might want to see that you are accomplishing your work goals and getting along with your boss and co-workers.

Month 2, Week 2, Day 5

Retire to your sacred place and practice a relaxation exercise. Inhale for four seconds. Hold the breath for four seconds. Exhale for four seconds. Hold the exhalation for four seconds. Repeat the process for as many times as possible.

Count from 100 backwards that is 100, 99, 88, etc, until you reach 1. Now count the normal way from 1 to 100. Next try counting from 1 to 200 and from 200 to 1. Concentrate on your counting and see the figures in your mind's eye as you count.

Reflect on Equality. Examine it thoroughly and try to understand its meaning and implications. What does it mean to you? Look at equality in you family. Then consider equality in your city and country. What do you think? Now meditate on equality among the races? What do you think? What can you do to improve equality in your city?

Next take inventory of your activities today. Where did you go? What did you do? Who did you meet? What did you contribute? How did you affect your environment? How did the environment affect you?

Lastly visualize the next day of your life in the family and in the office or wherever you would be the next day. What do you want to see happen? For the family you might want harmony, understanding and unity. For work you might want to see that you are accomplishing your work goals and getting along with your boss and co-workers.

**Month 2, Week 2, Day 6**

Retire to your sacred place and practice a relaxation exercise. Inhale for four seconds. Hold the breath for four seconds. Exhale for four seconds. Hold the exhalation for four seconds. Repeat the process for as many times as possible.

Count from 100 backwards that is 100, 99, 88, etc, until you reach 1. Now count the normal way from 1 to 100. Next try counting from 1 to 200 and from 200 to 1. Concentrate on your counting and see the figures in your mind's eye as you count.

Meditate on walking into a nearby wood. See the trees, the flowers, the leaves, the plants and the squirrels. Remain quiet in one place preferably under a tree. Get out the nuts in your bag and begin to feed the squirrels. Be perfectly still with the knowledge that any slight move you make will scare away the squirrels. How many squirrels are you feeding now? How are you feeling? Stay there a while and continue to be still. You may leave as soon as you are done.

Next take inventory of your activities today. Where did you go? What did you do? Who did you meet? What did you contribute? How did you affect your environment? How did the environment affect you? Is there any thing you did that you could have done differently? How could you have done it next time?

Lastly visualize the next day of your life in the family and in the office or wherever you would be the next day. What do you want to see happen? For the family you might want harmony, understanding and unity. For work you might want to see that you are accomplishing your work goals and getting along with your boss and co-workers.

**Month 2, Week 2, Day 7**

Attend a church, a temple, or any other meeting that brings you together with people for a common goal. If you do not have one you may begin today and find one that meets your interest and inclination. If you want you could also organize a group of your own. For instance you could start an Awakened Living Study Program. You may contact UNISM for more information.

Retire to your sacred place and practice a relaxation exercise. Inhale for four seconds. Hold the breath for four seconds. Exhale for four seconds. Hold the exhalation for four seconds. Repeat the process for as many times as possible.

Choose your favorite meditation posture and practice using the posture. For instance, if you use supports for your back during meditation start practicing your favorite posture without any support.

Next take inventory of your activities today. Where did you go? What did you do? Who did you meet? What did you contribute? How did you affect your environment? How did the environment affect you? Is there any thing you did that you could have done differently? How could you have done it next time?

Lastly visualize the next day of your life in the family and in the office or wherever you would be the next day. What do you want to see happen? For the family you might want harmony, understanding and unity. For work you might want to see that you are accomplishing your work goals and getting along with your boss and co-workers.

**Month 2, Week 3, Day 1**

Retire to your sacred place and practice a relaxation exercise. Inhale for four seconds. Hold the breath for four seconds. Exhale for four seconds. Hold the exhalation for four seconds. Repeat the process for as many times as possible.

Count from 100 backwards that is 100, 99, 88, etc, until you reach 1. Now count the normal way from 1 to 100. Next try counting from 1 to 200 and from 200 to 1. Concentrate on your counting and see the figures in your mind's eye as you count.

Now consider your most favorite inspirational event. It could be the birth of your child, the day you got married, your favorite birthday ceremony, the day you went hiking or the day you went skiing. Think about the events of that day and let it consume you completely. Stay in that mode for as long as possible. Repeat as often as you want and use this event to replace your negative or unprogressive thoughts.

Next take inventory of your activities today. Where did you go? What did you do? Who did you meet? What did you

contribute? How did you affect your environment? How did the environment affect you?

Lastly visualize the next day of your life in the family and in the office or wherever you would be the next day. What do you want to see happen? For the family you might want harmony, understanding and unity. For work you might want to see that you are accomplishing your work goals and getting along with your boss and co-workers.

**Month 2, Week 3, Day 2**

Retire to your sacred place and practice a relaxation exercise. Inhale for four seconds. Hold the breath for four seconds. Exhale for four seconds. Hold the exhalation for four seconds. Repeat the process for as many times as possible.

Count from 100 backwards that is 100, 99, 88, etc, until you reach 1. Now count the normal way from 1 to 100. Next try counting from 1 to 200 and from 200 to 1. Concentrate on your counting and see the figures in your mind's eye as you count.

Now visualize the following: Get a hold of your crabbing nets and go crabbing. Pick your favorite spot. Get out the nets and place the baits in them. Now cast the nets and wait. Look around you. Who else is there? What are they doing? Walk around the place and see what else you can find. Now come back to your nets and pull them. How many crabs did you catch? What kinds of crabs are they? Now put them gently back into the water and return home.

Next take inventory of your activities today. Where did you go? What did you do? Who did you meet? What did you contribute? How did you affect your environment? How did the environment affect you?

Lastly visualize the next day of your life in the family and in the office or wherever you would be the next day. What do you want to see happen? For the family you might want harmony, understanding and unity. For work you might want to see that you are accomplishing your work goals and getting along with your boss and co-workers.

**Month 2, Week 3, Day 3**

Retire to your sacred place and practice a relaxation exercise. Inhale for four seconds. Hold the breath for four seconds. Exhale for four seconds. Hold the exhalation for four seconds. Repeat the process for as many times as possible.

Count from 100 backwards that is 100, 99, 88, etc, until you reach 1. Now count the normal way from 1 to 100. Next try counting from 1 to 200 and from 200 to 1. Concentrate on your counting and see the figures in your mind's eye as you count.

Consider your most favorite birthday celebration. Think about the events of that day from the beginning to the end. See the whole activity in your mind's eye and feel the joy and happiness. Recall the special things you did including the contributions of all the people present. You may use this exercise to counter negative or unprogressive thoughts in your life!

Next take inventory of your activities today. Where did you go? What did you do? Who did you meet? What did you contribute? How did you affect your environment? How did the environment affect you?

Lastly visualize the next day of your life in the family and in the office or wherever you would be the next day. What do you want to see happen? For the family you might want harmony, understanding and unity. For work you might want to see that you

are accomplishing your work goals and getting along with your boss and co-workers.

### Month 2, Week 3, Day 4

Retire to your sacred place and practice a relaxation exercise. Inhale for four seconds. Hold the breath for four seconds. Exhale for four seconds. Hold the exhalation for four seconds. Repeat the process for as many times as possible.

Count from 100 backwards that is 100, 99, 88, etc, until you reach 1. Now count the normal way from 1 to 100. Next try counting from 1 to 200 and from 200 to 1. Concentrate on your counting and see the figures in your mind's eye as you count.

Consider a sodium atom consisting of an electron on its outermost shell, eight electrons on its second shell, two electrons on its innermost shell and a nucleus. Visualize the sodium atom and remove the components one by one beginning with the nucleus. Next remove the two electrons on the innermost shell followed by the shell. Next remove the eight electrons on the second shell followed by the shell. Finally remove the electron on the outermost shell. What you have now is only the outermost shell with nothing in it. Now remove the outermost shell and you have nothing. Remain in this nothingness for a while and reflect on it. How do you feel?

Next take inventory of your activities today. Where did you go? What did you do? Who did you meet? What did you contribute? How did you affect your environment? How did the environment affect you?

Lastly visualize the next day of your life in the family and in the office or wherever you would be the next day. What do you want to see happen? For the family you might want harmony, understanding and unity. For work you might want to see that you

are accomplishing your work goals and getting along with your boss and co-workers.

**Month 2, Week 3, Day 5**

Retire to your sacred place and practice a relaxation exercise. Inhale for four seconds. Hold the breath for four seconds. Exhale for four seconds. Hold the exhalation for four seconds. Repeat the process for as many times as possible.

Count from 100 backwards that is 100, 99, 88, etc, until you reach 1. Now count the normal way from 1 to 100. Next try counting from 1 to 200 and from 200 to 1. Concentrate on your counting and see the figures in your mind's eye as you count.

Go fishing at your favorite creek. You have your hook and bait and are ready. Visualize that you are driving down to the creek. Observe the things you see on the way. Drive carefully and make sure you have put on your seatbelt. When you arrive at the place choose your favorite spot. Now put the bait on the hook and begin to fish. What is going through your mind? Try to remain focused on your fishing. How many fishes did you catch? Name the fishes you caught. Now put them back into the water and return home.

Next take inventory of your activities today. Where did you go? What did you do? Who did you meet? What did you contribute? How did you affect your environment? How did the environment affect you?

Lastly visualize the next day of your life in the family and in the office or wherever you would be the next day. What do you want to see happen? For the family you might want harmony, understanding and unity. For work you might want to see that you are accomplishing your work goals and getting along with your boss and co-workers.

### Month 2, Week 3, Day 6

Retire to your sacred place and practice a relaxation exercise. Inhale for four seconds. Hold the breath for four seconds. Exhale for four seconds. Hold the exhalation for four seconds. Repeat the process for as many times as possible.

Count from 100 backwards that is 100, 99, 88, etc, until you reach 1. Now count the normal way from 1 to 100. Next try counting from 1 to 200 and from 200 to 1. Concentrate on your counting and see the figures in your mind's eye as you count.

Next consider your financial goals. What are your financial goals? How much do you want to save for your retirement? How much do you need for recreation, travels and entertainment? How are you going to make the income? Meditate on these questions and write down your financial goals.

Next take inventory of your activities today. Where did you go? What did you do? Who did you meet? What did you contribute? How did you affect your environment? How did the environment affect you? Is there any thing you did that you could have done differently? How could you have done it next time?

Lastly visualize the next day of your life in the family and in the office or wherever you would be the next day. What do you want to see happen? For the family you might want harmony, understanding and unity. For work you might want to see that you are accomplishing your work goals and getting along with your boss and co-workers.

### Month 2, Week 3, Day 7

Attend a church, a temple, or any other meeting that brings you together with people for a common goal. If you do not have one you may begin today and find one that meets your interest and inclination. If you want you could also organize a group of your own. For instance you could start an Awakened Living Study Program. You may contact UNISM for more information.

Retire to your sacred place and practice a relaxation exercise. Inhale for four seconds. Hold the breath for four seconds. Exhale for four seconds. Hold the exhalation for four seconds. Repeat the process for as many times as possible.

Choose your favorite meditation posture and practice using the posture. For instance, if you use supports for your back during meditation start practicing your favorite posture without any support.

Next take inventory of your activities today. Where did you go? What did you do? Who did you meet? What did you contribute? How did you affect your environment? How did the environment affect you? Is there any thing you did that you could have done differently? How could you have done it next time?

Lastly visualize the next day of your life in the family and in the office or wherever you would be the next day. What do you want to see happen? For the family you might want harmony, understanding and unity. For work you might want to see that you are accomplishing your work goals and getting along with your boss and co-workers.

**Month 2, Week 4, Day 1**

Retire to your sacred place and practice a relaxation exercise. Inhale for four seconds. Hold the breath for four seconds. Exhale for four seconds. Hold the exhalation for four seconds. Repeat the process for as many times as possible.

Count from 100 backwards that is 100, 99, 88, etc, until you reach 1. Now count the normal way from 1 to 100. Next try

counting from 1 to 200 and from 200 to 1. Concentrate on your counting and see the figures in your mind's eye as you count.

Now reflect on Universal Love as the love you ought to have for your fellow creatures. When was the last time you demonstrated unconditional love towards a person or another creature? What did you do? Reflect on your action. The idea is to reach out in such a way that it feels like your last chance to make a difference on the creature. Do you think you met this requirement in your action? What could you have done differently next time?

Next take inventory of your activities today. Where did you go? What did you do? Who did you meet? What did you contribute? How did you affect your environment? How did the environment affect you?

Lastly visualize the next day of your life in the family and in the office or wherever you would be the next day. What do you want to see happen? For the family you might want harmony, understanding and unity. For work you might want to see that you are accomplishing your work goals and getting along with your boss and co-workers.

### Month 2, Week 4, Day 2

Retire to your sacred place and practice a relaxation exercise. Inhale for four seconds. Hold the breath for four seconds. Exhale for four seconds. Hold the exhalation for four seconds. Repeat the process for as many times as possible.

Count from 100 backwards that is 100, 99, 88, etc, until you reach 1. Now count the normal way from 1 to 100. Next try counting from 1 to 200 and from 200 to 1. Concentrate on your counting and see the figures in your mind's eye as you count.

Now reflect on Freedom by Paul Brunton: Outwardly one's life may suffer every kind of limitation, from bodily paralysis to miserable surroundings, but inwardly it is free in meditation to reach out to a sphere of light, beauty, truth, love, and power.

Next take inventory of your activities today. Where did you go? What did you do? Who did you meet? What did you contribute? How did you affect your environment? How did the environment affect you?

Lastly visualize the next day of your life in the family and in the office or wherever you would be the next day. What do you want to see happen? For the family you might want harmony, understanding and unity. For work you might want to see that you are accomplishing your work goals and getting along with your boss and co-workers.

## Month 2, Week 4, Day 3

Retire to your sacred place and practice a relaxation exercise. Inhale for four seconds. Hold the breath for four seconds. Exhale for four seconds. Hold the exhalation for four seconds. Repeat the process for as many times as possible.

Count from 100 backwards that is 100, 99, 88, etc, until you reach 1. Now count the normal way from 1 to 100. Next try counting from 1 to 200 and from 200 to 1. Concentrate on your counting and see the figures in your mind's eye as you count.

Now reflect on the following: The wise man should surrender his words to his mind; and this he should surrender to the Knowing Self; and the Knowing Self he should surrender to the Great Self; and that he should surrender to the Peaceful Self. Hinduism. Katha Upanishad 3.13

Next take inventory of your activities today. Where did you go? What did you do? Who did you meet? What did you contribute? How did you affect your environment? How did the environment affect you?

Lastly visualize the next day of your life in the family and in the office or wherever you would be the next day. What do you want to see happen? For the family you might want harmony, understanding and unity. For work you might want to see that you are accomplishing your work goals and getting along with your boss and co-workers.

**Month 2, Week 4, Day 4**

Retire to your sacred place and practice a relaxation exercise. Inhale for four seconds. Hold the breath for four seconds. Exhale for four seconds. Hold the exhalation for four seconds. Repeat the process for as many times as possible.

Count from 100 backwards that is 100, 99, 88, etc, until you reach 1. Now count the normal way from 1 to 100. Next try counting from 1 to 200 and from 200 to 1. Concentrate on your counting and see the figures in your mind's eye as you count.

Meditate on getting into your boat and going for a ride on your favorite river. Observe the environment around you. What did you see? Check out the birds, ducks, and the people. What are they doing? Are there people fishing? Are they catching any fishes? What kind of fish are they catching? They are fishing for fun and they put the fishes back into the water after they catch them. Meditate on the joy of the fishes as they are released into the water. Return home at the end of your meditation.

Next take inventory of your activities today. Where did you go? What did you do? Who did you meet? What did you contribute? How did you affect your environment? How did the environment affect you?

Lastly visualize the next day of your life in the family and in the office or wherever you would be the next day. What do you want to see happen? For the family you might want harmony,

understanding and unity. For work you might want to see that you are accomplishing your work goals and getting along with your boss and co-workers.

**Month 2, Week 4, Day 5**

Retire to your sacred place and practice a relaxation exercise. Inhale for four seconds. Hold the breath for four seconds. Exhale for four seconds. Hold the exhalation for four seconds. Repeat the process for as many times as possible.

Count from 100 backwards that is 100, 99, 88, etc, until you reach 1. Now count the normal way from 1 to 100. Next try counting from 1 to 200 and from 200 to 1. Concentrate on your counting and see the figures in your mind's eye as you count.

Visualize that you are in a boat at the middle of a turbulent sea. The waves rise and fall and you feel like being swallowed by the sea. Gradually visualize the turbulent sea calming down. The sea becomes so calm that you could not even imagine there was ever a storm on that sea.

Next take inventory of your activities today. Where did you go? What did you do? Who did you meet? What did you contribute? How did you affect your environment? How did the environment affect you?

Lastly visualize the next day of your life in the family and in the office or wherever you would be the next day. What do you want to see happen? For the family you might want harmony, understanding and unity. For work you might want to see that you are accomplishing your work goals and getting along with your boss and co-workers.

Month 2, Week 4, Day 6

Retire to your sacred place and practice a relaxation exercise. Inhale for four seconds. Hold the breath for four seconds.

Exhale for four seconds. Hold the exhalation for four seconds. Repeat the process for as many times as possible.

Count from 100 backwards that is 100, 99, 88, etc, until you reach 1. Now count the normal way from 1 to 100. Next try counting from 1 to 200 and from 200 to 1. Concentrate on your counting and see the figures in your mind's eye as you count.

Now reflect on the following: Wherever there is a human being there is an opportunity for kindness. Seneca

Next take inventory of your activities today. Where did you go? What did you do? Who did you meet? What did you contribute? How did you affect your environment? How did the environment affect you? Is there any thing you did that you could have done differently? How could you have done it next time?

Lastly visualize the next day of your life in the family and in the office or wherever you would be the next day. What do you want to see happen? For the family you might want harmony, understanding and unity. For work you might want to see that you are accomplishing your work goals and getting along with your boss and co-workers.

**Month 2, Week 4, Day 7**

Attend a church, a temple, or any other meeting that brings you together with people for a common goal. If you do not have one you may begin today and find one that meets your interest and inclination. If you want you could also organize a group of your own. For instance you could start an Awakened Living Study Program. You may contact UNISM for more information.

Retire to your sacred place and practice a relaxation exercise. Inhale for four seconds. Hold the breath for four seconds. Exhale for four seconds. Hold the exhalation for four seconds. Repeat the process for as many times as possible.

Choose your favorite meditation posture and practice using the posture. For instance, if you use supports for your back during meditation start practicing your favorite posture without any support.

Next take inventory of your activities today. Where did you go? What did you do? Who did you meet? What did you contribute? How did you affect your environment? How did the environment affect you? Is there any thing you did that you could have done differently? How could you have done it next time?

Lastly visualize the next day of your life in the family and in the office or wherever you would be the next day. What do you want to see happen? For the family you might want harmony, understanding and unity. For work you might want to see that you are accomplishing your work goals and getting along with your boss and co-workers.

# Individual Meditation: Third Month

Goal

The goal of the third month of meditation is to give. Give a smile when next you meet another human being. Appreciate a flower on your way to work. Play with a squirrel the next time you visit a park. Volunteer your time for your favorite cause. Produce something for the benefit of humanity. Note that none of these activities really requires you to have anything to make a difference. Some people go through life thinking that they could only make a difference if they have material resources such as money. But in this view having money is not important. The true giver gives with money or without it! Learn to give and see the difference!

**Month 3, Week 1, Day 1**

Retire to your sacred place and practice a relaxation exercise. Inhale for four seconds. Hold the breath for four seconds. Exhale for four seconds. Hold the exhalation for four seconds. Repeat the process for as many times as possible.

Count from 50 backwards that is 50, 49, 48, etc, until you reach 1. Now count the normal way from 1 to 50. Next try counting from 1 to 100 and from 100 to 1. Concentrate on your counting and see the figures in your mind's eye as you count.

Now re-examine your life in the light of your successes and failures; your negative and positive actions and your contributions. Considering everything would you say your life is a success, a failure or just balanced? Where do you go from here?

Next take inventory of your activities today. Where did you go? What did you do? Who did you meet? What did you contribute? How did you affect your environment? How did the environment affect you?

Lastly visualize the next day of your life in the family and in the office or wherever you would be the next day. What do you want to see happen? For the family you might want harmony, understanding and unity. For work you might want to see that you are accomplishing your work goals and getting along with your boss and co-workers.

**Month 3, Week 1, Day 2**

Retire to your sacred place and practice a relaxation exercise. Inhale for four seconds. Hold the breath for four seconds. Exhale for four seconds. Hold the exhalation for four seconds. Repeat the process for as many times as possible.

Count from 50 backwards that is 50, 49, 48, etc, until you reach 1. Now count the normal way from 1 to 50. Next try counting from 1 to 100 and from 100 to 1. Concentrate on your counting and see the figures in your mind's eye as you count.

Now visualize that you are in a flower garden. How many flowers are there? What are the kinds of flowers? Choose one flower and meditate on it. Consider the sepals, petals, stigma, styles, ovaries and ovules. Reflect on the beauty of the flower and consider the quality that makes it so attractive to insects and people. Now meditate on an attractive quality within you and let it bring joy and happiness to all around you!

Next take inventory of your activities today. Where did you go? What did you do? Who did you meet? What did you contribute? How did you affect your environment? How did the environment affect you?

Lastly visualize the next day of your life in the family and in the office or wherever you would be the next day. What do you want to see happen? For the family you might want harmony, understanding and unity. For work you might want to see that you

are accomplishing your work goals and getting along with your boss and co-workers.

### Month 3, Week 1, Day 3

Retire to your sacred place and practice a relaxation exercise. Inhale for four seconds. Hold the breath for four seconds. Exhale for four seconds. Hold the exhalation for four seconds. Repeat the process for as many times as possible.

Count from 50 backwards that is 50, 49, 48, etc, until you reach 1. Now count the normal way from 1 to 50. Next try counting from 1 to 100 and from 100 to 1. Concentrate on your counting and see the figures in your mind's eye as you count.

Now reflect on **Human Development by Krishnamurti:** "For the total development of the human being, solitude as a means of cultivating sensitivity becomes a necessity. One has to know what it means to be alone, what it is to meditate, what it is to die; and the implications of solitude, of meditation, of death, can be known only by seeking them out. These implications cannot be taught, they must be learned."

Next take inventory of your activities today. Where did you go? What did you do? Who did you meet? What did you contribute? How did you affect your environment? How did the environment affect you?

Lastly visualize the next day of your life in the family and in the office or wherever you would be the next day. What do you want to see happen? For the family you might want harmony, understanding and unity. For work you might want to see that you are accomplishing your work goals and getting along with your boss and co-workers.

### Month 3, Week 1, Day 4

Retire to your sacred place and practice a relaxation exercise. Inhale for four seconds. Hold the breath for four seconds. Exhale for four seconds. Hold the exhalation for four seconds. Repeat the process for as many times as possible.

Count from 50 backwards that is 50, 49, 48, etc, until you reach 1. Now count the normal way from 1 to 50. Next try counting from 1 to 100 and from 100 to 1. Concentrate on your counting and see the figures in your mind's eye as you count.

Now think about someone you have neglected for a long time; someone who lives in another part of the country or the Earth. It could be a parent or a friend. Reflect on your time together and relive the experiences you had together. Shower the person with your love and tell him or her that he is still in your mind. The next day send a card to the person and share how you feel.

Next take inventory of your activities today. Where did you go? What did you do? Who did you meet? What did you contribute? How did you affect your environment? How did the environment affect you?

Lastly visualize the next day of your life in the family and in the office or wherever you would be the next day. What do you want to see happen? For the family you might want harmony, understanding and unity. For work you might want to see that you are accomplishing your work goals and getting along with your boss and co-workers.

### Month 3, Week 1, Day 5

Retire to your sacred place and practice a relaxation exercise. Inhale for four seconds. Hold the breath for four seconds.

Exhale for four seconds. Hold the exhalation for four seconds. Repeat the process for as many times as possible.

*Retire to your sacred place. Count from 50 backwards that is 50, 49, 48, etc, until you reach 1. Now count the normal way from 1 to 50. Next try counting from 1 to 100 and from 100 to 1. Concentrate on your counting and see the figures in your mind's eye as you count.*

Next reflect on the Secret of Life **by the Buddha:** The whole secret of existence is to have no fear. Never fear what will become of you, depend on no one. Only the moment you reject all help are you freed.

Next take inventory of your activities today. Where did you go? What did you do? Who did you meet? What did you contribute? How did you affect your environment? How did the environment affect you?

Lastly visualize the next day of your life in the family and in the office or wherever you would be the next day. What do you want to see happen? For the family you might want harmony, understanding and unity. For work you might want to see that you are accomplishing your work goals and getting along with your boss and co-workers.

**Month 3, Week 1, Day 6**

Retire to your sacred place and practice a relaxation exercise. Inhale for four seconds. Hold the breath for four seconds. Exhale for four seconds. Hold the exhalation for four seconds. Repeat the process for as many times as possible.

Count from 50 backwards that is 50, 49, 48, etc, until you reach 1. Now count the normal way from 1 to 50. Next try counting from 1 to 100 and from 100 to 1. Concentrate on your counting and see the figures in your mind's eye as you count.

Now reflect on the following: **Compassion is a feeling of pity for the suffering of your neighbor coupled with a desire to relieve the suffering. Dr. Sonari**

Next take inventory of your activities today. Where did you go? What did you do? Who did you meet? What did you contribute? How did you affect your environment? How did the environment affect you? Is there any thing you did that you could have done differently? How could you have done it next time?

Lastly visualize the next day of your life in the family and in the office or wherever you would be the next day. What do you want to see happen? For the family you might want harmony, understanding and unity. For work you might want to see that you are accomplishing your work goals and getting along with your boss and co-workers.

### Month 3, Week 1, Day 7

Attend a church, a temple, or any other meeting that brings you together with people for a common goal. If you do not have one you may begin today and find one that meets your interest and inclination. If you want you could also organize a group of your own. For instance you could start an Awakened Living Study Program. You may contact UNISM for more information.

Retire to your sacred place and practice a relaxation exercise. Inhale for four seconds. Hold the breath for four seconds. Exhale for four seconds. Hold the exhalation for four seconds. Repeat the process for as many times as possible.

Choose your favorite meditation posture and practice using the posture. For instance, if you use supports for your back during meditation start practicing your favorite posture without any support.

Next take inventory of your activities today. Where did you go? What did you do? Who did you meet? What did you contribute? How did you affect your environment? How did the environment affect you? Is there any thing you did that you could have done differently? How could you have done it next time?

Lastly visualize the next day of your life in the family and in the office or wherever you would be the next day. What do you want to see happen? For the family you might want harmony, understanding and unity. For work you might want to see that you are accomplishing your work goals and getting along with your boss and co-workers.

**Month 3, Week 2, Day 1**

Retire to your sacred place and practice a relaxation exercise. Inhale for four seconds. Hold the breath for four seconds. Exhale for four seconds. Hold the exhalation for four seconds. Repeat the process for as many times as possible.

Count from 50 backwards that is 50, 49, 48, etc, until you reach 1. Now count the normal way from 1 to 50. Next try counting from 1 to 100 and from 100 to 1. Concentrate on your counting and see the figures in your mind's eye as you count.

Next reflect on the good things that have happened to you since you were born. What are they? Pick one of them and relieve the experience. Then reflect on how you could live your life for the good of others more especially those that are in unfortunate circumstances.

Next take inventory of your activities today. Where did you go? What did you do? Who did you meet? What did you contribute? How did you affect your environment? How did the environment affect you?

Lastly visualize the next day of your life in the family and in the office or wherever you would be the next day. What do you want to see happen? For the family you might want harmony, understanding and unity. For work you might want to see that you are accomplishing your work goals and getting along with your boss and co-workers.

**Month 3, Week 2, Day 2**
Retire to your sacred place and practice a relaxation exercise. Inhale for four seconds. Hold the breath for four seconds. Exhale for four seconds. Hold the exhalation for four seconds. Repeat the process for as many times as possible.

Count from 50 backwards that is 50, 49, 48, etc, until you reach 1. Now count the normal way from 1 to 50. Next try counting from 1 to 100 and from 100 to 1. Concentrate on your counting and see the figures in your mind's eye as you count.

Now visualize the route you normally take to your office, school, or any place you frequently visit. Leave your home and start walking or driving or riding whatever your means of transportation might be. Stop at the stop signs and note all the things that you see on your way. Greet the people, the squirrels and the flowers on your way. On arrival pack your means of transportation and walk into the building or location. If you walked to the place just go right in. Note what people are doing. Get to your workplace and begin your work for the day. Note all your activities including your relationship with customers, your boss and co-workers. Sign off at the end of the day and return home noting all the important sights on your way. Visualization, when used in advance of an activity, helps the activity to go like clock work. An invisible hand seems to guide your activities. You may bring order to your daily life by practicing visualization in advance of all your activities.

Next take inventory of your activities today. Where did you go? What did you do? Who did you meet? What did you contribute? How did you affect your environment? How did the environment affect you?

Lastly visualize the next day of your life in the family and in the office or wherever you would be the next day. What do you want to see happen? For the family you might want harmony, understanding and unity. For work you might want to see that you are accomplishing your work goals and getting along with your boss and co-workers.

### Month 3, Week 2, Day 3

Retire to your sacred place and practice a relaxation exercise. Inhale for four seconds. Hold the breath for four seconds. Exhale for four seconds. Hold the exhalation for four seconds. Repeat the process for as many times as possible.

Count from 50 backwards that is 50, 49, 48, etc, until you reach 1. Now count the normal way from 1 to 50. Next try counting from 1 to 100 and from 100 to 1. Concentrate on your counting and see the figures in your mind's eye as you count.

Consider your most favorite inspirational event. It could be the birth of your child, the day you got married, your favorite birthday ceremony, the day you went hiking or the day you went skiing. Think about the events of that day and let it consume you completely. Stay in that mode for as long as possible. Repeat as often as you want and use this event to replace your negative or unprogressive thoughts.

Next take inventory of your activities today. Where did you go? What did you do? Who did you meet? What did you

contribute? How did you affect your environment? How did the environment affect you?

Lastly visualize the next day of your life in the family and in the office or wherever you would be the next day. What do you want to see happen? For the family you might want harmony, understanding and unity. For work you might want to see that you are accomplishing your work goals and getting along with your boss and co-workers.

## Month 3, Week 2, Day 4

Retire to your sacred place and practice a relaxation exercise. Inhale for four seconds. Hold the breath for four seconds. Exhale for four seconds. Hold the exhalation for four seconds. Repeat the process for as many times as possible.

Count from 50 backwards that is 50, 49, 48, etc, until you reach 1. Now count the normal way from 1 to 50. Next try counting from 1 to 100 and from 100 to 1. Concentrate on your counting and see the figures in your mind's eye as you count.

Now think about your contribution to the planet. What is it? Is it the way you relate to people? Is it the way you do your work? Is it the way your share your resources? Whatever it is, reflect on it to see if you could even do more.

Next take inventory of your activities today. Where did you go? What did you do? Who did you meet? What did you contribute? How did you affect your environment? How did the environment affect you?

Lastly visualize the next day of your life in the family and in the office or wherever you would be the next day. What do you want to see happen? For the family you might want harmony, understanding and unity. For work you might want to see that you

are accomplishing your work goals and getting along with your boss and co-workers.

### Month 3, Week 2, Day 5

Retire to your sacred place and practice a relaxation exercise. Inhale for four seconds. Hold the breath for four seconds. Exhale for four seconds. Hold the exhalation for four seconds. Repeat the process for as many times as possible.

Count from 50 backwards that is 50, 49, 48, etc, until you reach 1. Now count the normal way from 1 to 50. Next try counting from 1 to 100 and from 100 to 1. Concentrate on your counting and see the figures in your mind's eye as you count.

Now reflect on **Happiness by Kalidisa**:

Listen to the Exhortation of the Dawn!
Look to this Day!
For it is Life, the very Life of Life.
In its brief course lie all the
Verities and Realities of your Existence.
The Bliss of Growth,
The Glory of Action,
The Splendor of Beauty;
For Yesterday is but a Dream,
And To-morrow is only a Vision;
But To-day well lived makes
Every Yesterday a Dream of Happiness,
And every Tomorrow a Vision of Hope.
Look well therefore to this Day!
Such is the Salutation of the Dawn!

Next take inventory of your activities today. Where did you go? What did you do? Who did you meet? What did you

contribute? How did you affect your environment? How did the environment affect you?

Lastly visualize the next day of your life in the family and in the office or wherever you would be the next day. What do you want to see happen? For the family you might want harmony, understanding and unity. For work you might want to see that you are accomplishing your work goals and getting along with your boss and co-workers.

**Month 3, Week 2, Day 6**

Retire to your sacred place and practice a relaxation exercise. Inhale for four seconds. Hold the breath for four seconds. Exhale for four seconds. Hold the exhalation for four seconds. Repeat the process for as many times as possible.

Count from 50 backwards that is 50, 49, 48, etc, until you reach 1. Now count the normal way from 1 to 50. Next try counting from 1 to 100 and from 100 to 1. Concentrate on your counting and see the figures in your mind's eye as you count.

Now reflect on the following: Our task must be to free ourselves by widening our circle of compassion to embrace all living creatures and the whole of nature and its beauty. **Albert Einstein**

Next take inventory of your activities today. Where did you go? What did you do? Who did you meet? What did you contribute? How did you affect your environment? How did the environment affect you? Is there any thing you did that you could have done differently? How could you have done it next time?

Lastly visualize the next day of your life in the family and in the office or wherever you would be the next day. What do you want to see happen? For the family you might want harmony, understanding and unity. For work you might want to see that you

are accomplishing your work goals and getting along with your boss and co-workers.

**Month 3, Week 2, Day 7**

Attend a church, a temple, or any other meeting that brings you together with people for a common goal. If you do not have one you may begin today and find one that meets your interest and inclination. If you want you could also organize a group of your own. For instance you could start an Awakened Living Study Program. You may contact UNISM for more information.

Retire to your sacred place and practice a relaxation exercise. Inhale for four seconds. Hold the breath for four seconds. Exhale for four seconds. Hold the exhalation for four seconds. Repeat the process for as many times as possible.

Choose your favorite meditation posture and practice using the posture. For instance, if you use supports for your back during meditation start practicing your favorite posture without any support.

Next take inventory of your activities today. Where did you go? What did you do? Who did you meet? What did you contribute? How did you affect your environment? How did the environment affect you? Is there any thing you did that you could have done differently? How could you have done it next time?

Lastly visualize the next day of your life in the family and in the office or wherever you would be the next day. What do you want to see happen? For the family you might want harmony, understanding and unity. For work you might want to see that you are accomplishing your work goals and getting along with your boss and co-workers.

### Month 3, Week 3, Day 1

Retire to your sacred place and practice a relaxation exercise. Inhale for four seconds. Hold the breath for four seconds. Exhale for four seconds. Hold the exhalation for four seconds. Repeat the process for as many times as possible.

Count from 50 backwards that is 50, 49, 48, etc, until you reach 1. Now count the normal way from 1 to 50. Next try counting from 1 to 100 and from 100 to 1. Concentrate on your counting and see the figures in your mind's eye as you count.

Now consider some of the choices you made that taught you life lessons. Which of them improved your life? Relive the experience and consider ways to use that experience to help others in similar circumstances.

Next take inventory of your activities today. Where did you go? What did you do? Who did you meet? What did you contribute? How did you affect your environment? How did the environment affect you?

Lastly visualize the next day of your life in the family and in the office or wherever you would be the next day. What do you want to see happen? For the family you might want harmony, understanding and unity. For work you might want to see that you are accomplishing your work goals and getting along with your boss and co-workers.

### Month 3, Week 3, Day 2

Retire to your sacred place and practice a relaxation exercise. Inhale for four seconds. Hold the breath for four seconds. Exhale for four seconds. Hold the exhalation for four seconds. Repeat the process for as many times as possible.

Count from 50 backwards that is 50, 49, 48, etc, until you reach 1. Now count the normal way from 1 to 50. Next try

counting from 1 to 100 and from 100 to 1. Concentrate on your counting and see the figures in your mind's eye as you count.

Concentrate on the word "LOVE". Try to see the word in your mind's eye. Reflect on it. Explore it. Examine it thoroughly and try to understand all the aspects of LOVE. What does it mean to you? What is your concept of LOVE? What is the spiritual concept of LOVE? Compare both concepts and open your mind to all the streams of thoughts on LOVE. What do you know now about LOVE?

Next take inventory of your activities today. Where did you go? What did you do? Who did you meet? What did you contribute? How did you affect your environment? How did the environment affect you?

Lastly visualize the next day of your life in the family and in the office or wherever you would be the next day. What do you want to see happen? For the family you might want harmony, understanding and unity. For work you might want to see that you are accomplishing your work goals and getting along with your boss and co-workers.

### Month 3, Week 3, Day 3

Retire to your sacred place and practice a relaxation exercise. Inhale for four seconds. Hold the breath for four seconds. Exhale for four seconds. Hold the exhalation for four seconds. Repeat the process for as many times as possible.

Count from 50 backwards that is 50, 49, 48, etc, until you reach 1. Now count the normal way from 1 to 50. Next try counting from 1 to 100 and from 100 to 1. Concentrate on your counting and see the figures in your mind's eye as you count.

Next reflect on the Everlasting Life **by the Buddha**: Thousands of candles can be lighted from a single candle, and the life of the candle will not be shortened.

Next take inventory of your activities today. Where did you go? What did you do? Who did you meet? What did you contribute? How did you affect your environment? How did the environment affect you?

Lastly visualize the next day of your life in the family and in the office or wherever you would be the next day. What do you want to see happen? For the family you might want harmony, understanding and unity. For work you might want to see that you are accomplishing your work goals and getting along with your boss and co-workers.

## Month 3, Week 3, Day 4

Retire to your sacred place and practice a relaxation exercise. Inhale for four seconds. Hold the breath for four seconds. Exhale for four seconds. Hold the exhalation for four seconds. Repeat the process for as many times as possible.

Count from 50 backwards that is 50, 49, 48, etc, until you reach 1. Now count the normal way from 1 to 50. Next try counting from 1 to 100 and from 100 to 1. Concentrate on your counting and see the figures in your mind's eye as you count.

Next reflect on Believing **by the Buddha:** Believe nothing, no matter where you read it, or who said it, no matter if I have said it, unless it agrees with your own reason and your own common sense.

Next take inventory of your activities today. Where did you go? What did you do? Who did you meet? What did you contribute? How did you affect your environment? How did the environment affect you?

Lastly visualize the next day of your life in the family and in the office or wherever you would be the next day. What do you want to see happen? For the family you might want harmony, understanding and unity. For work you might want to see that you are accomplishing your work goals and getting along with your boss and co-workers.

**Month 3, Week 3, Day 5**

Retire to your sacred place and practice a relaxation exercise. Inhale for four seconds. Hold the breath for four seconds. Exhale for four seconds. Hold the exhalation for four seconds. Repeat the process for as many times as possible.

Count from 50 backwards that is 50, 49, 48, etc, until you reach 1. Now count the normal way from 1 to 50. Next try counting from 1 to 100 and from 100 to 1. Concentrate on your counting and see the figures in your mind's eye as you count.

Now reflect on **Learning by Anonymous**: Those who remember always that they know nothing, and who have become willing to learn everything, will learn it. But whenever they trust themselves, they will not learn. They have destroyed their motivation for learning by thinking they already know.

Next take inventory of your activities today. Where did you go? What did you do? Who did you meet? What did you contribute? How did you affect your environment? How did the environment affect you?

Lastly visualize the next day of your life in the family and in the office or wherever you would be the next day. What do you want to see happen? For the family you might want harmony, understanding and unity. For work you might want to see that you are accomplishing your work goals and getting along with your boss and co-workers.

### Month 3, Week 3, Day 6

Retire to your sacred place and practice a relaxation exercise. Inhale for four seconds. Hold the breath for four seconds. Exhale for four seconds. Hold the exhalation for four seconds. Repeat the process for as many times as possible.

Count from 50 backwards that is 50, 49, 48, etc, until you reach 1. Now count the normal way from 1 to 50. Next try counting from 1 to 100 and from 100 to 1. Concentrate on your counting and see the figures in your mind's eye as you count.

Now reflect on the following: The purpose of human life is to serve, and to show compassion and the will to help others.
**Albert Schweitzer**

Next take inventory of your activities today. Where did you go? What did you do? Who did you meet? What did you contribute? How did you affect your environment? How did the environment affect you? Is there any thing you did that you could have done differently? How could you have done it next time?

Lastly visualize the next day of your life in the family and in the office or wherever you would be the next day. What do you want to see happen? For the family you might want harmony, understanding and unity. For work you might want to see that you are accomplishing your work goals and getting along with your boss and co-workers.

### Month 3, Week 3, Day 7

Attend a church, a temple, or any other meeting that brings you together with people for a common goal. If you do not have one you may begin today and find one that meets your interest and inclination. If you want you could also organize a group of your own. For instance you could start an Awakened Living Study Program. You may contact UNISM for more information.

Retire to your sacred place and practice a relaxation exercise. Inhale for four seconds. Hold the breath for four seconds. Exhale for four seconds. Hold the exhalation for four seconds. Repeat the process for as many times as possible.

Choose your favorite meditation posture and practice using the posture. For instance, if you use supports for your back during meditation start practicing your favorite posture without any support.

Next take inventory of your activities today. Where did you go? What did you do? Who did you meet? What did you contribute? How did you affect your environment? How did the environment affect you? Is there any thing you did that you could have done differently? How could you have done it next time?

Lastly visualize the next day of your life in the family and in the office or wherever you would be the next day. What do you want to see happen? For the family you might want harmony, understanding and unity. For work you might want to see that you are accomplishing your work goals and getting along with your boss and co-workers.

### Month 3, Week 4, Day 1

Retire to your sacred place and practice a relaxation exercise. Inhale for four seconds. Hold the breath for four seconds. Exhale for four seconds. Hold the exhalation for four seconds. Repeat the process for as many times as possible.

Count from 50 backwards that is 50, 49, 48, etc, until you reach 1. Now count the normal way from 1 to 50. Next try counting from 1 to 100 and from 100 to 1. Concentrate on your counting and see the figures in your mind's eye as you count.

Take a specific problem to your meditation with the intent of solving it. Concentrate on the problem intensely. Examine the problem in an out and reflect on why you have not been able to find a solution to the problem. Now open up your mind for inspiration.

Next take inventory of your activities today. Where did you go? What did you do? Who did you meet? What did you contribute? How did you affect your environment? How did the environment affect you?

Lastly visualize the next day of your life in the family and in the office or wherever you would be the next day. What do you want to see happen? For the family you might want harmony, understanding and unity. For work you might want to see that you are accomplishing your work goals and getting along with your boss and co-workers.

## Month 3, Week 4, Day 2

Retire to your sacred place and practice a relaxation exercise. Inhale for four seconds. Hold the breath for four seconds. Exhale for four seconds. Hold the exhalation for four seconds. Repeat the process for as many times as possible.

Count from 50 backwards that is 50, 49, 48, etc, until you reach 1. Now count the normal way from 1 to 50. Next try counting from 1 to 100 and from 100 to 1. Concentrate on your counting and see the figures in your mind's eye as you count.

Next reflect on the Independence **by the Buddha:** "Therefore, be islands unto yourselves. Be your own refuge. Have recourse to none else for refuge. Hold fast to the Dharma as a refuge. Resort to no other refuge. Whosoever, either now or after I am gone, shall be islands unto themselves, shall seek no eternal refuge, it is they, among my disciples who shall reach the very topmost height! But they must be keen to progress."

Next take inventory of your activities today. Where did you go? What did you do? Who did you meet? What did you contribute? How did you affect your environment? How did the environment affect you?

Lastly visualize the next day of your life in the family and in the office or wherever you would be the next day. What do you want to see happen? For the family you might want harmony, understanding and unity. For work you might want to see that you are accomplishing your work goals and getting along with your boss and co-workers.

### Month 3, Week 4, Day 3

Retire to your sacred place and practice a relaxation exercise. Inhale for four seconds. Hold the breath for four seconds. Exhale for four seconds. Hold the exhalation for four seconds. Repeat the process for as many times as possible.

Count from 50 backwards that is 50, 49, 48, etc, until you reach 1. Now count the normal way from 1 to 50. Next try counting from 1 to 100 and from 100 to 1. Concentrate on your counting and see the figures in your mind's eye as you count.

Now reflect of the following: A generous heart, kind speech, and a life of service and compassion are the things which renew humanity. **The Buddha**

Next take inventory of your activities today. Where did you go? What did you do? Who did you meet? What did you contribute? How did you affect your environment? How did the environment affect you?

Lastly visualize the next day of your life in the family and in the office or wherever you would be the next day. What do you want to see happen? For the family you might want harmony, understanding and unity. For work you might want to see that you

are accomplishing your work goals and getting along with your boss and co-workers.

**Month 3, Week 4, Day 4**

Retire to your sacred place and practice a relaxation exercise. Inhale for four seconds. Hold the breath for four seconds. Exhale for four seconds. Hold the exhalation for four seconds. Repeat the process for as many times as possible.

Count from 50 backwards that is 50, 49, 48, etc, until you reach 1. Now count the normal way from 1 to 50. Next try counting from 1 to 100 and from 100 to 1. Concentrate on your counting and see the figures in your mind's eye as you count.

Now consider the nature of life that involves killing and eating. How does that make you feel? How do you reconcile this act of killing for food with something good? One way is to consider the victim as a voluntary sacrifice for your life. In this way you feel gratitude for the sacrifice and at the same time feel an obligation to live your life in such a way as befits the sacrifice. Meditate on this thought on how best to live your life.

Next take inventory of your activities today. Where did you go? What did you do? Who did you meet? What did you contribute? How did you affect your environment? How did the environment affect you?

Lastly visualize the next day of your life in the family and in the office or wherever you would be the next day. What do you want to see happen? For the family you might want harmony, understanding and unity. For work you might want to see that you are accomplishing your work goals and getting along with your boss and co-workers.

**Month 3, Week 4, Day 5**

Retire to your sacred place and practice a relaxation exercise. Inhale for four seconds. Hold the breath for four seconds. Exhale for four seconds. Hold the exhalation for four seconds. Repeat the process for as many times as possible.

Count from 50 backwards that is 50, 49, 48, etc, until you reach 1. Now count the normal way from 1 to 50. Next try counting from 1 to 100 and from 100 to 1. Concentrate on your counting and see the figures in your mind's eye as you count.

Now reflect on **I Promise myself by Christian D Larson:**

**I Promise Myself**

To forget the mistakes of the past and press on
to the greater achievements of the future.
To wear a cheerful expression at all times
and give a smile to every living creature I meet.
To give so much time to improving myself
that I have no time to criticize others.
To be too large for worry, too noble for anger,
too strong for fear, and too happy to permit the presence of trouble.
To think well of myself and to proclaim this fact to the world,
not in loud words, but in great deeds.
To live in the faith that the whole world is on my side,
so long as I am true to the best that is in me.

Next take inventory of your activities today. Where did you go? What did you do? Who did you meet? What did you contribute? How did you affect your environment? How did the environment affect you?

Lastly visualize the next day of your life in the family and in the office or wherever you would be the next day. What do you want to see happen? For the family you might want harmony, understanding and unity. For work you might want to see that you

are accomplishing your work goals and getting along with your boss and co-workers.

### Month 3, Week 4, Day 6

Retire to your sacred place and practice a relaxation exercise. Inhale for four seconds. Hold the breath for four seconds. Exhale for four seconds. Hold the exhalation for four seconds. Repeat the process for as many times as possible.

Count from 50 backwards that is 50, 49, 48, etc, until you reach 1. Now count the normal way from 1 to 50. Next try counting from 1 to 100 and from 100 to 1. Concentrate on your counting and see the figures in your mind's eye as you count.

Now reflect on the following: To forgive is to set a prisoner free and discover that the prisoner was you. **Lewis B. Smedes**

Next take inventory of your activities today. Where did you go? What did you do? Who did you meet? What did you contribute? How did you affect your environment? How did the environment affect you? Is there any thing you did that you could have done differently? How could you have done it next time?

Lastly visualize the next day of your life in the family and in the office or wherever you would be the next day. What do you want to see happen? For the family you might want harmony, understanding and unity. For work you might want to see that you are accomplishing your work goals and getting along with your boss and co-workers.

### Month 3, Week 4, Day 7

Attend a church, a temple, or any other meeting that brings you together with people for a common goal. If you do not have one you may begin today and find one that meets your interest and inclination. If you want you could also organize a group of your

own. For instance you could start an Awakened Living Study Program. You may contact UNISM for more information.

Retire to your sacred place and practice a relaxation exercise. Inhale for four seconds. Hold the breath for four seconds. Exhale for four seconds. Hold the exhalation for four seconds. Repeat the process for as many times as possible.

Choose your favorite meditation posture and practice using the posture. For instance, if you use supports for your back during meditation start practicing your favorite posture without any support.

Next take inventory of your activities today. Where did you go? What did you do? Who did you meet? What did you contribute? How did you affect your environment? How did the environment affect you? Is there any thing you did that you could have done differently? How could you have done it next time?

Lastly visualize the next day of your life in the family and in the office or wherever you would be the next day. What do you want to see happen? For the family you might want harmony, understanding and unity. For work you might want to see that you are accomplishing your work goals and getting along with your boss and co-workers.

## Individual Meditation: Fourth Month

Goal

The goal of the fourth month of meditation is to know the Earth. How often have you paid attention to the soil, grasses, flowers, plants and trees around your home? When last did you observe a river, a lake, a sea or an ocean? Have you ever wondered about the wood or forest in your area? What about the wind, waterfall, rain, the snow and the sunshine? Lastly do not forget the hills and the mountains.

Month 4, Week 1, Day 1

Retire to your sacred place and practice a relaxation exercise. Inhale for four seconds. Hold the breath for four seconds. Exhale for four seconds. Hold the exhalation for four seconds. Repeat the process for as many times as possible.

Count from 50 backwards that is 50, 49, 48, etc, until you reach 1. Now count the normal way from 1 to 50. Next try counting from 1 to 100 and from 100 to 1. Concentrate on your counting and see the figures in your mind's eye as you count.

Now imagine getting out to your backyard on a Sunday morning bare feet. Feel the soil under your feet. Feel the grass under your feet. Reflect on what you feel. Touch the grass with your hand. Touch the soil with your hand. Reflect on what you feel. Do it for real when you feel like it.

Next take inventory of your activities today. Where did you go? What did you do? Who did you meet? What did you contribute? How did you affect your environment? How did the environment affect you?

Lastly visualize the next day of your life in the family and in the office or wherever you would be the next day. What do you

want to see happen? For the family you might want harmony, understanding and unity. For work you might want to see that you are accomplishing your work goals and getting along with your boss and co-workers.

### Month 4, Week 1, Day 2

Retire to your sacred place and practice a relaxation exercise. Inhale for four seconds. Hold the breath for four seconds. Exhale for four seconds. Hold the exhalation for four seconds. Repeat the process for as many times as possible.

Count from 50 backwards that is 50, 49, 48, etc, until you reach 1. Now count the normal way from 1 to 50. Next try counting from 1 to 100 and from 100 to 1. Concentrate on your counting and see the figures in your mind's eye as you count.

Consider climbing a mountain. You have all your climbing materials. Just put them on and begin to climb. Which mountain are you climbing? Who else is climbing with you? Observe the birds, plants, flowers and trees. When you reach the summit sit down and reflect on your climb from the beginning to the end. Consider the obstacles. What kept you going? Relate your thoughts to a real life experience.

Next take inventory of your activities today. Where did you go? What did you do? Who did you meet? What did you contribute? How did you affect your environment? How did the environment affect you?

Lastly visualize the next day of your life in the family and in the office or wherever you would be the next day. What do you want to see happen? For the family you might want harmony, understanding and unity. For work you might want to see that you are accomplishing your work goals and getting along with your boss and co-workers.

### Month 4, Week 1, Day 3

Retire to your sacred place and practice a relaxation exercise. Inhale for four seconds. Hold the breath for four seconds. Exhale for four seconds. Hold the exhalation for four seconds. Repeat the process for as many times as possible.

Count from 50 backwards that is 50, 49, 48, etc, until you reach 1. Now count the normal way from 1 to 50. Next try counting from 1 to 100 and from 100 to 1. Concentrate on your counting and see the figures in your mind's eye as you count.

Meditate visiting your neighbor. Have a gift with you. It could be a card or something you made. Walk to your neighbor's home and knock at the door. Your neighbor opens the door with a smile. Give the gift and note the reaction. What did he say? What did she say? How do you feel? Do this in real life!

Next take inventory of your activities today. Where did you go? What did you do? Who did you meet? What did you contribute? How did you affect your environment? How did the environment affect you?

Lastly visualize the next day of your life in the family and in the office or wherever you would be the next day. What do you want to see happen? For the family you might want harmony, understanding and unity. For work you might want to see that you are accomplishing your work goals and getting along with your boss and co-workers.

### Month 4, Week 1, Day 4

Retire to your sacred place and practice a relaxation exercise. Inhale for four seconds. Hold the breath for four seconds. Exhale for four seconds. Hold the exhalation for four seconds. Repeat the process for as many times as possible.

Count from 50 backwards that is 50, 49, 48, etc, until you reach 1. Now count the normal way from 1 to 50. Next try counting from 1 to 100 and from 100 to 1. Concentrate on your counting and see the figures in your mind's eye as you count.

Get into your boat on a Saturday morning and begin to drift with the tide on your favorite river. Name the river. Do not do anything. Just sit down in one place in the boat and observe. What do you see? How does it feel? How far did you go? You can also do this in real life.

Next take inventory of your activities today. Where did you go? What did you do? Who did you meet? What did you contribute? How did you affect your environment? How did the environment affect you?

Lastly visualize the next day of your life in the family and in the office or wherever you would be the next day. What do you want to see happen? For the family you might want harmony, understanding and unity. For work you might want to see that you are accomplishing your work goals and getting along with your boss and co-workers.

**Month 4, Week 1, Day 5**

Retire to your sacred place and practice a relaxation exercise. Inhale for four seconds. Hold the breath for four seconds. Exhale for four seconds. Hold the exhalation for four seconds. Repeat the process for as many times as possible.

Count from 50 backwards that is 50, 49, 48, etc, until you reach 1. Now count the normal way from 1 to 50. Next try counting from 1 to 100 and from 100 to 1. Concentrate on your counting and see the figures in your mind's eye as you count.

Now meditate on the parable of the Precious Gift by Anonymous: A wise woman who was traveling in the mountains found a precious stone in a stream. The next day she met another traveler who was hungry, and the wise woman opened her bag to share her food. The hungry traveler saw the precious stone and asked the woman to give it to him. She did so without hesitation. The traveler left rejoicing in his good fortune. He knew the stone was worth enough to give him security for a lifetime. But, a few days later, he came back to return the stone to the wise woman. "I've been thinking," he said. "I know how valuable this stone is, but I give it back in the hope that you can give me something even more precious. Give me what you have within you that enabled you to give me this stone. "Sometimes it's not the wealth you have but what's inside you that others need."

Next take inventory of your activities today. Where did you go? What did you do? Who did you meet? What did you contribute? How did you affect your environment? How did the environment affect you?

Lastly visualize the next day of your life in the family and in the office or wherever you would be the next day. What do you want to see happen? For the family you might want harmony, understanding and unity. For work you might want to see that you are accomplishing your work goals and getting along with your boss and co-workers.

**Month 4, Week 1, Day 6**

Retire to your sacred place and practice a relaxation exercise. Inhale for four seconds. Hold the breath for four seconds. Exhale for four seconds. Hold the exhalation for four seconds. Repeat the process for as many times as possible.

Count from 50 backwards that is 50, 49, 48, etc, until you reach 1. Now count the normal way from 1 to 50. Next try

counting from 1 to 100 and from 100 to 1. Concentrate on your counting and see the figures in your mind's eye as you count.

Now reflect on the following: My son, observe the postage stamp! Its usefulness depends upon its ability to stick to one thing until it gets there. Henry Wheeler Shaw

Next take inventory of your activities today. Where did you go? What did you do? Who did you meet? What did you contribute? How did you affect your environment? How did the environment affect you? Is there any thing you did that you could have done differently? How could you have done it next time?

Lastly visualize the next day of your life in the family and in the office or wherever you would be the next day. What do you want to see happen? For the family you might want harmony, understanding and unity. For work you might want to see that you are accomplishing your work goals and getting along with your boss and co-workers.

**Month 4, Week 1, Day 7**

Attend a church, a temple, or any other meeting that brings you together with people for a common goal. If you do not have one you may begin today and find one that meets your interest and inclination. If you want you could also organize a group of your own. For instance you could start an Awakened Living Study Program. You may contact UNISM for more information.

Retire to your sacred place and practice a relaxation exercise. Inhale for four seconds. Hold the breath for four seconds. Exhale for four seconds. Hold the exhalation for four seconds. Repeat the process for as many times as possible.

Choose your favorite meditation posture and practice using the posture. For instance, if you use supports for your back during

meditation start practicing your favorite posture without any support.

Next take inventory of your activities today. Where did you go? What did you do? Who did you meet? What did you contribute? How did you affect your environment? How did the environment affect you? Is there any thing you did that you could have done differently? How could you have done it next time?

Lastly visualize the next day of your life in the family and in the office or wherever you would be the next day. What do you want to see happen? For the family you might want harmony, understanding and unity. For work you might want to see that you are accomplishing your work goals and getting along with your boss and co-workers.

**Month 4, Week 2, Day 1**

Retire to your sacred place and practice a relaxation exercise. Inhale for four seconds. Hold the breath for four seconds. Exhale for four seconds. Hold the exhalation for four seconds. Repeat the process for as many times as possible.

Count from 50 backwards that is 50, 49, 48, etc, until you reach 1. Now count the normal way from 1 to 50. Next try counting from 1 to 100 and from 100 to 1. Concentrate on your counting and see the figures in your mind's eye as you count.

Next reflect on the Existence by **the Buddha:**
*"This existence of ours is as transient as autumn clouds,*
*To watch the birth and death of beings is like looking at the*
*Movements of dance,*
*A lifetime is like a flash of lightning in the sky,*
*Rushing by, like a torrent down a steep mountain.*

Next take inventory of your activities today. Where did you go? What did you do? Who did you meet? What did you

contribute? How did you affect your environment? How did the environment affect you?

Lastly visualize the next day of your life in the family and in the office or wherever you would be the next day. What do you want to see happen? For the family you might want harmony, understanding and unity. For work you might want to see that you are accomplishing your work goals and getting along with your boss and co-workers.

### Month 4, Week 2, Day 2

Retire to your sacred place and practice a relaxation exercise. Inhale for four seconds. Hold the breath for four seconds. Exhale for four seconds. Hold the exhalation for four seconds. Repeat the process for as many times as possible.

Count from 50 backwards that is 50, 49, 48, etc, until you reach 1. Now count the normal way from 1 to 50. Next try counting from 1 to 100 and from 100 to 1. Concentrate on your counting and see the figures in your mind's eye as you count.

Imagine stepping outside very early in the morning and observing the darkness as it fades and is overtaken by the daylight. Visualize the Light passing through your body making you whole and enlightening your life. Direct this Light to the troubled areas of the world and to all people in darkness. Now see the Light illuminating the troubled areas of the world and enlightening people in darkness.

Next take inventory of your activities today. Where did you go? What did you do? Who did you meet? What did you contribute? How did you affect your environment? How did the environment affect you?

Now visualize the next day of your life in the family and in the office or wherever you would be the next day. What do you

want to see happen? For the family you might want harmony, understanding and unity. For work you might want to see that you are accomplishing your work goals and getting along with your boss and co-workers.

### Month 4, Week 2, Day 3

Retire to your sacred place and practice a relaxation exercise. Inhale for four seconds. Hold the breath for four seconds. Exhale for four seconds. Hold the exhalation for four seconds. Repeat the process for as many times as possible.

Count from 50 backwards that is 50, 49, 48, etc, until you reach 1. Now count the normal way from 1 to 50. Next try counting from 1 to 100 and from 100 to 1. Concentrate on your counting and see the figures in your mind's eye as you count.

Meditate on stepping outside very early in the morning and looking up toward heaven. Observe the sky as the darkness fades. Reflect on the beauty and wonder of the limitless heaven. Place your faith in heaven and have faith in yourself.

Next take inventory of your activities today. Where did you go? What did you do? Who did you meet? What did you contribute? How did you affect your environment? How did the environment affect you?

Now visualize the next day of your life in the family and in the office or wherever you would be the next day. What do you want to see happen? For the family you might want harmony, understanding and unity. For work you might want to see that you are accomplishing your work goals and getting along with your boss and co-workers.

**Month 4, Week 2, Day 4**

Retire to your sacred place and practice a relaxation exercise. Inhale for four seconds. Hold the breath for four seconds. Exhale for four seconds. Hold the exhalation for four seconds. Repeat the process for as many times as possible.

Count from 50 backwards that is 50, 49, 48, etc, until you reach 1. Now count the normal way from 1 to 50. Next try counting from 1 to 100 and from 100 to 1. Concentrate on your counting and see the figures in your mind's eye as you count.

Imagine visiting a park by a river. Consider a turbulent ocean and a peaceful river. Compare the turbulent ocean to the calm river. Think about the whole expanse of water. Reflect on the flowing and the ebbing of river, seas and oceans. How does this relate to your life?

Next take inventory of your activities today. Where did you go? What did you do? Who did you meet? What did you contribute? How did you affect your environment? How did the environment affect you?

Now visualize the next day of your life in the family and in the office or wherever you would be the next day. What do you want to see happen? For the family you might want harmony, understanding and unity. For work you might want to see that you are accomplishing your work goals and getting along with your boss and co-workers.

**Month 4, Week 2, Day 5**

Retire to your sacred place and practice a relaxation exercise. Inhale for four seconds. Hold the breath for four seconds. Exhale for four seconds. Hold the exhalation for four seconds. Repeat the process for as many times as possible.

Count from 50 backwards that is 50, 49, 48, etc, until you reach 1. Now count the normal way from 1 to 50. Next try counting from 1 to 100 and from 100 to 1. Concentrate on your counting and see the figures in your mind's eye as you count.

Now meditate on Awakening Compassion by Ken McLeod: As compassion deepens, we find ourselves developing a nobility of the heart. Increasingly, and often to our surprise, we respond to difficult situations with calmness, clarity and directness. A quiet fearlessness or confidence is present as we no longer fear that we will compromise our own integrity. We find, too, a joy which arises from the knowledge that our every act is meaningful and helpful to the world.

Next take inventory of your activities today. Where did you go? What did you do? Who did you meet? What did you contribute? How did you affect your environment? How did the environment affect you?

Now visualize the next day of your life in the family and in the office or wherever you would be the next day. What do you want to see happen? For the family you might want harmony, understanding and unity. For work you might want to see that you are accomplishing your work goals and getting along with your boss and co-workers.

**Month 2, Week 2, Day 6**

Retire to your sacred place and practice a relaxation exercise. Inhale for four seconds. Hold the breath for four seconds. Exhale for four seconds. Hold the exhalation for four seconds. Repeat the process for as many times as possible.

Count from 50 backwards that is 50, 49, 48, etc, until you reach 1. Now count the normal way from 1 to 50. Next try

counting from 1 to 100 and from 100 to 1. Concentrate on your counting and see the figures in your mind's eye as you count.

Now reflect on the following: The mind is indeed restless, Arjuna: it is indeed hard to train. But by constant practice and by freedom from passions the mind in truth can be trained. Hinduism: Bhagavad Gita 6:35

Next take inventory of your activities today. Where did you go? What did you do? Who did you meet? What did you contribute? How did you affect your environment? How did the environment affect you? Is there any thing you did that you could have done differently? How could you have done it next time?

Lastly visualize the next day of your life in the family and in the office or wherever you would be the next day. What do you want to see happen? For the family you might want harmony, understanding and unity. For work you might want to see that you are accomplishing your work goals and getting along with your boss and co-workers.

**Month 4, Week 2, Day 7**

Attend a church, a temple, or any other meeting that brings you together with people for a common goal. If you do not have one you may begin today and find one that meets your interest and inclination. If you want you could also organize a group of your own. For instance you could start an Awakened Living Study Program. You may contact UNISM for more information.

Retire to your sacred place and practice a relaxation exercise. Inhale for four seconds. Hold the breath for four seconds. Exhale for four seconds. Hold the exhalation for four seconds. Repeat the process for as many times as possible.

Choose your favorite meditation posture and practice using the posture. For instance, if you use supports for your back during

meditation start practicing your favorite posture without any support.

Next take inventory of your activities today. Where did you go? What did you do? Who did you meet? What did you contribute? How did you affect your environment? How did the environment affect you? Is there any thing you did that you could have done differently? How could you have done it next time?

Lastly visualize the next day of your life in the family and in the office or wherever you would be the next day. What do you want to see happen? For the family you might want harmony, understanding and unity. For work you might want to see that you are accomplishing your work goals and getting along with your boss and co-workers.

**Month 4, Week 3, Day 1**

Retire to your sacred place and practice a relaxation exercise. Inhale for four seconds. Hold the breath for four seconds. Exhale for four seconds. Hold the exhalation for four seconds. Repeat the process for as many times as possible.

Count from 50 backwards that is 50, 49, 48, etc, until you reach 1. Now count the normal way from 1 to 50. Next try counting from 1 to 100 and from 100 to 1. Concentrate on your counting and see the figures in your mind's eye as you count.

Visit a lake. Sit in a comfortable place where you could observe the lake. Notice the calm atmosphere around the lake. Reflect on the calmness and try to merge with it. In other words bring the same calmness to your world.

Next take inventory of your activities today. Where did you go? What did you do? Who did you meet? What did you contribute? How did you affect your environment? How did the environment affect you?

Now visualize the next day of your life in the family and in the office or wherever you would be the next day. What do you want to see happen? For the family you might want harmony, understanding and unity. For work you might want to see that you are accomplishing your work goals and getting along with your boss and co-workers.

**Month 4, Week 3, Day 2**

Retire to your sacred place and practice a relaxation exercise. Inhale for four seconds. Hold the breath for four seconds. Exhale for four seconds. Hold the exhalation for four seconds. Repeat the process for as many times as possible.

Count from 50 backwards that is 50, 49, 48, etc, until you reach 1. Now count the normal way from 1 to 50. Next try counting from 1 to 100 and from 100 to 1. Concentrate on your counting and see the figures in your mind's eye as you count.

Imagine stepping outside very early in the morning and observing the plants, flowers and trees. Consider a plant and reflect on its life. How does it live without human care? How does it grow? Where did it get the magnificent colors of the flowers? What is the partnership between land, sea, and plants? Enjoy the peacefulness of the environment. Visualize this peace as present in your life and in the world.

Next take inventory of your activities today. Where did you go? What did you do? Who did you meet? What did you contribute? How did you affect your environment? How did the environment affect you?

Now visualize the next day of your life in the family and in the office or wherever you would be the next day. What do you want to see happen? For the family you might want harmony, understanding and unity. For work you might want to see that you

are accomplishing your work goals and getting along with your boss and co-workers.

**Month 4, Week 3, Day 3**

Retire to your sacred place and practice a relaxation exercise. Inhale for four seconds. Hold the breath for four seconds. Exhale for four seconds. Hold the exhalation for four seconds. Repeat the process for as many times as possible.

Count from 50 backwards that is 50, 49, 48, etc, until you reach 1. Now count the normal way from 1 to 50. Next try counting from 1 to 100 and from 100 to 1. Concentrate on your counting and see the figures in your mind's eye as you count.

Imagine stepping outside very early in the morning before the sun rises. Watch the sky as the sun rises. Name the benefits of the sun to the earth. Reflect on an Earth without a sun. What do you see? Reflect on the very nature of the sun.

Next take inventory of your activities today. Where did you go? What did you do? Who did you meet? What did you contribute? How did you affect your environment? How did the environment affect you?

Now visualize the next day of your life in the family and in the office or wherever you would be the next day. What do you want to see happen? For the family you might want harmony, understanding and unity. For work you might want to see that you are accomplishing your work goals and getting along with your boss and co-workers.

**Month 4, Week 3, Day 4**

Retire to your sacred place and practice a relaxation exercise. Inhale for four seconds. Hold the breath for four seconds.

Exhale for four seconds. Hold the exhalation for four seconds. Repeat the process for as many times as possible.

Count from 50 backwards that is 50, 49, 48, etc, until you reach 1. Now count the normal way from 1 to 50. Next try counting from 1 to 100 and from 100 to 1. Concentrate on your counting and see the figures in your mind's eye as you count.

Imagine stepping into a night of moon and stars. Observe the constellations, the brightness and the number of stars. Who lights the stars?

Next take inventory of your activities today. Where did you go? What did you do? Who did you meet? What did you contribute? How did you affect your environment? How did the environment affect you?

Now visualize the next day of your life in the family and in the office or wherever you would be the next day. What do you want to see happen? For the family you might want harmony, understanding and unity. For work you might want to see that you are accomplishing your work goals and getting along with your boss and co-workers.

### Month 4, Week 3, Day 5

Retire to your sacred place and practice a relaxation exercise. Inhale for four seconds. Hold the breath for four seconds. Exhale for four seconds. Hold the exhalation for four seconds. Repeat the process for as many times as possible.

Count from 50 backwards that is 50, 49, 48, etc, until you reach 1. Now count the normal way from 1 to 50. Next try counting from 1 to 100 and from 100 to 1. Concentrate on your counting and see the figures in your mind's eye as you count.

Now meditate on Acts of Kindness Benefit Everyone by The Dalai Lama:

Do you really want to be happy? Everyone says yes, but the gateway to happiness makes some of us frown. The gateway to happiness, is giving to others. Think about this: "If you want others to be happy, practice compassion. If you want to be happy, practice compassion."

Next take inventory of your activities today. Where did you go? What did you do? Who did you meet? What did you contribute? How did you affect your environment? How did the environment affect you?

Now visualize the next day of your life in the family and in the office or wherever you would be the next day. What do you want to see happen? For the family you might want harmony, understanding and unity. For work you might want to see that you are accomplishing your work goals and getting along with your boss and co-workers.

**Month 4, Week 3, Day 6**

Retire to your sacred place and practice a relaxation exercise. Inhale for four seconds. Hold the breath for four seconds. Exhale for four seconds. Hold the exhalation for four seconds. Repeat the process for as many times as possible.

Count from 50 backwards that is 50, 49, 48, etc, until you reach 1. Now count the normal way from 1 to 50. Next try counting from 1 to 100 and from 100 to 1. Concentrate on your counting and see the figures in your mind's eye as you count.

Now reflect on the following: Prosperity forsakes those who always dream of fate and favors those who persevere. One should therefore always be active and alert. Hinduism: Matsya Purana 221.2

Next take inventory of your activities today. Where did you go? What did you do? Who did you meet? What did you

contribute? How did you affect your environment? How did the environment affect you? Is there any thing you did that you could have done differently? How could you have done it next time?

Lastly visualize the next day of your life in the family and in the office or wherever you would be the next day. What do you want to see happen? For the family you might want harmony, understanding and unity. For work you might want to see that you are accomplishing your work goals and getting along with your boss and co-workers.

**Month 4, Week 3, Day 7**

Attend a church, a temple, or any other meeting that brings you together with people for a common goal. If you do not have one you may begin today and find one that meets your interest and inclination. If you want you could also organize a group of your own. For instance you could start an Awakened Living Study Program. You may contact UNISM for more information.

Retire to your sacred place and practice a relaxation exercise. Inhale for four seconds. Hold the breath for four seconds. Exhale for four seconds. Hold the exhalation for four seconds. Repeat the process for as many times as possible.

Choose your favorite meditation posture and practice using the posture. For instance, if you use supports for your back during meditation start practicing your favorite posture without any support.

Next take inventory of your activities today. Where did you go? What did you do? Who did you meet? What did you contribute? How did you affect your environment? How did the environment affect you? Is there any thing you did that you could have done differently? How could you have done it next time?

Lastly visualize the next day of your life in the family and in the office or wherever you would be the next day. What do you want to see happen? For the family you might want harmony, understanding and unity. For work you might want to see that you are accomplishing your work goals and getting along with your boss and co-workers.

**Month 4, Week 4, Day 1**

Retire to your sacred place and practice a relaxation exercise. Inhale for four seconds. Hold the breath for four seconds. Exhale for four seconds. Hold the exhalation for four seconds. Repeat the process for as many times as possible.

Count from 50 backwards that is 50, 49, 48, etc, until you reach 1. Now count the normal way from 1 to 50. Next try counting from 1 to 100 and from 100 to 1. Concentrate on your counting and see the figures in your mind's eye as you count.

Imagine stepping out into a night of moon and stars. Reflect on the moon. Why does it wax and wane? Who lights the moon? Reflect on when time started. How does time affect your life on Earth? Reflect on the fact that your time is limited on Earth.

Next take inventory of your activities today. Where did you go? What did you do? Who did you meet? What did you contribute? How did you affect your environment? How did the environment affect you?

Now visualize the next day of your life in the family and in the office or wherever you would be the next day. What do you want to see happen? For the family you might want harmony, understanding and unity. For work you might want to see that you are accomplishing your work goals and getting along with your boss and co-workers.

**Month 4, Week 4, Day 2**

Retire to your sacred place and practice a relaxation exercise. Inhale for four seconds. Hold the breath for four seconds. Exhale for four seconds. Hold the exhalation for four seconds. Repeat the process for as many times as possible.

Count from 50 backwards that is 50, 49, 48, etc, until you reach 1. Now count the normal way from 1 to 50. Next try counting from 1 to 100 and from 100 to 1. Concentrate on your counting and see the figures in your mind's eye as you count.

Imagine visiting a nearby river or lake where you could see fishes in their natural habitat. Reflect on the life of a fish. It swims, eats and reproduces without human intervention. What is the driving force behind the fish? Compare the life of a fish with your life. How are they similar? How are they different?

Next take inventory of your activities today. Where did you go? What did you do? Who did you meet? What did you contribute? How did you affect your environment? How did the environment affect you?

Now visualize the next day of your life in the family and in the office or wherever you would be the next day. What do you want to see happen? For the family you might want harmony, understanding and unity. For work you might want to see that you are accomplishing your work goals and getting along with your boss and co-workers.

**Month 4, Week 4, Day 3**

Retire to your sacred place and practice a relaxation exercise. Inhale for four seconds. Hold the breath for four seconds. Exhale for four seconds. Hold the exhalation for four seconds. Repeat the process for as many times as possible.

Count from 50 backwards that is 50, 49, 48, etc, until you reach 1. Now count the normal way from 1 to 50. Next try counting from 1 to 100 and from 100 to 1. Concentrate on your counting and see the figures in your mind's eye as you count.

Imagine visiting an aviary or any place where you could observe the birds of the air. They neither sow nor reap yet they live. They fly, eat, reproduce and take care of their young ones. What is the power behind their lives? Compare the life of a bird with your life. How are they similar? How are they different?

Next take inventory of your activities today. Where did you go? What did you do? Who did you meet? What did you contribute? How did you affect your environment? How did the environment affect you?

Now visualize the next day of your life in the family and in the office or wherever you would be the next day. What do you want to see happen? For the family you might want harmony, understanding and unity. For work you might want to see that you are accomplishing your work goals and getting along with your boss and co-workers.

**Month 4, Week 4, Day 4**

Retire to your sacred place and practice a relaxation exercise. Inhale for four seconds. Hold the breath for four seconds. Exhale for four seconds. Hold the exhalation for four seconds. Repeat the process for as many times as possible.

Count from 50 backwards that is 50, 49, 48, etc, until you reach 1. Now count the normal way from 1 to 50. Next try counting from 1 to 100 and from 100 to 1. Concentrate on your counting and see the figures in your mind's eye as you count.

Imagine visiting a zoo or any place where you could observe an animal. They walk, run, eat, reproduce and take care of their young ones. What is the power behind their lives? Compare the life of an animal with your life. How are they similar? How are they different?

Next take inventory of your activities today. Where did you go? What did you do? Who did you meet? What did you contribute? How did you affect your environment? How did the environment affect you?

Now visualize the next day of your life in the family and in the office or wherever you would be the next day. What do you want to see happen? For the family you might want harmony, understanding and unity. For work you might want to see that you are accomplishing your work goals and getting along with your boss and co-workers.

**Month 4, Week 4, Day 5**

Retire to your sacred place and practice a relaxation exercise. Inhale for four seconds. Hold the breath for four seconds. Exhale for four seconds. Hold the exhalation for four seconds. Repeat the process for as many times as possible.

Count from 50 backwards that is 50, 49, 48, etc, until you reach 1. Now count the normal way from 1 to 50. Next try counting from 1 to 100 and from 100 to 1. Concentrate on your counting and see the figures in your mind's eye as you count.

Now meditate on In Heaven we Feed each other by ValerieT: There is an ancient Chinese parable about an old man who knew he would die soon. He wanted to know what Heaven and hell were like. He visited a wise man in his village to ask "Can you tell me what Heaven and hell are like?" The wise man led him down a strange path, deep into the countryside. Finally they came upon a large house with many rooms and went inside. Inside they found lots of people and many enormous tables with an incredible array of food. Then the old man noticed a strange thing, the people, all thin and hungry were holding chopsticks 12 feet long. They tried to feed themselves, but of course could not get the food to their mouths with such long chopsticks. The old man then said to the wise man "Now I know what hell looks like, will you please show me what Heaven looks like?" The wise man led him down the same path a little further until they came upon another large house similar to the first. They went inside and saw many people well fed and happy, they too had chopsticks 12 feet long. This puzzled the old man and he asked, "I see all of these people have 12 feet chopsticks too, yet they are well fed and happy, please explain this to me. The wise man replied, "in Heaven we feed each other"

Next take inventory of your activities today. Where did you go? What did you do? Who did you meet? What did you contribute? How did you affect your environment? How did the environment affect you?

Now visualize the next day of your life in the family and in the office or wherever you would be the next day. What do you want to see happen? For the family you might want harmony, understanding and unity. For work you might want to see that you are accomplishing your work goals and getting along with your boss and co-workers.

**Month 4, Week 4, Day 6**

Retire to your sacred place and practice a relaxation exercise. Inhale for four seconds. Hold the breath for four seconds. Exhale for four seconds. Hold the exhalation for four seconds. Repeat the process for as many times as possible.

Count from 50 backwards that is 50, 49, 48, etc, until you reach 1. Now count the normal way from 1 to 50. Next try

counting from 1 to 100 and from 100 to 1. Concentrate on your counting and see the figures in your mind's eye as you count.

Now reflect on the following: Every sunrise is an invitation for us to arise and brighten someone's day." Richelle E. Goodrich

Next take inventory of your activities today. Where did you go? What did you do? Who did you meet? What did you contribute? How did you affect your environment? How did the environment affect you? Is there any thing you did that you could have done differently? How could you have done it next time?

Lastly visualize the next day of your life in the family and in the office or wherever you would be the next day. What do you want to see happen? For the family you might want harmony, understanding and unity. For work you might want to see that you are accomplishing your work goals and getting along with your boss and co-workers.

**Month 4, Week 4, Day 7**

Attend a church, a temple, or any other meeting that brings you together with people for a common goal. If you do not have one you may begin today and find one that meets your interest and inclination. If you want you could also organize a group of your own. For instance you could start an Awakened Living Study Program. You may contact UNISM for more information.

Retire to your sacred place and practice a relaxation exercise. Inhale for four seconds. Hold the breath for four seconds. Exhale for four seconds. Hold the exhalation for four seconds. Repeat the process for as many times as possible.

Choose your favorite meditation posture and practice using the posture. For instance, if you use supports for your back during meditation start practicing your favorite posture without any support.

Next take inventory of your activities today. Where did you go? What did you do? Who did you meet? What did you contribute? How did you affect your environment? How did the environment affect you? Is there any thing you did that you could have done differently? How could you have done it next time?

Lastly visualize the next day of your life in the family and in the office or wherever you would be the next day. What do you want to see happen? For the family you might want harmony, understanding and unity. For work you might want to see that you are accomplishing your work goals and getting along with your boss and co-workers.

# Individual Meditation: Fifth Month

**Goal**

The fifth month of meditation is to know your fellow creatures. The plants, trees, insects, birds, fishes, animals and all the numerous creatures that share the Earth with us are also important. As chief Seattle said they are our brothers and sisters. What have you done to know them? How have you helped them? This is your chance to learn about them and know that you are one!

**Month 5, Week 1, Day 1**

Retire to your sacred place and practice a relaxation exercise. Inhale for four seconds. Hold the breath for four seconds. Exhale for four seconds. Hold the exhalation for four seconds. Repeat the process for as many times as possible.

Count from 50 backwards that is 50, 49, 48, etc, until you reach 1. Now count the normal way from 1 to 50. Next try counting from 1 to 100 and from 100 to 1. Concentrate on your counting and see the figures in your mind's eye as you count.

Visualize paying a visit to your neighbor. Have a gift with you. It could be a card or something you made. Walk to each neighbor's home and knock at the door. Your neighbor opens the door with a smile. Say something like "I just came to say 'Hi' and I am happy with you as my neighbor" Be creative. Give the gift and note the reaction. What did he say? What did she say? How do you feel? Do this in real life!

Next take inventory of your activities today. Where did you go? What did you do? Who did you meet? What did you contribute? How did you affect your environment? How did the environment affect you?

Now visualize the next day of your life in the family and in the office or wherever you would be the next day. What do you want to see happen? For the family you might want harmony, understanding and unity. For work you might want to see that you are accomplishing your work goals and getting along with your boss and co-workers.

**Month 5, Week 1, Day 2**

Retire to your sacred place and practice a relaxation exercise. Inhale for four seconds. Hold the breath for four seconds. Exhale for four seconds. Hold the exhalation for four seconds. Repeat the process for as many times as possible.

Count from 50 backwards that is 50, 49, 48, etc, until you reach 1. Now count the normal way from 1 to 50. Next try counting from 1 to 100 and from 100 to 1. Concentrate on your counting and see the figures in your mind's eye as you count.

Next visualize that you are in a wood playing with squirrels. First a squirrel follows you as you walk through the wood. Then you stop and get some nuts from your bag to feed the squirrel. As you feed the squirrel other squirrels begin to join the feast. You get more nuts from your bag to feed them but finally ran out of nuts. Now count the number of squirrels you fed. Wait for squirrels in your backyard and feed them in real life.

Next take inventory of your activities today. Where did you go? What did you do? Who did you meet? What did you contribute? How did you affect your environment? How did the environment affect you?

Now visualize the next day of your life in the family and in the office or wherever you would be the next day. What do you want to see happen? For the family you might want harmony, understanding and unity. For work you might want to see that you

are accomplishing your work goals and getting along with your boss and co-workers.

### Month 5, Week 1, Day 3

Retire to your sacred place and practice a relaxation exercise. Inhale for four seconds. Hold the breath for four seconds. Exhale for four seconds. Hold the exhalation for four seconds. Repeat the process for as many times as possible.

Count from 50 backwards that is 50, 49, 48, etc, until you reach 1. Now count the normal way from 1 to 50. Next try counting from 1 to 100 and from 100 to 1. Concentrate on your counting and see the figures in your mind's eye as you count.

Next visualize that you are in at the coast and feeding seagulls. You have a bag of breadcrumbs with you to feed the birds. When you are ready begin by throwing the breadcrumbs into the air. That attracts a seagull. As you continue to do that more and more seagulls begin to come and enjoy the feast. But soon you ran out of breadcrumbs. Now count the number of seagulls you fed. Do this in real life.

Next take inventory of your activities today. Where did you go? What did you do? Who did you meet? What did you contribute? How did you affect your environment? How did the environment affect you?

Now visualize the next day of your life in the family and in the office or wherever you would be the next day. What do you want to see happen? For the family you might want harmony, understanding and unity. For work you might want to see that you are accomplishing your work goals and getting along with your boss and co-workers.

### Month 5, Week 1, Day 4

Retire to your sacred place and practice a relaxation exercise. Inhale for four seconds. Hold the breath for four seconds. Exhale for four seconds. Hold the exhalation for four seconds. Repeat the process for as many times as possible.

Count from 50 backwards that is 50, 49, 48, etc, until you reach 1. Now count the normal way from 1 to 50. Next try counting from 1 to 100 and from 100 to 1. Concentrate on your counting and see the figures in your mind's eye as you count.

Next reflect on Mindfulness by **the Buddha**

When things are going well, be mindful of adversity
When prosperous, be mindful of poverty
When loved, be mindful of thoughtfulness
When respected, be mindful of humility

Next take inventory of your activities today. Where did you go? What did you do? Who did you meet? What did you contribute? How did you affect your environment? How did the environment affect you?

Now visualize the next day of your life in the family and in the office or wherever you would be the next day. What do you want to see happen? For the family you might want harmony, understanding and unity. For work you might want to see that you are accomplishing your work goals and getting along with your boss and co-workers.

### Month 5, Week 1, Day 5

Retire to your sacred place and practice a relaxation exercise. Inhale for four seconds. Hold the breath for four seconds. Exhale for four seconds. Hold the exhalation for four seconds. Repeat the process for as many times as possible.

Count from 50 backwards that is 50, 49, 48, etc, until you reach 1. Now count the normal way from 1 to 50. Next try counting from 1 to 100 and from 100 to 1. Concentrate on your counting and see the figures in your mind's eye as you count.

Now meditate on the New Testament: 1 Corinthians 13:1-7: If I speak in the tongues of men or of angels, but do not have love, I am only a resounding gong or a clanging cymbal. If I have the gift of prophecy and can fathom all mysteries and all knowledge, and if I have a faith that can move mountains, but do not have love, I am nothing. If I give all I possess to the poor and give over my body to hardship that I may boast, but do not have love, I gain nothing. Love is patient, love is kind. It does not envy, it does not boast, it is not proud. It does not dishonor others, it is not self-seeking, it is not easily angered, it keeps no record of wrongs. Love does not delight in evil but rejoices with the truth. It always protects, always trusts, always hopes, always perseveres.

Next take inventory of your activities today. Where did you go? What did you do? Who did you meet? What did you contribute? How did you affect your environment? How did the environment affect you?

Now visualize the next day of your life in the family and in the office or wherever you would be the next day. What do you want to see happen? For the family you might want harmony, understanding and unity. For work you might want to see that you are accomplishing your work goals and getting along with your boss and co-workers.

**Month 5, Week 1, Day 6**
Retire to your sacred place and practice a relaxation exercise. Inhale for four seconds. Hold the breath for four seconds.

Exhale for four seconds. Hold the exhalation for four seconds. Repeat the process for as many times as possible.

Count from 50 backwards that is 50, 49, 48, etc, until you reach 1. Now count the normal way from 1 to 50. Next try counting from 1 to 100 and from 100 to 1. Concentrate on your counting and see the figures in your mind's eye as you count.

Now reflect on the following: Just as treasures are uncovered from the earth, so virtue appears from good deeds, and wisdom appears from a pure and peaceful mind. To walk safely through the maze of human life, one needs the light of wisdom and the guidance of virtue. Buddha

Next take inventory of your activities today. Where did you go? What did you do? Who did you meet? What did you contribute? How did you affect your environment? How did the environment affect you? Is there any thing you did that you could have done differently? How could you have done it next time?

Lastly visualize the next day of your life in the family and in the office or wherever you would be the next day. What do you want to see happen? For the family you might want harmony, understanding and unity. For work you might want to see that you are accomplishing your work goals and getting along with your boss and co-workers.

**Month 5, Week 1, Day 7**

Attend a church, a temple, or any other meeting that brings you together with people for a common goal. If you do not have one you may begin today and find one that meets your interest and inclination. If you want you could also organize a group of your own. For instance you could start an Awakened Living Study Program. You may contact UNISM for more information.

Retire to your sacred place and practice a relaxation exercise. Inhale for four seconds. Hold the breath for four seconds. Exhale for four seconds. Hold the exhalation for four seconds. Repeat the process for as many times as possible.

Choose your favorite meditation posture and practice using the posture. For instance, if you use supports for your back during meditation start practicing your favorite posture without any support.

Next take inventory of your activities today. Where did you go? What did you do? Who did you meet? What did you contribute? How did you affect your environment? How did the environment affect you? Is there any thing you did that you could have done differently? How could you have done it next time?

Lastly visualize the next day of your life in the family and in the office or wherever you would be the next day. What do you want to see happen? For the family you might want harmony, understanding and unity. For work you might want to see that you are accomplishing your work goals and getting along with your boss and co-workers.

### Month 5, Week 2, Day 1

Retire to your sacred place and practice a relaxation exercise. Inhale for four seconds. Hold the breath for four seconds. Exhale for four seconds. Hold the exhalation for four seconds. Repeat the process for as many times as possible.

Count from 50 backwards that is 50, 49, 48, etc, until you reach 1. Now count the normal way from 1 to 50. Next try counting from 1 to 100 and from 100 to 1. Concentrate on your counting and see the figures in your mind's eye as you count.

Imagine having a walk with a friend to find out more about the person. Meet with your friend at a pre-arranged place and begin your walk from there. Begin a conversation to learn more about your friend's life. Find out about work, finances, health, the future and life in general. Render help if needed. Do this in real life. It will mean a lot to your friend.

Next take inventory of your activities today. Where did you go? What did you do? Who did you meet? What did you contribute? How did you affect your environment? How did the environment affect you?

Now visualize the next day of your life in the family and in the office or wherever you would be the next day. What do you want to see happen? For the family you might want harmony, understanding and unity. For work you might want to see that you are accomplishing your work goals and getting along with your boss and co-workers.

**Month 5, Week 2, Day 2**

Retire to your sacred place and practice a relaxation exercise. Inhale for four seconds. Hold the breath for four seconds. Exhale for four seconds. Hold the exhalation for four seconds. Repeat the process for as many times as possible.

Count from 50 backwards that is 50, 49, 48, etc, until you reach 1. Now count the normal way from 1 to 50. Next try counting from 1 to 100 and from 100 to 1. Concentrate on your counting and see the figures in your mind's eye as you count.

Imagine volunteering your time to help the homeless. Get the necessary permit from your city Government and set up a table with packaged food, bottled water, motivational greeting cards, tissue paper, and some cash. Also have a list of homeless shelters as well as government programs for the homeless. Place a sign to let people know what you are doing. The sign could say "HOMELESS? We can Help!" or "HOMELESS STAND". As the homeless stop by the stand give them the freedom to take one of each of what you have. Stop your meditation as soon as you are done. Do this in real life.

Next take inventory of your activities today. Where did you go? What did you do? Who did you meet? What did you contribute? How did you affect your environment? How did the environment affect you?

Now visualize the next day of your life in the family and in the office or wherever you would be the next day. What do you want to see happen? For the family you might want harmony, understanding and unity. For work you might want to see that you are accomplishing your work goals and getting along with your boss and co-workers.

**Month 5, Week 2, Day 3**

Retire to your sacred place and practice a relaxation exercise. Inhale for four seconds. Hold the breath for four seconds. Exhale for four seconds. Hold the exhalation for four seconds. Repeat the process for as many times as possible.

Count from 50 backwards that is 50, 49, 48, etc, until you reach 1. Now count the normal way from 1 to 50. Next try counting from 1 to 100 and from 100 to 1. Concentrate on your counting and see the figures in your mind's eye as you count.

Imagine going to a nearby wood on a Sunday morning. Look for a comfortable place preferably under a tree and sit quietly and listen. Listen to the music of the earth as the sound of animals, birds, insects, trees, plants and flowers come alive. Reflect on the sound and merge with it.

Next take inventory of your activities today. Where did you go? What did you do? Who did you meet? What did you

contribute? How did you affect your environment? How did the environment affect you?

Now visualize the next day of your life in the family and in the office or wherever you would be the next day. What do you want to see happen? For the family you might want harmony, understanding and unity. For work you might want to see that you are accomplishing your work goals and getting along with your boss and co-workers.

**Month 5, Week 2, Day 4**

Retire to your sacred place and practice a relaxation exercise. Inhale for four seconds. Hold the breath for four seconds. Exhale for four seconds. Hold the exhalation for four seconds. Repeat the process for as many times as possible.

Count from 50 backwards that is 50, 49, 48, etc, until you reach 1. Now count the normal way from 1 to 50. Next try counting from 1 to 100 and from 100 to 1. Concentrate on your counting and see the figures in your mind's eye as you count.

Life is lived by killing and eating. The birds, fishes and animals are our brothers and sisters but we kill and eat them. When next you eat show gratitude to the animal or fish for the sacrifice. The animal is a willing sacrifice for you to eat and live but in return it is your responsibility to live an exemplary life to benefit others. In this way the sacrifice yields fruits for future generations. Reflect on the sacrifice and note the teachings.

Next take inventory of your activities today. Where did you go? What did you do? Who did you meet? What did you contribute? How did you affect your environment? How did the environment affect you?

Now visualize the next day of your life in the family and in the office or wherever you would be the next day. What do you

want to see happen? For the family you might want harmony, understanding and unity. For work you might want to see that you are accomplishing your work goals and getting along with your boss and co-workers.

**Month 5, Week 2, Day 5**

Retire to your sacred place and practice a relaxation exercise. Inhale for four seconds. Hold the breath for four seconds. Exhale for four seconds. Hold the exhalation for four seconds. Repeat the process for as many times as possible.

Count from 50 backwards that is 50, 49, 48, etc, until you reach 1. Now count the normal way from 1 to 50. Next try counting from 1 to 100 and from 100 to 1. Concentrate on your counting and see the figures in your mind's eye as you count.

Now meditate on The Power of One by Anonymous:

One SONG can spark a moment
One FLOWER can wake the dream
One TREE can start a forest
One BIRD can herald spring
One SMILE begins a friendship
One HANDCLASP lifts a soul
One STAR can guide a ship at sea
One WORD can frame the goal
One VOTE can change a nation
One SUNBEAM lights a room
One CANDLE wipes out darkness
One LAUGH will conquer gloom
One STEP must start each journey
One WORD must start a prayer
One HOPE will raise our spirits
One TOUCH can show you care

One VOICE can speak with wisdom
One HEART can know what is true
One LIFE can make a difference
You see, it's up to you.

Next take inventory of your activities today. Where did you go? What did you do? Who did you meet? What did you contribute? How did you affect your environment? How did the environment affect you?

Now visualize the next day of your life in the family and in the office or wherever you would be the next day. What do you want to see happen? For the family you might want harmony, understanding and unity. For work you might want to see that you are accomplishing your work goals and getting along with your boss and co-workers.

**Month 5, Week 2, Day 6**

Retire to your sacred place and practice a relaxation exercise. Inhale for four seconds. Hold the breath for four seconds. Exhale for four seconds. Hold the exhalation for four seconds. Repeat the process for as many times as possible.

Count from 50 backwards that is 50, 49, 48, etc, until you reach 1. Now count the normal way from 1 to 50. Next try counting from 1 to 100 and from 100 to 1. Concentrate on your counting and see the figures in your mind's eye as you count.

Now reflect on the following: Birth does not lead to greatness; but cultivation of numerous virtues by a man leads him to greatness. It is a pearl that possesses real greatness and not the pair of shells in which it is produced. Jainism. Vajjalagam 687

Next take inventory of your activities today. Where did you go? What did you do? Who did you meet? What did you contribute? How did you affect your environment? How did the

environment affect you? Is there any thing you did that you could have done differently? How could you have done it next time?

Lastly visualize the next day of your life in the family and in the office or wherever you would be the next day. What do you want to see happen? For the family you might want harmony, understanding and unity. For work you might want to see that you are accomplishing your work goals and getting along with your boss and co-workers.

### Month 5, Week 2, Day 7

Attend a church, a temple, or any other meeting that brings you together with people for a common goal. If you do not have one you may begin today and find one that meets your interest and inclination. If you want you could also organize a group of your own. For instance you could start an Awakened Living Study Program. You may contact UNISM for more information.

Retire to your sacred place and practice a relaxation exercise. Inhale for four seconds. Hold the breath for four seconds. Exhale for four seconds. Hold the exhalation for four seconds. Repeat the process for as many times as possible.

Choose your favorite meditation posture and practice using the posture. For instance, if you use supports for your back during meditation start practicing your favorite posture without any support.

Next take inventory of your activities today. Where did you go? What did you do? Who did you meet? What did you contribute? How did you affect your environment? How did the environment affect you? Is there any thing you did that you could have done differently? How could you have done it next time?

Lastly visualize the next day of your life in the family and in the office or wherever you would be the next day. What do you

want to see happen? For the family you might want harmony, understanding and unity. For work you might want to see that you are accomplishing your work goals and getting along with your boss and co-workers.

### Month 5, Week 3, Day 1

Retire to your sacred place and practice a relaxation exercise. Inhale for four seconds. Hold the breath for four seconds. Exhale for four seconds. Hold the exhalation for four seconds. Repeat the process for as many times as possible.

Count from 50 backwards that is 50, 49, 48, etc, until you reach 1. Now count the normal way from 1 to 50. Next try counting from 1 to 100 and from 100 to 1. Concentrate on your counting and see the figures in your mind's eye as you count.

Imagine that you are in a foreign land where the culture is different from your culture. What problems are you facing? How are you addressing the challenges? What are you learning about the people? How have you grown because of this experience?

Next take inventory of your activities today. Where did you go? What did you do? Who did you meet? What did you contribute? How did you affect your environment? How did the environment affect you?

Now visualize the next day of your life in the family and in the office or wherever you would be the next day. What do you want to see happen? For the family you might want harmony, understanding and unity. For work you might want to see that you are accomplishing your work goals and getting along with your boss and co-workers.

### Month 5, Week 3, Day 2

Retire to your sacred place and practice a relaxation exercise. Inhale for four seconds. Hold the breath for four seconds. Exhale for four seconds. Hold the exhalation for four seconds. Repeat the process for as many times as possible.

Count from 50 backwards that is 50, 49, 48, etc, until you reach 1. Now count the normal way from 1 to 50. Next try counting from 1 to 100 and from 100 to 1. Concentrate on your counting and see the figures in your mind's eye as you count.

Imagine that you are very rich with a mansion and luxurious vehicles at your disposal. Invite a poor family to your home for dinner. The aim is to show them the possibilities of life. You pick them up with a limo and take them to your mansion. Share the message of hope and possibilities without overwhelming them with your riches. Do this in real life.

Next take inventory of your activities today. Where did you go? What did you do? Who did you meet? What did you contribute? How did you affect your environment? How did the environment affect you?

Now visualize the next day of your life in the family and in the office or wherever you would be the next day. What do you want to see happen? For the family you might want harmony, understanding and unity. For work you might want to see that you are accomplishing your work goals and getting along with your boss and co-workers.

### Month 5, Week 3, Day 3

Retire to your sacred place and practice a relaxation exercise. Inhale for four seconds. Hold the breath for four seconds. Exhale for four seconds. Hold the exhalation for four seconds. Repeat the process for as many times as possible.

Count from 50 backwards that is 50, 49, 48, etc, until you reach 1. Now count the normal way from 1 to 50. Next try counting from 1 to 100 and from 100 to 1. Concentrate on your counting and see the figures in your mind's eye as you count.

Meditate on visiting a prison in your city. You see different people imprisoned for different crimes. Some of these people are innocent of the crimes for which they are imprisoned. With that fact it dawns on you that you could also be one of them. How do you feel? What could we do to minimize wrongful imprisonments? What could we do to minimize crime? You may visit a prison for real.

Next take inventory of your activities today. Where did you go? What did you do? Who did you meet? What did you contribute? How did you affect your environment? How did the environment affect you?

Now visualize the next day of your life in the family and in the office or wherever you would be the next day. What do you want to see happen? For the family you might want harmony, understanding and unity. For work you might want to see that you are accomplishing your work goals and getting along with your boss and co-workers.

## Month 5, Week 3, Day 4

Retire to your sacred place and practice a relaxation exercise. Inhale for four seconds. Hold the breath for four seconds. Exhale for four seconds. Hold the exhalation for four seconds. Repeat the process for as many times as possible.

Count from 50 backwards that is 50, 49, 48, etc, until you reach 1. Now count the normal way from 1 to 50. Next try counting from 1 to 100 and from 100 to 1. Concentrate on your counting and see the figures in your mind's eye as you count.

Meditate on your favorite pet. Consider the importance of pets to humans. Recount the different ways in which pets have been used to assist people. They do their work and perform tricks with joy, without pay and with full cooperation. What can you learn from them?

Next take inventory of your activities today. Where did you go? What did you do? Who did you meet? What did you contribute? How did you affect your environment? How did the environment affect you?

Now visualize the next day of your life in the family and in the office or wherever you would be the next day. What do you want to see happen? For the family you might want harmony, understanding and unity. For work you might want to see that you are accomplishing your work goals and getting along with your boss and co-workers.

**Month 5, Week 3, Day 5**

Retire to your sacred place and practice a relaxation exercise. Inhale for four seconds. Hold the breath for four seconds. Exhale for four seconds. Hold the exhalation for four seconds. Repeat the process for as many times as possible.

Count from 50 backwards that is 50, 49, 48, etc, until you reach 1. Now count the normal way from 1 to 50. Next try counting from 1 to 100 and from 100 to 1. Concentrate on your counting and see the figures in your mind's eye as you count.

Now meditate on Who is the Rich man by Anonymous: One day a wealthy father took his son on a trip to the country so that the son could see how the poor lived. They spent a day and a night at the farm of a very poor family. When they got back from their trip, the father asked his son, "How was the trip?" "Very good, Dad!" "Did you see how poor people can be?" "Yeah!" "And what did you learn?" The son answered, "I saw that we have a dog at home, and they have four. We have a pool that reaches to the middle of the garden; they have a creek that has no end. We have imported lamps in the house; they have the stars. Our patio reaches to the front yard; they have the whole horizon." When the little boy was finished, the father was speechless. His son then added, "Thanks Dad for showing me how poor we are!"

Next take inventory of your activities today. Where did you go? What did you do? Who did you meet? What did you contribute? How did you affect your environment? How did the environment affect you?

Now visualize the next day of your life in the family and in the office or wherever you would be the next day. What do you want to see happen? For the family you might want harmony, understanding and unity. For work you might want to see that you are accomplishing your work goals and getting along with your boss and co-workers.

**Month 5, Week 3, Day 6**

Retire to your sacred place and practice a relaxation exercise. Inhale for four seconds. Hold the breath for four seconds. Exhale for four seconds. Hold the exhalation for four seconds. Repeat the process for as many times as possible.

Count from 50 backwards that is 50, 49, 48, etc, until you reach 1. Now count the normal way from 1 to 50. Next try counting from 1 to 100 and from 100 to 1. Concentrate on your counting and see the figures in your mind's eye as you count.

Now reflect on the following: First keep the peace within yourself, then you can also bring peace to others. Thomas A. Kempis

Next take inventory of your activities today. Where did you go? What did you do? Who did you meet? What did you contribute? How did you affect your environment? How did the environment affect you? Is there any thing you did that you could have done differently? How could you have done it next time?

Lastly visualize the next day of your life in the family and in the office or wherever you would be the next day. What do you want to see happen? For the family you might want harmony, understanding and unity. For work you might want to see that you are accomplishing your work goals and getting along with your boss and co-workers.

### Month 5, Week 3, Day 7

Attend a church, a temple, or any other meeting that brings you together with people for a common goal. If you do not have one you may begin today and find one that meets your interest and inclination. If you want you could also organize a group of your own. For instance you could start an Awakened Living Study Program. You may contact UNISM for more information.

Retire to your sacred place and practice a relaxation exercise. Inhale for four seconds. Hold the breath for four seconds. Exhale for four seconds. Hold the exhalation for four seconds. Repeat the process for as many times as possible.

Choose your favorite meditation posture and practice using the posture. For instance, if you use supports for your back during meditation start practicing your favorite posture without any support.

Next take inventory of your activities today. Where did you go? What did you do? Who did you meet? What did you contribute? How did you affect your environment? How did the

environment affect you? Is there any thing you did that you could have done differently? How could you have done it next time?

Lastly visualize the next day of your life in the family and in the office or wherever you would be the next day. What do you want to see happen? For the family you might want harmony, understanding and unity. For work you might want to see that you are accomplishing your work goals and getting along with your boss and co-workers.

**Month 5, Week 4, Day 1**

Retire to your sacred place and practice a relaxation exercise. Inhale for four seconds. Hold the breath for four seconds. Exhale for four seconds. Hold the exhalation for four seconds. Repeat the process for as many times as possible.

Count from 50 backwards that is 50, 49, 48, etc, until you reach 1. Now count the normal way from 1 to 50. Next try counting from 1 to 100 and from 100 to 1. Concentrate on your counting and see the figures in your mind's eye as you count.

Imagine that you saw a homeless pet and took it home. There was an instant bonding between the two of you. Begin to study the needs of the pet and help it to meet those needs. What did you find? How are you helping the pet to meet its needs? What are you learning about pets? What are the similarities in behavior between your pet and humans? What are the differences? What have you learned about pets and people?

Next take inventory of your activities today. Where did you go? What did you do? Who did you meet? What did you contribute? How did you affect your environment? How did the environment affect you?

Now visualize the next day of your life in the family and in the office or wherever you would be the next day. What do you

want to see happen? For the family you might want harmony, understanding and unity. For work you might want to see that you are accomplishing your work goals and getting along with your boss and co-workers.

### Month 5, Week 4, Day 2

Retire to your sacred place and practice a relaxation exercise. Inhale for four seconds. Hold the breath for four seconds. Exhale for four seconds. Hold the exhalation for four seconds. Repeat the process for as many times as possible.

Count from 50 backwards that is 50, 49, 48, etc, until you reach 1. Now count the normal way from 1 to 50. Next try counting from 1 to 100 and from 100 to 1. Concentrate on your counting and see the figures in your mind's eye as you count.

Imagine volunteering your time to a homeless shelter. The homeless come to the shelter for food daily. You may be helping in preparing the food, cooking the food, doing the dishes, setting up the table, cleaning the table and interacting with the people. What are you doing? What did you learn from the homeless people that you talked to? How do you feel abut the experience?

Next take inventory of your activities today. Where did you go? What did you do? Who did you meet? What did you contribute? How did you affect your environment? How did the environment affect you?

Now visualize the next day of your life in the family and in the office or wherever you would be the next day. What do you want to see happen? For the family you might want harmony, understanding and unity. For work you might want to see that you are accomplishing your work goals and getting along with your boss and co-workers.

### Month 5, Week 4, Day 3

Retire to your sacred place and practice a relaxation exercise. Inhale for four seconds. Hold the breath for four seconds. Exhale for four seconds. Hold the exhalation for four seconds. Repeat the process for as many times as possible.

Count from 50 backwards that is 50, 49, 48, etc, until you reach 1. Now count the normal way from 1 to 50. Next try counting from 1 to 100 and from 100 to 1. Concentrate on your counting and see the figures in your mind's eye as you count.

Meditate on visiting a retirement home in your city. What are the amenities in the home? What do the people do for recreation? What is the age range of the people? What did you learn about retirement homes and about life?

Next take inventory of your activities today. Where did you go? What did you do? Who did you meet? What did you contribute? How did you affect your environment? How did the environment affect you?

Now visualize the next day of your life in the family and in the office or wherever you would be the next day. What do you want to see happen? For the family you might want harmony, understanding and unity. For work you might want to see that you are accomplishing your work goals and getting along with your boss and co-workers.

### Month 5, Week 4, Day 4

Retire to your sacred place and practice a relaxation exercise. Inhale for four seconds. Hold the breath for four seconds. Exhale for four seconds. Hold the exhalation for four seconds. Repeat the process for as many times as possible.

Count from 50 backwards that is 50, 49, 48, etc, until you reach 1. Now count the normal way from 1 to 50. Next try

counting from 1 to 100 and from 100 to 1. Concentrate on your counting and see the figures in your mind's eye as you count.

Next reflect on the Compassion by **the Buddha:** We already have perfect compassion, perfect wisdom, perfect joy. We only need to settle our minds so they can arise from deep within us. Develop the quiet, even state of mind. When praised by some and condemned by others, free the mind from hate and pride, and gently go your way in peace.

Next take inventory of your activities today. Where did you go? What did you do? Who did you meet? What did you contribute? How did you affect your environment? How did the environment affect you?

Now visualize the next day of your life in the family and in the office or wherever you would be the next day. What do you want to see happen? For the family you might want harmony, understanding and unity. For work you might want to see that you are accomplishing your work goals and getting along with your boss and co-workers.

### Month 5, Week 4, Day 5

Retire to your sacred place and practice a relaxation exercise. Inhale for four seconds. Hold the breath for four seconds. Exhale for four seconds. Hold the exhalation for four seconds. Repeat the process for as many times as possible.

Count from 50 backwards that is 50, 49, 48, etc, until you reach 1. Now count the normal way from 1 to 50. Next try counting from 1 to 100 and from 100 to 1. Concentrate on your counting and see the figures in your mind's eye as you count.

Now meditate on Do Something Meaningful by Ann Druyan: I remember that one time Carl [Sagan] was giving a talk, and he spelled out, in a kind of withering succession, these great theories of demotion that science has dealt us, all of the ways in which science is telling us we are not who we would like to believe we are. At the end of it, a young man came up to him and he said: "What do you give us in return? Now that you've taken everything from us? What meaning is left, if everything that I've been taught since I was a child turns out to be untrue?" Carl looked at him and said, "Do something meaningful."

Next take inventory of your activities today. Where did you go? What did you do? Who did you meet? What did you contribute? How did you affect your environment? How did the environment affect you?

Now visualize the next day of your life in the family and in the office or wherever you would be the next day. What do you want to see happen? For the family you might want harmony, understanding and unity. For work you might want to see that you are accomplishing your work goals and getting along with your boss and co-workers.

**Month 5, Week 4, Day 6**

Retire to your sacred place and practice a relaxation exercise. Inhale for four seconds. Hold the breath for four seconds. Exhale for four seconds. Hold the exhalation for four seconds. Repeat the process for as many times as possible.

Count from 50 backwards that is 50, 49, 48, etc, until you reach 1. Now count the normal way from 1 to 50. Next try counting from 1 to 100 and from 100 to 1. Concentrate on your counting and see the figures in your mind's eye as you count.

Now reflect on the following: Nobody can bring you peace but yourself. Ralph Waldo Emerson

Next take inventory of your activities today. Where did you go? What did you do? Who did you meet? What did you

contribute? How did you affect your environment? How did the environment affect you? Is there any thing you did that you could have done differently? How could you have done it next time?

Lastly visualize the next day of your life in the family and in the office or wherever you would be the next day. What do you want to see happen? For the family you might want harmony, understanding and unity. For work you might want to see that you are accomplishing your work goals and getting along with your boss and co-workers.

## Month 5, Week 4, Day 7

Attend a church, a temple, or any other meeting that brings you together with people for a common goal. If you do not have one you may begin today and find one that meets your interest and inclination. If you want you could also organize a group of your own. For instance you could start an Awakened Living Study Program. You may contact UNISM for more information.

Retire to your sacred place and practice a relaxation exercise. Inhale for four seconds. Hold the breath for four seconds. Exhale for four seconds. Hold the exhalation for four seconds. Repeat the process for as many times as possible.

Choose your favorite meditation posture and practice using the posture. For instance, if you use supports for your back during meditation start practicing your favorite posture without any support.

Next take inventory of your activities today. Where did you go? What did you do? Who did you meet? What did you contribute? How did you affect your environment? How did the environment affect you? Is there any thing you did that you could have done differently? How could you have done it next time?

Lastly visualize the next day of your life in the family and in the office or wherever you would be the next day. What do you want to see happen? For the family you might want harmony, understanding and unity. For work you might want to see that you are accomplishing your work goals and getting along with your boss and co-workers.

## Individual Meditation: Sixth Month

Goal

The goal of the sixth month of meditation is to develop your spiritual qualities. One of the most important spiritual realizations is the connection we share with all creatures. From this awareness comes the knowledge that you are not alone. You are connected with your fellow humans as well as with the rest of creation. If you are thus connected what does that mean. It means that you are here to take care of each other. In order to take care of each other you would learn to give and receive; you would learn to think before you act; you would learn to open up to the Universal Spirit; you would learn to create for the benefit of all creatures; you would learn to act without the benefit of rewards and you would learn to realize your purpose in life.

### Month 6, Week 1, Day 1

Retire to your sacred place and practice a relaxation exercise. Inhale for four seconds. Hold the breath for four seconds. Exhale for four seconds. Hold the exhalation for four seconds. Repeat the process for as many times as possible.

Count from 50 backwards that is 50, 49, 48, etc, until you reach 1. Now count the normal way from 1 to 50. Next try counting from 1 to 100 and from 100 to 1. Concentrate on your counting and see the figures in your mind's eye as you count.

Next reflect on Wisdom by **the Buddha:**

Those who are truly wise will remain unmoved by feelings of happiness and suffering, fame and disgrace, praise and blame, gain and loss. They will remain calm like the eye of a hurricane.

Next take inventory of your activities today. Where did you go? What did you do? Who did you meet? What did you

contribute? How did you affect your environment? How did the environment affect you?

Now visualize the next day of your life in the family and in the office or wherever you would be the next day. What do you want to see happen? For the family you might want harmony, understanding and unity. For work you might want to see that you are accomplishing your work goals and getting along with your boss and co-workers.

**Month 6, Week 1, Day 2**

Retire to your sacred place and practice a relaxation exercise. Inhale for four seconds. Hold the breath for four seconds. Exhale for four seconds. Hold the exhalation for four seconds. Repeat the process for as many times as possible.

Count from 50 backwards that is 50, 49, 48, etc, until you reach 1. Now count the normal way from 1 to 50. Next try counting from 1 to 100 and from 100 to 1. Concentrate on your counting and see the figures in your mind's eye as you count.

Reflect on the doctrine of receiving. For a gift to be given there must be a receiver. So both giving and receiving are important. Imagine a situation in which there is a gift but no person to accept it. How does it feel? What lessons have you learned? As a practical exercise pay a compliment to at least seven creatures including people, animals, fishes, insects, plants, flowers, trees and birds. You may say, "Hi, nice sweater, great complexion, good scent, great height, or great personality. And be there to receive the return gift of "Thank you" How does it feel?

Next take inventory of your activities today. Where did you go? What did you do? Who did you meet? What did you contribute? How did you affect your environment? How did the environment affect you?

Now visualize the next day of your life in the family and in the office or wherever you would be the next day. What do you want to see happen? For the family you might want harmony, understanding and unity. For work you might want to see that you are accomplishing your work goals and getting along with your boss and co-workers.

**Month 6, Week 1, Day 3**

Retire to your sacred place and practice a relaxation exercise. Inhale for four seconds. Hold the breath for four seconds. Exhale for four seconds. Hold the exhalation for four seconds. Repeat the process for as many times as possible.

Count from 50 backwards that is 50, 49, 48, etc, until you reach 1. Now count the normal way from 1 to 50. Next try counting from 1 to 100 and from 100 to 1. Concentrate on your counting and see the figures in your mind's eye as you count.

Imagine buying a greeting card to wish someone well. You may write your favorite affirmation or prayer to wish the person a great day and enclose a gift and take it with you during the day. Give the card and gift to the first homeless person you meet. In the card you might write, "Dear partner, may you have a wonderful day and may all your days be encouraging and fruitful!" Who did you meet? What were they doing when you met him or her? What was the reaction when you gave the card? What did you learn from your experience?

Next take inventory of your activities today. Where did you go? What did you do? Who did you meet? What did you contribute? How did you affect your environment? How did the environment affect you?

Now visualize the next day of your life in the family and in the office or wherever you would be the next day. What do you

want to see happen? For the family you might want harmony, understanding and unity. For work you might want to see that you are accomplishing your work goals and getting along with your boss and co-workers.

## Month 6, Week 1, Day 4

Retire to your sacred place and practice a relaxation exercise. Inhale for four seconds. Hold the breath for four seconds. Exhale for four seconds. Hold the exhalation for four seconds. Repeat the process for as many times as possible.

Count from 50 backwards that is 50, 49, 48, etc, until you reach 1. Now count the normal way from 1 to 50. Next try counting from 1 to 100 and from 100 to 1. Concentrate on your counting and see the figures in your mind's eye as you count.

Imagine going into a nearby wood. Enjoy the flowers and plants; listen to the birds; and observe the squirrels. How do you feel?

Next take inventory of your activities today. Where did you go? What did you do? Who did you meet? What did you contribute? How did you affect your environment? How did the environment affect you?

Now visualize the next day of your life in the family and in the office or wherever you would be the next day. What do you want to see happen? For the family you might want harmony, understanding and unity. For work you might want to see that you are accomplishing your work goals and getting along with your boss and co-workers.

## Month 6, Week 1, Day 5

Retire to your sacred place and practice a relaxation exercise. Inhale for four seconds. Hold the breath for four seconds.

Exhale for four seconds. Hold the exhalation for four seconds. Repeat the process for as many times as possible.

Count from 50 backwards that is 50, 49, 48, etc, until you reach 1. Now count the normal way from 1 to 50. Next try counting from 1 to 100 and from 100 to 1. Concentrate on your counting and see the figures in your mind's eye as you count.

Now meditate on The Deserving by Khalil Gibran:

You often say, "I would give, but only to the deserving."
The trees in your orchard say not so, nor the flocks in your pasture.
They give that they may live, for to withhold is to perish.
Surely he who is worthy to receive his day and his nights, is
worthy of all else from you.
And he who has deserved to drink from the ocean of life deserves
to fill his cup from your little stream.
And what desert greater shall there be, than that which lies in the
courage and the confidence, nay the charity, of receiving?
And who are you that men should rend their bosom and unveil
their pride, that you may see their worth naked and their pride
unabashed?
See first that you yourself deserve to be a giver, and an instrument
of giving.

For in truth it is life that gives unto life--while you, who deem yourself a giver, are but a witness.

Next take inventory of your activities today. Where did you go? What did you do? Who did you meet? What did you contribute? How did you affect your environment? How did the environment affect you?

Now visualize the next day of your life in the family and in the office or wherever you would be the next day. What do you want to see happen? For the family you might want harmony, understanding and unity. For work you might want to see that you

are accomplishing your work goals and getting along with your boss and co-workers.

**Month 6, Week 1, Day 6**

Retire to your sacred place and practice a relaxation exercise. Inhale for four seconds. Hold the breath for four seconds. Exhale for four seconds. Hold the exhalation for four seconds. Repeat the process for as many times as possible.

Count from 50 backwards that is 50, 49, 48, etc, until you reach 1. Now count the normal way from 1 to 50. Next try counting from 1 to 100 and from 100 to 1. Concentrate on your counting and see the figures in your mind's eye as you count.

Now reflect on the following: I love you my brother whoever you are whether you worship in your church, kneel in your temple, or pray in your mosque. You and I are all children of one faith for the diverse paths of religion are fingers of the loving hand of one Supreme Being, a hand extended to all, offering completeness of spirit to all, eager to receive all. Kahil Gibran

Next take inventory of your activities today. Where did you go? What did you do? Who did you meet? What did you contribute? How did you affect your environment? How did the environment affect you? Is there any thing you did that you could have done differently? How could you have done it next time?

Lastly visualize the next day of your life in the family and in the office or wherever you would be the next day. What do you want to see happen? For the family you might want harmony, understanding and unity. For work you might want to see that you are accomplishing your work goals and getting along with your boss and co-workers.

### Month 6, Week 1, Day 7

Attend a church, a temple, or any other meeting that brings you together with people for a common goal. If you do not have one you may begin today and find one that meets your interest and inclination. If you want you could also organize a group of your own. For instance you could start an Awakened Living Study Program. You may contact UNISM for more information.

Retire to your sacred place and practice a relaxation exercise. Inhale for four seconds. Hold the breath for four seconds. Exhale for four seconds. Hold the exhalation for four seconds. Repeat the process for as many times as possible.

Choose your favorite meditation posture and practice using the posture. For instance, if you use supports for your back during meditation start practicing your favorite posture without any support.

Next take inventory of your activities today. Where did you go? What did you do? Who did you meet? What did you contribute? How did you affect your environment? How did the environment affect you? Is there any thing you did that you could have done differently? How could you have done it next time?

Lastly visualize the next day of your life in the family and in the office or wherever you would be the next day. What do you want to see happen? For the family you might want harmony, understanding and unity. For work you might want to see that you are accomplishing your work goals and getting along with your boss and co-workers.

### Month 6, Week 2, Day 1

Retire to your sacred place and practice a relaxation exercise. Inhale for four seconds. Hold the breath for four seconds.

Exhale for four seconds. Hold the exhalation for four seconds. Repeat the process for as many times as possible.

Count from 50 backwards that is 50, 49, 48, etc, until you reach 1. Now count the normal way from 1 to 50. Next try counting from 1 to 100 and from 100 to 1. Concentrate on your counting and see the figures in your mind's eye as you count.

Patience is a quality of holding ones center in conflict, provocation or suffering. How does patience apply to your life? Have you been patient with your children? Have you been patient with your spouse? Have you been patient with your parents? Have you been patient with your friends? Have you been patient with your neighbors? Have you been patient with strangers? Have you been patient in your interactions with your environment? Reflect on these thoughts?

Next take inventory of your activities today. Where did you go? What did you do? Who did you meet? What did you contribute? How did you affect your environment? How did the environment affect you?

Now visualize the next day of your life in the family and in the office or wherever you would be the next day. What do you want to see happen? For the family you might want harmony, understanding and unity. For work you might want to see that you are accomplishing your work goals and getting along with your boss and co-workers.

**Month 6, Week 2, Day 2**

Retire to your sacred place and practice a relaxation exercise. Inhale for four seconds. Hold the breath for four seconds. Exhale for four seconds. Hold the exhalation for four seconds. Repeat the process for as many times as possible.

Count from 50 backwards that is 50, 49, 48, etc, until you reach 1. Now count the normal way from 1 to 50. Next try counting from 1 to 100 and from 100 to 1. Concentrate on your counting and see the figures in your mind's eye as you count.

Compassion is a feeling of pity for the suffering of your neighbor coupled with a desire to relieve the suffering. Are you compassionate? Recall the instances in which you have been compassionate to a person or an animal. Which experience stands out? What happened? What did you do? What did you learn from the experience?

Next take inventory of your activities today. Where did you go? What did you do? Who did you meet? What did you contribute? How did you affect your environment? How did the environment affect you?

Now visualize the next day of your life in the family and in the office or wherever you would be the next day. What do you want to see happen? For the family you might want harmony, understanding and unity. For work you might want to see that you are accomplishing your work goals and getting along with your boss and co-workers.

**Month 6, Week 2, Day 3**

Retire to your sacred place and practice a relaxation exercise. Inhale for four seconds. Hold the breath for four seconds. Exhale for four seconds. Hold the exhalation for four seconds. Repeat the process for as many times as possible.

Count from 50 backwards that is 50, 49, 48, etc, until you reach 1. Now count the normal way from 1 to 50. Next try counting from 1 to 100 and from 100 to 1. Concentrate on your counting and see the figures in your mind's eye as you count.

Honesty is a quality of being upright, plain, truthful and sincere in our dealings with our environment. Consider your life and trace the instances in which you have been honest with your environment. Which experience stands out? What happened? What did you do? What have you learned about life?

Next take inventory of your activities today. Where did you go? What did you do? Who did you meet? What did you contribute? How did you affect your environment? How did the environment affect you?

Now visualize the next day of your life in the family and in the office or wherever you would be the next day. What do you want to see happen? For the family you might want harmony, understanding and unity. For work you might want to see that you are accomplishing your work goals and getting along with your boss and co-workers.

## Month 6, Week 2, Day 4

Retire to your sacred place and practice a relaxation exercise. Inhale for four seconds. Hold the breath for four seconds. Exhale for four seconds. Hold the exhalation for four seconds. Repeat the process for as many times as possible.

Count from 50 backwards that is 50, 49, 48, etc, until you reach 1. Now count the normal way from 1 to 50. Next try counting from 1 to 100 and from 100 to 1. Concentrate on your counting and see the figures in your mind's eye as you count.

Forgiveness is the act of ceasing to be angry at someone or feeling resentful of someone for wrongs they committed against you. Trace the number of times you have forgiven those who wronged you or took advantage of you. When was the last time you forgave someone? What happened? What are you learning about life?

Next take inventory of your activities today. Where did you go? What did you do? Who did you meet? What did you contribute? How did you affect your environment? How did the environment affect you?

Now visualize the next day of your life in the family and in the office or wherever you would be the next day. What do you want to see happen? For the family you might want harmony, understanding and unity. For work you might want to see that you are accomplishing your work goals and getting along with your boss and co-workers.

**Month 6, Week 2, Day 5**

Retire to your sacred place and practice a relaxation exercise. Inhale for four seconds. Hold the breath for four seconds. Exhale for four seconds. Hold the exhalation for four seconds. Repeat the process for as many times as possible.

Count from 50 backwards that is 50, 49, 48, etc, until you reach 1. Now count the normal way from 1 to 50. Next try counting from 1 to 100 and from 100 to 1. Concentrate on your counting and see the figures in your mind's eye as you count.

Now meditate on A Smile by Anonymous: A smile costs nothing but gives much. It enriches those who receive without making poorer those who give. It takes but a moment, but the memory of it sometimes lasts forever. None is so rich or mighty that he cannot get along without it and none is so poor that he cannot be made rich by it. Yet a smile cannot be bought, begged, borrowed, or stolen, for it is something that is of no value to anyone until it is given away. Some people are too tired to give you a smile. Give them one of yours, as none needs a smile so much as he who has no more to give.

Next take inventory of your activities today. Where did you go? What did you do? Who did you meet? What did you contribute? How did you affect your environment? How did the environment affect you?

Now visualize the next day of your life in the family and in the office or wherever you would be the next day. What do you want to see happen? For the family you might want harmony, understanding and unity. For work you might want to see that you are accomplishing your work goals and getting along with your boss and co-workers.

## Month 6, Week 2, Day 6

Retire to your sacred place and practice a relaxation exercise. Inhale for four seconds. Hold the breath for four seconds. Exhale for four seconds. Hold the exhalation for four seconds. Repeat the process for as many times as possible.

Count from 50 backwards that is 50, 49, 48, etc, until you reach 1. Now count the normal way from 1 to 50. Next try counting from 1 to 100 and from 100 to 1. Concentrate on your counting and see the figures in your mind's eye as you count.

Now reflect on the following: No heaven can come to us unless our hearts find rest in it today. Take heaven! No peace lies in the future that is not hidden in this present little instant. Take peace! The gloom of the world is but a shadow. Behind it, yet within our reach, is joy. There is radiance and glory in the darkness, could we but see, and to see we have only to look. Life is so generous a giver, but we, judging the gifts by their covering, cast them away as ugly, or heavy, or hard. Remove the covering and you find beneath it a living splendor, woven of love, by wisdom with power. Welcome it, grasp it and you touch the angel's hand that brings it to you. Everything we call a trial, a sorrow, or a duty, believe me, that angel's hand is there; the gift is there and the wonder of an overshadowing Presence. Our joys, too, be not content with them as joys. They, too, conceal diviner gifts. Life is so full of meaning and purpose, so full of beauty beneath its covering, that you will find earth that cloaks your heaven. Courage, then, to claim it; that is all! But courage you have and the knowledge that we are pilgrims together, wending through unknown country, home. Fra Giovanni

Next take inventory of your activities today. Where did you go? What did you do? Who did you meet? What did you contribute? How did you affect your environment? How did the environment affect you? Is there any thing you did that you could have done differently? How could you have done it next time?

Lastly visualize the next day of your life in the family and in the office or wherever you would be the next day. What do you want to see happen? For the family you might want harmony, understanding and unity. For work you might want to see that you are accomplishing your work goals and getting along with your boss and co-workers.

**Month 6, Week 2, Day 7**

Attend a church, a temple, or any other meeting that brings you together with people for a common goal. If you do not have one you may begin today and find one that meets your interest and inclination. If you want you could also organize a group of your own. For instance you could start an Awakened Living Study Program. You may contact UNISM for more information.

Retire to your sacred place and practice a relaxation exercise. Inhale for four seconds. Hold the breath for four seconds. Exhale for four seconds. Hold the exhalation for four seconds. Repeat the process for as many times as possible.

Choose your favorite meditation posture and practice using the posture. For instance, if you use supports for your back during meditation start practicing your favorite posture without any support.

Next take inventory of your activities today. Where did you go? What did you do? Who did you meet? What did you contribute? How did you affect your environment? How did the environment affect you? Is there any thing you did that you could have done differently? How could you have done it next time?

Lastly visualize the next day of your life in the family and in the office or wherever you would be the next day. What do you want to see happen? For the family you might want harmony, understanding and unity. For work you might want to see that you are accomplishing your work goals and getting along with your boss and co-workers.

**Month 6, Week 3, Day 1**

Retire to your sacred place and practice a relaxation exercise. Inhale for four seconds. Hold the breath for four seconds. Exhale for four seconds. Hold the exhalation for four seconds. Repeat the process for as many times as possible.

Count from 50 backwards that is 50, 49, 48, etc, until you reach 1. Now count the normal way from 1 to 50. Next try counting from 1 to 100 and from 100 to 1. Concentrate on your counting and see the figures in your mind's eye as you count.

Contentment is the quality of being at peace with your life and happy with who you are and what you have. Are you contented? Reflect on your life and remember the times you were discontented and the times you were contented. What changed and what have you learned?

Next take inventory of your activities today. Where did you go? What did you do? Who did you meet? What did you contribute? How did you affect your environment? How did the environment affect you?

Now visualize the next day of your life in the family and in the office or wherever you would be the next day. What do you want to see happen? For the family you might want harmony, understanding and unity. For work you might want to see that you are accomplishing your work goals and getting along with your boss and co-workers.

## Month 6, Week 3, Day 2

Retire to your sacred place and practice a relaxation exercise. Inhale for four seconds. Hold the breath for four seconds. Exhale for four seconds. Hold the exhalation for four seconds. Repeat the process for as many times as possible.

Count from 50 backwards that is 50, 49, 48, etc, until you reach 1. Now count the normal way from 1 to 50. Next try counting from 1 to 100 and from 100 to 1. Concentrate on your counting and see the figures in your mind's eye as you count.

Reflect on the following: Love the whole world as a mother loves her only child. **Buddha**

Next take inventory of your activities today. Where did you go? What did you do? Who did you meet? What did you contribute? How did you affect your environment? How did the environment affect you?

Now visualize the next day of your life in the family and in the office or wherever you would be the next day. What do you want to see happen? For the family you might want harmony, understanding and unity. For work you might want to see that you

are accomplishing your work goals and getting along with your boss and co-workers.

### Month 6, Week 3, Day 3

Retire to your sacred place and practice a relaxation exercise. Inhale for four seconds. Hold the breath for four seconds. Exhale for four seconds. Hold the exhalation for four seconds. Repeat the process for as many times as possible.

Count from 50 backwards that is 50, 49, 48, etc, until you reach 1. Now count the normal way from 1 to 50. Next try counting from 1 to 100 and from 100 to 1. Concentrate on your counting and see the figures in your mind's eye as you count.

Belief is a condition or state of mind in which one trusts or has confident in a person or a thing. Do you believe in an underlying Mystery within the universe? Do you believe in people? Do you believe in your family? Do you believe in your self? Reflect on these questions as they affect your life.

Next take inventory of your activities today. Where did you go? What did you do? Who did you meet? What did you contribute? How did you affect your environment? How did the environment affect you?

Now visualize the next day of your life in the family and in the office or wherever you would be the next day. What do you want to see happen? For the family you might want harmony, understanding and unity. For work you might want to see that you are accomplishing your work goals and getting along with your boss and co-workers.

### Month 6, Week 3, Day 4

Retire to your sacred place and practice a relaxation exercise. Inhale for four seconds. Hold the breath for four seconds.

Exhale for four seconds. Hold the exhalation for four seconds. Repeat the process for as many times as possible.

Count from 50 backwards that is 50, 49, 48, etc, until you reach 1. Now count the normal way from 1 to 50. Next try counting from 1 to 100 and from 100 to 1. Concentrate on your counting and see the figures in your mind's eye as you count.

Peace is a state of harmony, order or tranquility. Are you at peace? Reflect on your life and sort out the areas of conflict. Choose one particular area and meditate on it. What is it? What happened? What have you done to achieve balance?

Next take inventory of your activities today. Where did you go? What did you do? Who did you meet? What did you contribute? How did you affect your environment? How did the environment affect you?

Now visualize the next day of your life in the family and in the office or wherever you would be the next day. What do you want to see happen? For the family you might want harmony, understanding and unity. For work you might want to see that you are accomplishing your work goals and getting along with your boss and co-workers.

**Month 6, Week 3, Day 5**

Retire to your sacred place and practice a relaxation exercise. Inhale for four seconds. Hold the breath for four seconds. Exhale for four seconds. Hold the exhalation for four seconds. Repeat the process for as many times as possible.

Count from 50 backwards that is 50, 49, 48, etc, until you reach 1. Now count the normal way from 1 to 50. Next try counting from 1 to 100 and from 100 to 1. Concentrate on your counting and see the figures in your mind's eye as you count.

Now meditate on Giving by Khalil Gibran:

Then said a rich man, Speak to us of Giving.
And he answered:
You give but little when you give of your possessions.
It is when you give of yourself that you truly give.
For what are your possessions but things you keep and guard for fear you may need them tomorrow?
And tomorrow, what shall tomorrow bring to the over-prudent dog burying bones in the trackless sand as he follows the pilgrims to the holy city?
And what is fear of need but need itself?
Is not dread of thirst when your well is full, the thirst that is unquenchable?
There are those who give little of the much which they have-- and they give it for recognition and their hidden desire makes their gifts unwholesome.
And there are those who have little and give it all.
These are the believers in life and the bounty of life, and their coffer is never empty.
There are those who give with joy, and that joy is their reward.
And there are those who give with pain, and that pain is their baptism.
And there are those who give and know not pain in giving, nor do they seek joy, nor give with mindfulness of virtue;
They give as in yonder valley the myrtle breathes its fragrance into space.
Through the hands of such as these God speaks, and from behind their eyes He smiles upon the earth.

Next take inventory of your activities today. Where did you go? What did you do? Who did you meet? What did you contribute? How did you affect your environment? How did the environment affect you?

Now visualize the next day of your life in the family and in the office or wherever you would be the next day. What do you want to see happen? For the family you might want harmony, understanding and unity. For work you might want to see that you are accomplishing your work goals and getting along with your boss and co-workers.

**Month 3, Week 3, Day 6**

Retire to your sacred place and practice a relaxation exercise. Inhale for four seconds. Hold the breath for four seconds. Exhale for four seconds. Hold the exhalation for four seconds. Repeat the process for as many times as possible.

Count from 50 backwards that is 50, 49, 48, etc, until you reach 1. Now count the normal way from 1 to 50. Next try counting from 1 to 100 and from 100 to 1. Concentrate on your counting and see the figures in your mind's eye as you count.

Now reflect on the following: He who conquers others is strong; he who conquers himself is mighty. Lao Tzu

Next take inventory of your activities today. Where did you go? What did you do? Who did you meet? What did you contribute? How did you affect your environment? How did the environment affect you? Is there any thing you did that you could have done differently? How could you have done it next time?

Lastly visualize the next day of your life in the family and in the office or wherever you would be the next day. What do you want to see happen? For the family you might want harmony, understanding and unity. For work you might want to see that you are accomplishing your work goals and getting along with your boss and co-workers.

### Month 3, Week 3, Day 7

Attend a church, a temple, or any other meeting that brings you together with people for a common goal. If you do not have one you may begin today and find one that meets your interest and inclination. If you want you could also organize a group of your own. For instance you could start an Awakened Living Study Program. You may contact UNISM for more information.

Retire to your sacred place and practice a relaxation exercise. Inhale for four seconds. Hold the breath for four seconds. Exhale for four seconds. Hold the exhalation for four seconds. Repeat the process for as many times as possible.

Choose your favorite meditation posture and practice using the posture. For instance, if you use supports for your back during meditation start practicing your favorite posture without any support.

Next take inventory of your activities today. Where did you go? What did you do? Who did you meet? What did you contribute? How did you affect your environment? How did the environment affect you? Is there any thing you did that you could have done differently? How could you have done it next time?

Lastly visualize the next day of your life in the family and in the office or wherever you would be the next day. What do you want to see happen? For the family you might want harmony, understanding and unity. For work you might want to see that you are accomplishing your work goals and getting along with your boss and co-workers.

### Month 6, Week 4, Day 1

Retire to your sacred place and practice a relaxation exercise. Inhale for four seconds. Hold the breath for four seconds.

Exhale for four seconds. Hold the exhalation for four seconds. Repeat the process for as many times as possible.

Count from 50 backwards that is 50, 49, 48, etc, until you reach 1. Now count the normal way from 1 to 50. Next try counting from 1 to 100 and from 100 to 1. Concentrate on your counting and see the figures in your mind's eye as you count.

Love is an emotion of good feeling but in practice you love people when you are sincere with them, when you are patient with them, when you take time to understand who they are and why they are different from you, when you appreciate their contributions for the general good, when you let your light shine on them, when you help them without counting the costs, when you share your good fortune with them, when you share their sorrows, when you are kind to them, when you rejoice in their successes and when you have their interests in your mind. Reflect on this type of love as it affects your life.

Next take inventory of your activities today. Where did you go? What did you do? Who did you meet? What did you contribute? How did you affect your environment? How did the environment affect you?

Now visualize the next day of your life in the family and in the office or wherever you would be the next day. What do you want to see happen? For the family you might want harmony, understanding and unity. For work you might want to see that you are accomplishing your work goals and getting along with your boss and co-workers.

**Month 6, Week 4, Day 2**

Retire to your sacred place and practice a relaxation exercise. Inhale for four seconds. Hold the breath for four seconds.

Exhale for four seconds. Hold the exhalation for four seconds. Repeat the process for as many times as possible.

Count from 50 backwards that is 50, 49, 48, etc, until you reach 1. Now count the normal way from 1 to 50. Next try counting from 1 to 100 and from 100 to 1. Concentrate on your counting and see the figures in your mind's eye as you count.

Take a specific problem to your meditation with the intent of solving it. Concentrate on the problem intensely. Examine the problem in and out and reflect on why you have not been able to find a solution to the problem. Now open up your mind to suggestions from the Universe.

Next take inventory of your activities today. Where did you go? What did you do? Who did you meet? What did you contribute? How did you affect your environment? How did the environment affect you?

Now visualize the next day of your life in the family and in the office or wherever you would be the next day. What do you want to see happen? For the family you might want harmony, understanding and unity. For work you might want to see that you are accomplishing your work goals and getting along with your boss and co-workers.

**Month 6, Week 4, Day 3**

Retire to your sacred place and practice a relaxation exercise. Inhale for four seconds. Hold the breath for four seconds. Exhale for four seconds. Hold the exhalation for four seconds. Repeat the process for as many times as possible.

Count from 50 backwards that is 50, 49, 48, etc, until you reach 1. Now count the normal way from 1 to 50. Next try counting from 1 to 100 and from 100 to 1. Concentrate on your counting and see the figures in your mind's eye as you count.

Who are you and what is your purpose in life? Reflect on this question. Open up to LIFE and live a life of purpose!

Next take inventory of your activities today. Where did you go? What did you do? Who did you meet? What did you contribute? How did you affect your environment? How did the environment affect you?

Now visualize the next day of your life in the family and in the office or wherever you would be the next day. What do you want to see happen? For the family you might want harmony, understanding and unity. For work you might want to see that you are accomplishing your work goals and getting along with your boss and co-workers.

**Month 6, Week 4, Day 4**

Retire to your sacred place and practice a relaxation exercise. Inhale for four seconds. Hold the breath for four seconds. Exhale for four seconds. Hold the exhalation for four seconds. Repeat the process for as many times as possible.

Count from 50 backwards that is 50, 49, 48, etc, until you reach 1. Now count the normal way from 1 to 50. Next try counting from 1 to 100 and from 100 to 1. Concentrate on your counting and see the figures in your mind's eye as you count.

Now reflect on the following: You cannot control what happens to you, but you can control your attitude toward what happens to you, and in that, you will be mastering change rather than allowing it to master you. Brian Tracy

Next take inventory of your activities today. Where did you go? What did you do? Who did you meet? What did you contribute? How did you affect your environment? How did the environment affect you?

Now visualize the next day of your life in the family and in the office or wherever you would be the next day. What do you want to see happen? For the family you might want harmony, understanding and unity. For work you might want to see that you are accomplishing your work goals and getting along with your boss and co-workers.

**Month 6, Week 4, Day 5**

Retire to your sacred place and practice a relaxation exercise. Inhale for four seconds. Hold the breath for four seconds. Exhale for four seconds. Hold the exhalation for four seconds. Repeat the process for as many times as possible.

Count from 50 backwards that is 50, 49, 48, etc, until you reach 1. Now count the normal way from 1 to 50. Next try counting from 1 to 100 and from 100 to 1. Concentrate on your counting and see the figures in your mind's eye as you count.

Now meditate on The Mysterious by Albert Einstein:

The most beautiful and deepest experience a man can have is the sense of the mysterious. It is the underlying principle of religion as well as all serious endeavor in art and science. He who never had this experience seems to me, if not dead, then at least blind. To sense that behind anything that can be experienced there is a something that our mind cannot grasp and whose beauty and sublimity reaches us only indirectly and as a feeble reflection, this is religiousness. In this sense I am religious. To me it suffices to wonder at these secrets and to attempt humbly to grasp with my mind a mere image of the lofty structure of all that there is.

Next take inventory of your activities today. Where did you go? What did you do? Who did you meet? What did you contribute? How did you affect your environment? How did the environment affect you?

Now visualize the next day of your life in the family and in the office or wherever you would be the next day. What do you want to see happen? For the family you might want harmony, understanding and unity. For work you might want to see that you are accomplishing your work goals and getting along with your boss and co-workers.

**Month 6, Week 4, Day 6**

Retire to your sacred place and practice a relaxation exercise. Inhale for four seconds. Hold the breath for four seconds. Exhale for four seconds. Hold the exhalation for four seconds. Repeat the process for as many times as possible.

Count from 50 backwards that is 50, 49, 48, etc, until you reach 1. Now count the normal way from 1 to 50. Next try counting from 1 to 100 and from 100 to 1. Concentrate on your counting and see the figures in your mind's eye as you count.

Now reflect on the following: It is unwise to be too sure of one's own wisdom. It is healthy to be reminded that the strongest might weaken and the wisest might err. Mohandas K. Gandhi

Next take inventory of your activities today. Where did you go? What did you do? Who did you meet? What did you contribute? How did you affect your environment? How did the environment affect you? Is there any thing you did that you could have done differently? How could you have done it next time?

Lastly visualize the next day of your life in the family and in the office or wherever you would be the next day. What do you want to see happen? For the family you might want harmony, understanding and unity. For work you might want to see that you are accomplishing your work goals and getting along with your boss and co-workers.

### Month 6, Week 4, Day 7

Attend a church, a temple, or any other meeting that brings you together with people for a common goal. If you do not have one you may begin today and find one that meets your interest and inclination. If you want you could also organize a group of your own. For instance you could start an Awakened Living Study Program. You may contact UNISM for more information.

Retire to your sacred place and practice a relaxation exercise. Inhale for four seconds. Hold the breath for four seconds. Exhale for four seconds. Hold the exhalation for four seconds. Repeat the process for as many times as possible.

Choose your favorite meditation posture and practice using the posture. For instance, if you use supports for your back during meditation start practicing your favorite posture without any support.

Next take inventory of your activities today. Where did you go? What did you do? Who did you meet? What did you contribute? How did you affect your environment? How did the environment affect you? Is there any thing you did that you could have done differently? How could you have done it next time?

Lastly visualize the next day of your life in the family and in the office or wherever you would be the next day. What do you want to see happen? For the family you might want harmony, understanding and unity. For work you might want to see that you are accomplishing your work goals and getting along with your boss and co-workers.

Congratulations! This is the end of your meditation program. You may repeat this course for as often as you want. If you learned anything in this program one of them would be to make daily meditation part of your life. In this respect we encourage you to continue the practice for as long as you live. Thank you for letting us to introduce you to meditation.

# Family Meditation Program

*Supreme Bliss is the lot of the sage, whose mind attains Peace, whose passions subside, who is without sin and who becomes one with the Absolute. Thus, free from sin, abiding always in the Eternal, the saint enjoys without effort the Bliss which flows from realization of the Infinite.* Bhagavad Gita 6:27-28

**Introduction**

The main purpose of a family meditation program is to cultivate unity within the family. As a family we are united in mission and purpose. To be united means that we care for each other; we help each other; we protect each other; we look out for each other; and we love each other. As parents we put the needs of our children above our needs and we put the needs of our family above our individual needs. Family meditation helps us to internalize our family values. The values of love teach us to care for others. Caring for others is the beginning of the development of unity consciousness. The values of patience teach us to take time in our interactions with our environment. When we take time we give way to the forces of fulfillment to work in our favor. The values of honesty teach us to be straightforward with our environment. When we are straightforward we are truthful in our dealings. The values of work teach us to contribute to the good of society. Work enables us to use our talents for the good of all creatures and at the same time helps us to take care of our own needs. The values of cooperation help us to work together with others for the accomplishment of worthwhile purposes. Cooperating with others brings out the best in us that serves as the missing link in a group effort. The values of generosity teach us to give without expecting anything in return. When we are generous with our time, talents and wealth we attract similar efforts from our environment for our good. These values are necessary not only for the growth and stability of our families but also for the growth and stability of society in general.

Family meditation also helps us to develop peace of mind. Raising children could sometimes be a daunting task but through daily meditation and disclosure we could reduce the stress of parenting. Meditation calms us down and helps us to be realistic with our environment. It helps children to divert their attention from the demands of life and focus on worthwhile goals. This diversion could be a tonic for their peace of mind and well being. Peace of mind as you would expect is necessary to excel in school since they would be able to concentrate in class and do their homework. Disclosure as mentioned above helps the parent to tune into the life of the child in school and in day care. Children like to talk about their day and do not hesitate to include disclosure in your meditation schedule for the family. In this way you could detect potential problems before they materialize. These problems could be drug use, bullies and similar issues in the life of your child.

A typical family meditation session could begin around 8:00 PM in a room like the living room, the family room or any other room. You may use meditation mats or cushions and sit facing the North or the East. Sitting facing the North aligns you with the earth's magnetic field and sitting facing the East places you in the direction of the rising sun. You may also sit in a circle or semi circle depending on whether it is an individual meditation or group meditation. In an individual meditation each meditates on an assigned subject according to the person's preference. In a group meditation each follows a guided pattern of meditation. You may begin with a breathing exercise for about 5 minutes before beginning the meditation. Breathing helps to foster the state of mind necessary for meditation. Your meditation could be for about 5 minutes initially and gradually increase the duration as the family becomes more comfortable.

It is healthy to serve tea at the end of your meditation as a treat for the family. Let an adult make the tea. The children may take turns to serve tea to each member. When choosing tea for your enjoyment after meditation, consider tea with health benefits like green tea. Green tea is said to help in boosting the immune system, regulating cholesterol levels, fighting the build-up of sticky plaque in the arteries, interfering with the cancer process, assisting in weight loss, fighting harmful bacteria and viruses, protecting the body against free radical damage, etc. For all these benefits it is worth serving green tea and raise your children to make a healthy choice for their tea needs.

Make individual disclosure a part of your meditation program. This is a proactive way of finding out what is going on in your child's life when you are not there. Let them talk about their day with respect to their classmates, teachers and friends. Ask them what they did at school or in the day care. Find out about their relationship with their friends and their teachers. Find out if there are any bullies in their class. If there are bullies what is the school doing about them. Follow up with the teacher or principal immediately. Drug use, peer pressure and discrimination are some other areas to be concerned with your child's education and well-being.

Let the children first take turns to share what happened to them in school. If they go straight to the day care after school let them also talk about what happened at the day care. There should be complete silence as soon as sharing begins. Parents should pay particular attention to each child as he or she recounts what happened. Do not interrupt the presentation. Ask questions after each presentation. Parents should also share their day at work or wherever they went and what they did during the day. Encourage the children to also ask questions after each disclosure session.

You may use part of the meditation period to make presentations on books you read during the week. You could also observe family reading time on Saturday and Sunday evenings. Family reading is when the whole family reads for about 30 minutes. Set a family reading goal. For instance each member of the family may finish reading a book of about 100 pages every week. Encourage the family by rewarding those who meet this goal. A family award certificate, a treat at your son's or daughter's favorite restaurant, or a "well done" card are some of the ways to reward any one who meets his or her goal.

Further you may also use the period after meditation to draft, update or reconsider your family rules. Family rules are important to the family and should be a visible part of the family. Every family member should have a copy. While family rules are important lack of enforcement for violations will seem as if you have no rules at all. For an effective rule let all members of the family including the children make the rules and the children should also take part in the enforcement. Enforcement could be a dollar for each violation and the proceeds donated to a non-profit organization such as a homeless shelter or animal rescue center at the end of the year.

Lastly we cannot overlook the importance of food even in a program of meditation. According to the Bhagavad Gita **(Bhagavad Gita 6:16-17):** *Meditation is not for him who eats too much, nor for him who eats not at all; nor for him who is overmuch addicted to sleep, nor for him who is always awake. But for him who regulates his food and recreation, who is balanced in action, in sleeping and in waking, it shall dispel all unhappiness.* Further the United States Department of Agriculture (USDA) in Dietary Guidelines advises us to pay particular attention to the food in our plates and to eat less. You may get a copy of the USDA Dietary Guideline by going to the following website: https://www.nal.usda.gov/fnic/dietary-guidelines

## Family Meditation: First Month

**Goal**

The goal of the first month of meditation is to be in control of your thoughts. Instead of letting your thoughts going wild you try to choose what you want to think about. Replace for instance the bad things people did to you with good things that happened to you and how you could help others with your time and talent. Master your thoughts and choose what you think about. Change your life by the thoughts you hold because your thoughts have wings and you become what you think about.

**Month 1, Week 1, Day 1**

Turn off all sources of noise such as your television and go to your meditation room at the agreed upon time. Assume your meditation positions. You may sit on the floor, on meditation mats or on meditation cushions. You may sit facing the East, or the North. Alternatively you could sit forming a semi circle or a full circle.

Inhale for four seconds. Hold the breath for four seconds. Exhale for four seconds. Hold the exhalation for four seconds. Repeat the process for as many times as possible.

Now have your favorite picture before you. First look at the picture for thirty seconds and note how it looks like. Now put away the picture but see it in your mind's eye for about thirty seconds. If your mind wonders bring it back to the image until you could see it continuously for five minutes or more.

Now share your day with the rest of the family. This is the individual disclosure session. What happened to you, your friends and teachers during the day? What special role did you play in school? What contribution did you make in school? Did you get

hurt at work or in school? If you did how did it happen and who was responsible? What have you done to address the issue? What did others do to address the issue? How do you feel now?

Next take inventory of your activities today. Where did you go? What did you do? Who did you meet? What did you contribute? How did you affect your environment? How did the environment affect you? Is there any thing you did that you could have done differently? How could you have done it next time?

Next visualize the next day of your life in the family, at work or in school. What do you want to see happen? For the family you might want harmony, understanding and unity. For work you might want to accomplish your work goals and get along with your boss and co-workers. For school you might see that you are getting along with your teachers and fellow students. You are doing your schoolwork and getting good grades as well as participating in school activities and doing well.

**Month 1, Week 1, Day 2**

Retire to your sacred place and practice a relaxation exercise. Inhale for four seconds. Hold the breath for four seconds. Exhale for four seconds. Hold the exhalation for four seconds. Repeat the process for as many times as possible.

Now have a book before you. First look at the book for thirty seconds and note the shape, color and texture. Now put away the book but see it in your mind's eye for about thirty seconds. If your mind wonders bring it back to the image until you could see it continuously for five minutes or more.

Now share your day with the rest of the family. This is the individual disclosure session. What happened to you, your friends and teachers during the day? What special role did you play in school? What contribution did you make in school? Did you get

hurt at work or in school? If you did how did it happen and who was responsible? What have you done to address the issue? What did others do to address the issue? How do you feel now?

Next take inventory of your activities today. Where did you go? What did you do? Who did you meet? What did you contribute? How did you affect your environment? How did the environment affect you? Is there any thing you did that you could have done differently? How could you have done it next time?

Next visualize the next day of your life in the family, at work or in school. What do you want to see happen? For the family you might want harmony, understanding and unity. For work you might want to accomplish your work goals and get along with your boss and co-workers. For school you might see that you are getting along with your teachers and fellow students. You are doing your schoolwork and getting good grades as well as participating in school activities and doing well.

**Month 1, Week1, Day 3**

Retire to your sacred place and practice a relaxation exercise. Inhale for four seconds. Hold the breath for four seconds. Exhale for four seconds. Hold the exhalation for four seconds. Repeat the process for as many times as possible.

Reflect on an inspiring childhood incident that makes your day. What happened? Where did it happen? Who else is involved? What are they doing? What are you doing? What are they saying? What are you saying? What makes it memorable?

Now share your day with the rest of the family. This is the individual disclosure session. What happened to you, your friends and teachers during the day? What special role did you play in school? What contribution did you make in school? Did you get hurt at work or in school? If you did how did it happen and who

was responsible? What have you done to address the issue? What did others do to address the issue? How do you feel now?

Next take inventory of your activities today. Where did you go? What did you do? Who did you meet? What did you contribute? How did you affect your environment? How did the environment affect you? Is there any thing you did that you could have done differently? How could you have done it next time?

Next visualize the next day of your life in the family, at work or in school. What do you want to see happen? For the family you might want harmony, understanding and unity. For work you might want to accomplish your work goals and get along with your boss and co-workers. For school you might see that you are getting along with your teachers and fellow students. You are doing your schoolwork and getting good grades as well as participating in school activities and doing well.

**Month 1, Week 1, Day 4**

Retire to your sacred place and practice a relaxation exercise. Inhale for four seconds. Hold the breath for four seconds. Exhale for four seconds. Hold the exhalation for four seconds. Repeat the process for as many times as possible.

Now have an apple before you. First look at the apple for about thirty seconds and note the shape, color and texture. Now put away the apple but see it in your mind's eye for about thirty seconds. If your mind wonders bring it back to the image until you could see it continuously for five minutes or more.

Now share your day with the rest of the family. This is the individual disclosure session. What happened to you, your friends and teachers during the day? What special role did you play in school? What contribution did you make in school? Did you get hurt at work or in school? If you did how did it happen and who

was responsible? What have you done to address the issue? What did others do to address the issue? How do you feel now?

Next take inventory of your activities today. Where did you go? What did you do? Who did you meet? What did you contribute? How did you affect your environment? How did the environment affect you? Is there any thing you did that you could have done differently? How could you have done it next time?

Next visualize the next day of your life in the family, at work or in school. What do you want to see happen? For the family you might want harmony, understanding and unity. For work you might want to accomplish your work goals and get along with your boss and co-workers. For school you might see that you are getting along with your teachers and fellow students. You are doing your schoolwork and getting good grades as well as participating in school activities and doing well.

## Month 1, Week 1, Day 5

Retire to your sacred place and practice a relaxation exercise. Inhale for four seconds. Hold the breath for four seconds. Exhale for four seconds. Hold the exhalation for four seconds. Repeat the process for as many times as possible.

Now reflect on **Initiative by George Bernard Shaw**: People are always blaming their circumstances for what they are. I don't believe in circumstances. The people who get on in this world are the people who get up and look for the circumstances they want, and if they can't find them, they make them.

Now share your day with the rest of the family. This is the individual disclosure session. What happened to you, your friends and teachers during the day? What special role did you play in school? What contribution did you make in school? Did you get hurt at work or in school? If you did how did it happen and who

was responsible? What have you done to address the issue? What did others do to address the issue? How do you feel now?

Next take inventory of your activities today. Where did you go? What did you do? Who did you meet? What did you contribute? How did you affect your environment? How did the environment affect you? Is there any thing you did that you could have done differently? How could you have done it next time?

Next visualize the next day of your life in the family, at work or in school. What do you want to see happen? For the family you might want harmony, understanding and unity. For work you might want to accomplish your work goals and get along with your boss and co-workers. For school you might see that you are getting along with your teachers and fellow students. You are doing your schoolwork and getting good grades as well as participating in school activities and doing well.

**Month 1, Week 1, Day 6**

Retire to your sacred place and practice a relaxation exercise. Inhale for four seconds. Hold the breath for four seconds. Exhale for four seconds. Hold the exhalation for four seconds. Repeat the process for as many times as possible.

Now reflect on the following: THE FAMILY IS---
The Most important unit of society,
A Spiritual thread that connects us to the world,
A loving haven that has room for all creatures,
Strengthened by Universal Spiritual Values,
Perfected by discipline and unconditional Love,
The crucible in which life is made and nurtured,
Enduring and cannot be broken in any way,
The birthplace of character and humaneness,
Our first Love, our Home and our Support,

Bound by an invincible thread that stretches
From the beginning of time into eternity! **Dr. Sonari**

Next take inventory of your activities today. Where did you go? What did you do? Who did you meet? What did you contribute? How did you affect your environment? How did the environment affect you? Is there any thing you did that you could have done differently? How could you have done it next time?

Lastly visualize the next day of your life in the family, at work or in school. What do you want to see happen? For the family you might want harmony, understanding and unity. For work you might want to accomplish your work goals and get along with your boss and co-workers. For school you might see that you are getting along with your teachers and fellow students. You are doing your schoolwork and getting good grades as well as participating in school activities and doing well.

**Month 1, Week 1, Day 7**

Attend a church, a temple, or any other meeting that brings you together with people for a common goal. If you do not have one you may begin today and find one that meets your interest and inclination. If you want you could also organize a group of your own. For instance you could start an Awakened Living Study Program. You may contact UNISM for more information.

Retire to your sacred place and practice a relaxation exercise. Inhale for four seconds. Hold the breath for four seconds. Exhale for four seconds. Hold the exhalation for four seconds. Repeat the process for as many times as possible.

Choose your favorite meditation posture and practice using the posture. For instance, if you use supports for your back during meditation start practicing your favorite posture without any support.

Next take inventory of your activities today. Where did you go? What did you do? Who did you meet? What did you contribute? How did you affect your environment? How did the environment affect you? Is there any thing you did that you could have done differently? How could you have done it next time?

Lastly visualize the next day of your life in the family, at work or in school. What do you want to see happen? For the family you might want harmony, understanding and unity. For work you might want to accomplish your work goals and get along with your boss and co-workers. For school you might see that you are getting along with your teachers and fellow students. You are doing your schoolwork and getting good grades as well as participating in school activities and doing well.

**Month 1, Week 2, Day 1**

Assume the state of meditation by first practicing a relaxation exercise. Count from 100 backwards that is 100, 99, 88, etc, until you reach 1. Now count the normal way from 1 to 100. Concentrate on your counting and see the figures in your mind's eye as you count.

Now have a banana before you. First look at the banana for about thirty seconds and note the shape, color and texture. Now put away the banana but see it in your mind's eye for about thirty seconds. If your mind wonders bring it back to the image until you could see it continuously for five minutes or more.

Now share your day with the rest of the family. This is the individual disclosure session. What happened to you, your friends and teachers during the day? What special role did you play in school? What contribution did you make in school? Did you get hurt at work or in school? If you did how did it happen and who

was responsible? What have you done to address the issue? What did others do to address the issue? How do you feel now?

Next take inventory of your activities today. Where did you go? What did you do? Who did you meet? What did you contribute? How did you affect your environment? How did the environment affect you? Is there any thing you did that you could have done differently? How could you have done it next time?

Next visualize the next day of your life in the family, at work or in school. What do you want to see happen? For the family you might want harmony, understanding and unity. For work you might want to accomplish your work goals and get along with your boss and co-workers. For school you might see that you are getting along with your teachers and fellow students. You are doing your schoolwork and getting good grades as well as participating in school activities and doing well.

**Month 1, Week 2, Day 2**

Assume the state of meditation by first practicing a relaxation exercise. Count from 100 backwards that is 100, 99, 88, etc, until you reach 1. Now count the normal way from 1 to 100. Concentrate on your counting and see the figures in your mind's eye as you count.

Now check out your Desktop Computer. First look at the Computer for about sixty seconds and note the parts at the front and at the back. Now go back to your meditation room and see the computer in your mind's eye. Name the parts. How many parts did you recall? What are they?

Now share your day with the rest of the family. This is the individual disclosure session. What happened to you, your friends and teachers during the day? What special role did you play in school? What contribution did you make in school? Did you get

hurt at work or in school? If you did how did it happen and who was responsible? What have you done to address the issue? What did others do to address the issue? How do you feel now?

Next take inventory of your activities today. Where did you go? What did you do? Who did you meet? What did you contribute? How did you affect your environment? How did the environment affect you? Is there any thing you did that you could have done differently? How could you have done it next time?

Next visualize the next day of your life in the family, at work or in school. What do you want to see happen? For the family you might want harmony, understanding and unity. For work you might want to accomplish your work goals and get along with your boss and co-workers. For school you might see that you are getting along with your teachers and fellow students. You are doing your schoolwork and getting good grades as well as participating in school activities and doing well.

**Month 1, Week 2, Day 3**

Assume the state of meditation by first practicing a relaxation exercise. Count from 100 backwards that is 100, 99, 88, etc, until you reach 1. Now count the normal way from 1 to 100. Concentrate on your counting and see the figures in your mind's eye as you count.

Now check out your refrigerator and count what are in it. Go back to your meditation room and reflect on the refrigerator. Note the shape, color and the height. Now open it and count all the things in it. How many did you count? Compare your result with those of others. Compare your result with the actual count.

Now share your day with the rest of the family. This is the individual disclosure session. What happened to you, your friends and teachers during the day? What special role did you play in

school? What contribution did you make in school? Did you get hurt at work or in school? If you did how did it happen and who was responsible? What have you done to address the issue? What did others do to address the issue? How do you feel now?

Next take inventory of your activities today. Where did you go? What did you do? Who did you meet? What did you contribute? How did you affect your environment? How did the environment affect you? Is there any thing you did that you could have done differently? How could you have done it next time?

Next visualize the next day of your life in the family, at work or in school. What do you want to see happen? For the family you might want harmony, understanding and unity. For work you might want to accomplish your work goals and get along with your boss and co-workers. For school you might see that you are getting along with your teachers and fellow students. You are doing your schoolwork and getting good grades as well as participating in school activities and doing well.

**Month 1, Week 2, Day 4**

Assume the state of meditation by first practicing a relaxation exercise. Count from 100 backwards that is 100, 99, 88, etc, until you reach 1. Now count the normal way from 1 to 100. Concentrate on your counting and see the figures in your mind's eye as you count.

Now check out the guest restroom and note what is in it. Go back to your meditation room and reflect on the guest restroom. Note the shape, color and the size. Now go into the room and count all the things in it. How many did you count? Compare your result with those of others. Compare your result with the actual count.

Now share your day with the rest of the family. This is the individual disclosure session. What happened to you, your friends

and teachers during the day? What special role did you play in school? What contribution did you make in school? Did you get hurt at work or in school? If you did how did it happen and who was responsible? What have you done to address the issue? What did others do to address the issue? How do you feel now?

Next take inventory of your activities today. Where did you go? What did you do? Who did you meet? What did you contribute? How did you affect your environment? How did the environment affect you? Is there any thing you did that you could have done differently? How could you have done it next time?

Next visualize the next day of your life in the family, at work or in school. What do you want to see happen? For the family you might want harmony, understanding and unity. For work you might want to accomplish your work goals and get along with your boss and co-workers. For school you might see that you are getting along with your teachers and fellow students. You are doing your schoolwork and getting good grades as well as participating in school activities and doing well.

**Month 1, Week 2, Day 5**

Assume the state of meditation by first practicing a relaxation exercise. Count from 100 backwards that is 100, 99, 88, etc, until you reach 1. Now count the normal way from 1 to 100. Concentrate on your counting and see the figures in your mind's eye as you count.

Now reflect on the **Present by W.E.B. Du Bois**: "Now is the accepted time, not tomorrow, not some more convenient season. It is today that our best work can be done and not some future day or future year. It is today that we fit ourselves for the greater usefulness of tomorrow. Today is the seed time, now are the hours of work, and tomorrow comes the harvest and the playtime".

Now share your day with the rest of the family. This is the individual disclosure session. What happened to you, your friends and teachers during the day? What special role did you play in school? What contribution did you make in school? Did you get hurt at work or in school? If you did how did it happen and who was responsible? What have you done to address the issue? What did others do to address the issue? How do you feel now?

Next take inventory of your activities today. Where did you go? What did you do? Who did you meet? What did you contribute? How did you affect your environment? How did the environment affect you? Is there any thing you did that you could have done differently? How could you have done it next time?

Next visualize the next day of your life in the family, at work or in school. What do you want to see happen? For the family you might want harmony, understanding and unity. For work you might want to accomplish your work goals and get along with your boss and co-workers. For school you might see that you are getting along with your teachers and fellow students. You are doing your schoolwork and getting good grades as well as participating in school activities and doing well.

**Month 1, Week 2, Day 6**

Assume the state of meditation by first practicing a relaxation exercise. Count from 100 backwards that is 100, 99, 88, etc, until you reach 1. Now count the normal way from 1 to 100. Concentrate on your counting and see the figures in your mind's eye as you count.

Now reflect on the following: Families are the compass that guides us. They are the inspiration to reach great heights, and our comfort when we occasionally falter. **Brad Henry**

Next take inventory of your activities today. Where did you go? What did you do? Who did you meet? What did you contribute? How did you affect your environment? How did the environment affect you? Is there any thing you did that you could have done differently? How could you have done it next time?

Lastly visualize the next day of your life in the family, at work or in school. What do you want to see happen? For the family you might want harmony, understanding and unity. For work you might want to accomplish your work goals and get along with your boss and co-workers. For school you might see that you are getting along with your teachers and fellow students. You are doing your schoolwork and getting good grades as well as participating in school activities and doing well.

**Month 1, Week 2, Day 7**

Attend a church, a temple, or any other meeting that brings you together with people for a common goal. If you do not have one you may begin today and find one that meets your interest and inclination. If you want you could also organize a group of your own. For instance you could start an Awakened Living Study Program. You may contact UNISM for more information.

Retire to your sacred place and practice a relaxation exercise. Inhale for four seconds. Hold the breath for four seconds. Exhale for four seconds. Hold the exhalation for four seconds. Repeat the process for as many times as possible.

Choose your favorite meditation posture and practice using the posture. For instance, if you use supports for your back during

meditation start practicing your favorite posture without any support.

Next take inventory of your activities today. Where did you go? What did you do? Who did you meet? What did you contribute? How did you affect your environment? How did the environment affect you? Is there any thing you did that you could have done differently? How could you have done it next time?

Lastly visualize the next day of your life in the family, at work or in school. What do you want to see happen? For the family you might want harmony, understanding and unity. For work you might want to accomplish your work goals and get along with your boss and co-workers. For school you might see that you are getting along with your teachers and fellow students. You are doing your schoolwork and getting good grades as well as participating in school activities and doing well.

Month 1, Week 3, Day 1

Assume the state of meditation by first practicing a relaxation exercise. Count from 100 backwards that is 100, 99, 88, etc, until you reach 1. Now count the normal way from 1 to 100. Concentrate on your counting and see the figures in your mind's eye as you count.

Next visualize the route you normally take to your office, school, or any place you frequently visit. Leave your home and start walking or driving or riding whatever your means of transportation might be. Stop at the stop signs and note all the things that you see on your way. Greet the people, the squirrels and the flowers on your way. On arrival pack your means of transportation and walk into the building or location. If you walked to the place or had a ride just go right in. Note what people are doing. Get to your table and begin your work for the day. Note all your activities including your relationship with customers, your boss and co-workers. Sign off at the end of the day and return home noting all the important sights on your way back. Visualization, when used in advance of an activity, helps the activity to go like clock work. An invincible hand seems to guide your activities. You may bring order to your daily life by practicing visualization in advance of all your activities.

Now share your day with the rest of the family. This is the individual disclosure session. What happened to you, your friends and teachers during the day? What special role did you play in school? What contribution did you make in school? Did you get hurt at work or in school? If you did how did it happen and who was responsible? What have you done to address the issue? What did others do to address the issue? How do you feel now?

Next take inventory of your activities today. Where did you go? What did you do? Who did you meet? What did you contribute? How did you affect your environment? How did the environment affect you? Is there any thing you did that you could have done differently? How could you have done it next time?

Next visualize the next day of your life in the family, at work or in school. What do you want to see happen? For the family you might want harmony, understanding and unity. For work you might want to accomplish your work goals and get along with your boss and co-workers. For school you might see that you are getting along with your teachers and fellow students. You are doing your schoolwork and getting good grades as well as participating in school activities and doing well.

**Month 1, Week 3, Day 2**

Assume the state of meditation by first practicing a relaxation exercise. Count from 100 backwards that is 100, 99, 88, etc, until

you might want harmony, understanding and unity. For work you might want to accomplish your work goals and get along with your boss and co-workers. For school you might see that you are getting along with your teachers and fellow students. You are doing your schoolwork and getting good grades as well as participating in school activities and doing well.

**Month 1, Week 4, Day 1:**

Assume the state of meditation by first practicing a relaxation exercise. Count from 100 backwards that is 100, 99, 88, etc, until you reach 1. Now count the normal way from 1 to 100. Concentrate on your counting and see the figures in your mind's eye as you count.

Next visualize visiting a flower garden. You may visit a rose garden, a tulip garden, a rhododendron garden or any flower garden of your choice. Observe the design of the garden. What flowers are in the garden? Does the garden only have one kind of flower or several kinds? Name the flowers. Note their colors, shape and appeal. Reflect on how they came to be so colorful.

Now share your day with the rest of the family. This is the individual disclosure session. What happened to you, your friends and teachers during the day? What special role did you play in school? What contribution did you make in school? Did you get hurt at work or in school? If you did how did it happen and who was responsible? What have you done to address the issue? What did others do to address the issue? How do you feel now?

Next take inventory of your activities today. Where did you go? What did you do? Who did you meet? What did you contribute? How did you affect your environment? How did the environment affect you? Is there any thing you did that you could have done differently? How could you have done it next time?

Now visualize the next day of your life in the family, at work or in school. What do you want to see happen? For the family you might want harmony, understanding and unity. For work you might want to accomplish your work goals and get along with your boss and co-workers. For school you might see that you are getting along with your teachers and fellow students. You are doing your schoolwork and getting good grades as well as participating in school activities and doing well.

**Month 1, Week 4, Day 2**:
Assume the state of meditation by first practicing a relaxation exercise. Count from 100 backwards that is 100, 99, 88, etc, until you reach 1. Now count the normal way from 1 to 100. Concentrate on your counting and see the figures in your mind's eye as you count.

Reflect on the following quote from the Universal Holy Book: It may seem to you at this period that your peers love you more. But make no mistake about the love of your parents. You are part of your parents. You are not part of your peers. Your parents love you and they want the best for you. Your peers pretend to love you and they want to be the best. Your parents are a permanent part of you. You peers are a temporary part of you. You parents will be there for you at the end of the day. Your peers will go to their homes at the end of the day. You parents will be there for you for as long as they live. Your peers will not be there after this phase! **Universal Holy Book: The Book of Life 6:51-62**

Now share your day with the rest of the family. This is the individual disclosure session. What happened to you, your friends and teachers during the day? What special role did you play in school? What contribution did you make in school? Did you get hurt at work or in school? If you did how did it happen and who

was responsible? What have you done to address the issue? What did others do to address the issue? How do you feel now?

Next take inventory of your activities today. Where did you go? What did you do? Who did you meet? What did you contribute? How did you affect your environment? How did the environment affect you? Is there any thing you did that you could have done differently? How could you have done it next time?

Next visualize the next day of your life in the family, at work or in school. What do you want to see happen? For the family you might want harmony, understanding and unity. For work you might want to accomplish your work goals and get along with your boss and co-workers. For school you might see that you are getting along with your teachers and fellow students. You are doing your schoolwork and getting good grades as well as participating in school activities and doing well.

**Month 1, Week 4, Day 3**

Assume the state of meditation by first practicing a relaxation exercise. Count from 100 backwards that is 100, 99, 88, etc, until you reach 1. Now count the normal way from 1 to 100. Concentrate on your counting and see the figures in your mind's eye as you count.

Next visualize the route you normally take to the grocery store. Leave your home driving or as a passenger. Stop at the stop signs and note all the things that you see on your way. Pack your vehicle on arrival and walk into the store. Get a shopping cart and begin to shop. Observe the people around you. Note the arrangement of the goods. Walk through all the isles and note the things and people you see. Now go to the cashier and pay for your grocery. First place them on the checking stand one by one at your turn. Watch as the cashier scans them. Now pay for your grocery when she is done. Note the means of payment. Is it a credit card, check or cash? You may now put your grocery in bags and put the bags in the cart. In some stores the cashier or another person may bag the grocery for you. Note how the person does it. Finally you may push your cart to your vehicle and transfer the bags into your vehicle and return the cart to the cart stand. You may now drive home. Obey traffic rules on your way back and note all the important sights on your way. Once at home off load your grocery and arrange them in your refrigerator or pantry as the case may be.

Now share your day with the rest of the family. This is the individual disclosure session. What happened to you, your friends and teachers during the day? What special role did you play in school? What contribution did you make in school? Did you get hurt at work or in school? If you did how did it happen and who was responsible? What have you done to address the issue? What did others do to address the issue? How do you feel now?

Next take inventory of your activities today. Where did you go? What did you do? Who did you meet? What did you contribute? How did you affect your environment? How did the environment affect you? Is there any thing you did that you could have done differently? How could you have done it next time?

Next visualize the next day of your life in the family, at work or in school. What do you want to see happen? For the family you might want harmony, understanding and unity. For work you might want to accomplish your work goals and get along with your boss and co-workers. For school you might see that you are getting along with your teachers and fellow students. You are doing your schoolwork and getting good grades as well as participating in school activities and doing well.

**Month 1, Week 4, Day 4**

Assume the state of meditation by first practicing a relaxation exercise. Count from 100 backwards that is 100, 99, 88, etc, until you reach 1. Now count the normal way from 1 to 100. Concentrate on your counting and see the figures in your mind's eye as you count.

Next imagine the family room and see it in your mind's eye. Note the color of the walls and the dimensions. Now walk to your family room and sit on one of the chairs. Observe all the things in the family room and count the things in it starting with the television. How many did you count? Compare your result with those of others. Compare your result with the actual count.

Now share your day with the rest of the family. This is the individual disclosure session. What happened to you, your friends and teachers during the day? What special role did you play in school? What contribution did you make in school? Did you get hurt at work or in school? If you did how did it happen and who was responsible? What have you done to address the issue? What did others do to address the issue? How do you feel now?

Next take inventory of your activities today. Where did you go? What did you do? Who did you meet? What did you contribute? How did you affect your environment? How did the environment affect you? Is there any thing you did that you could have done differently? How could you have done it next time?

Next visualize the next day of your life in the family, at work or in school. What do you want to see happen? For the family you might want harmony, understanding and unity. For work you might want to accomplish your work goals and get along with your boss and co-workers. For school you might see that you are getting along with your teachers and fellow students. You are doing your

schoolwork and getting good grades as well as participating in school activities and doing well.

**Month 1, Week 4, Day 5**

Assume the state of meditation by first practicing a relaxation exercise. Count from 100 backwards that is 100, 99, 88, etc, until you reach 1. Now count the normal way from 1 to 100. Concentrate on your counting and see the figures in your mind's eye as you count.

Next reflect on the Life of **Benjamin Carson, Surgeon by The Resilience Project**

In the Fifth grade, Benjamin Carson thought he was one of the dumbest kids in his class. His classmates though he was one of the dumbest, his teacher thought he was one of the dumbest, and he thought he was one of the dumbest. Therefore, when he brought home a report that reflected poor progress, Benjamin was very philosophical about it. He told his mother, "Yah, you know it doesn't matter very much". His mother was a different opinion. Having only a third grade education, Mrs. Carson knew that her children's only chance to escape poverty was through a good education. Her two boys were not reaching their potential at school, and she knew that if they were going to get a good education, it would have to start at home. She began with three rules. Rule number one, the boys would only be allowed to watch two pre-selected TV shows per week. Rule number two, the two boys would have to finish all their homework before they could watch TV or even play outside. Rule number three, the boys would have to read two books from the library each week and write a book report on each of them. Benjamin was dismayed at these new rules and tried very hard to talk his mother out of them. She stood firm, and not thinking to disobey his mother, he followed her rules.

Before long he saw the fruits of his labor, when he was the only one who knew an answer to a question the teacher asked the class. Then there was a second question only he knew the answer to. His teacher and rest of his classmates were surprised that he knew the correct answer to such hard questions. He was even a little surprised himself, but he knew his knowledge came from the books was reading. He began to surmise that if he could learn just a few facts from books at the library he could learn anything. Benjamin continued on his road of growth and became an academic leader in his school. He had learned to love reading and realized that he could channel that love into learning. He did not let the labels and jeers of others, forever box him into an unproductive and unfulfilling future. Mrs. Carson did not settle for less then her boys were capable of being, she demanded that they take their education seriously and gave them a structured way they could do it. Today Benjamin Carson, the boy who thought he was the dumbest boy in his 5th grade class, is a world famous surgeon at the prestigious Johns Hopkins Hospital in Maryland.

    Now share your day with the rest of the family. This is the individual disclosure session. What happened to you, your friends and teachers during the day? What special role did you play in school? What contribution did you make in school? Did you get hurt at work or in school? If you did how did it happen and who was responsible? What have you done to address the issue? What did others do to address the issue? How do you feel now?

    Next take inventory of your activities today. Where did you go? What did you do? Who did you meet? What did you contribute? How did you affect your environment? How did the environment affect you? Is there any thing you did that you could have done differently? How could you have done it next time?

Next visualize the next day of your life in the family, at work or in school. What do you want to see happen? For the family you might want harmony, understanding and unity. For work you might want to accomplish your work goals and get along with your boss and co-workers. For school you might see that you are getting along with your teachers and fellow students. You are doing your schoolwork and getting good grades as well as participating in school activities and doing well.

### Month 1, Week 4, Day 6

Retire to your sacred place and practice a relaxation exercise. Inhale for four seconds. Hold the breath for four seconds. Exhale for four seconds. Hold the exhalation for four seconds. Repeat the process for as many times as possible.

Count from 100 backwards that is 100, 99, 88, etc, until you reach 1. Now count the normal way from 1 to 100. Concentrate on your counting and see the figures in your mind's eye as you count.

Now reflect on the following: Supporting one's father and mother, cherishing wife and children and a peaceful occupation; this is the greatest blessing. **Buddhism. Sutta Nipata 262**

Next take inventory of your activities today. Where did you go? What did you do? Who did you meet? What did you contribute? How did you affect your environment? How did the environment affect you? Is there any thing you did that you could have done differently? How could you have done it next time?

Lastly visualize the next day of your life in the family, at work or in school. What do you want to see happen? For the family you might want harmony, understanding and unity. For work you might want to accomplish your work goals and get along with your boss and co-workers. For school you might see that you are getting along with your teachers and fellow students. You are doing your

schoolwork and getting good grades as well as participating in school activities and doing well.

**Month 1, Week 4, Day 7**

Attend a church, a temple, or any other meeting that brings you together with people for a common goal. If you do not have one you may begin today and find one that meets your interest and inclination. If you want you could also organize a group of your own. For instance you could start an Awakened Living Study Program. You may contact UNISM for more information.

Retire to your sacred place and practice a relaxation exercise. Inhale for four seconds. Hold the breath for four seconds. Exhale for four seconds. Hold the exhalation for four seconds. Repeat the process for as many times as possible.

Choose your favorite meditation posture and practice using the posture. For instance, if you use supports for your back during meditation start practicing your favorite posture without any support.

Next take inventory of your activities today. Where did you go? What did you do? Who did you meet? What did you contribute? How did you affect your environment? How did the environment affect you? Is there any thing you did that you could have done differently? How could you have done it next time?

Lastly visualize the next day of your life in the family, at work or in school. What do you want to see happen? For the family you might want harmony, understanding and unity. For work you might want to accomplish your work goals and get along with your boss and co-workers. For school you might see that you are getting along with your teachers and fellow students. You are doing your schoolwork and getting good grades as well as participating in school activities and doing well.

# Family Meditation: Second Month

**Goal**

The goal of the second month of meditation is to improve your power of visualization. Visualization is seeing with your mind and it plays a significant role in creation. The statement that "if you can see it, you can create it" is not just a fancy phrase. All creation begins from within and the more you can focus the better you will be in creating the circumstances of your life. Train your mind to focus on the images you want to create and avoid the images that intrude on your mind.

**Month 2, Week 1, Day 1**

Assume the state of meditation by first practicing a relaxation exercise. Inhale for four seconds. Hold the breath for four seconds. Exhale for four seconds. Hold the exhalation for four seconds. Repeat the process for as many times as possible.

Count from 100 backwards that is 100, 99, 88, etc, until you reach 1. Now count the normal way from 1 to 100. Concentrate on your counting and see the figures in your mind's eye as you count.

Reflect on **Responsibility and Commitment by Eric Liu and Nick Hanauer:** Our commitment should be to leave our environment in better shape than when we found it, our nation's fiscal house in better order, our public infrastructure in better repair, and our people better educated and healthier. To indulge in immediate gratification and exploitation is an insult to previous generations, who sacrificed for us, and thievery from the next generation, who depend on our virtue.

Now share your day with the rest of the family. This is the individual disclosure session. What happened to you, your friends and teachers during the day? What special role did you play in

school? What contribution did you make in school? Did you get hurt at work or in school? If you did how did it happen and who was responsible? What have you done to address the issue? What did others do to address the issue? How do you feel now?

Next take inventory of your activities today. Where did you go? What did you do? Who did you meet? What did you contribute? How did you affect your environment? How did the environment affect you? Is there any thing you did that you could have done differently? How could you have done it next time?

Now visualize the next day of your life in the family, at work or in school. What do you want to see happen? For the family you might want harmony, understanding and unity. For work you might want to accomplish your work goals and get along with your boss and co-workers. For school you might see that you are getting along with your teachers and fellow students. You are doing your schoolwork and getting good grades as well as participating in school activities and doing well.

**Month 2, Week 1, Day 2**

Assume the state of meditation by first practicing a relaxation exercise. Inhale for four seconds. Hold the breath for four seconds. Exhale for four seconds. Hold the exhalation for four seconds. Repeat the process for as many times as possible.

Count from 100 backwards that is 100, 99, 88, etc, until you reach 1. Now count the normal way from 1 to 100. Concentrate on your counting and see the figures in your mind's eye as you count.

Reflect on **Life by Proverbs 23:19-21:** Listen, my son, and be wise, and set your heart on the right path: Do not join those who drink too much wine or gorge themselves on meat, for drunkards and gluttons become poor, and drowsiness clothes them in rags.

Now share your day with the rest of the family. This is the individual disclosure session. What happened to you, your friends and teachers during the day? What special role did you play in school? What contribution did you make in school? Did you get hurt at work or in school? If you did how did it happen and who was responsible? What have you done to address the issue? What did others do to address the issue? How do you feel now?

Next take inventory of your activities today. Where did you go? What did you do? Who did you meet? What did you contribute? How did you affect your environment? How did the environment affect you? Is there any thing you did that you could have done differently? How could you have done it next time?

Now visualize the next day of your life in the family, at work or in school. What do you want to see happen? For the family you might want harmony, understanding and unity. For work you might want to accomplish your work goals and get along with your boss and co-workers. For school you might see that you are getting along with your teachers and fellow students. You are doing your schoolwork and getting good grades as well as participating in school activities and doing well.

**Month 2, Week 1, Day 3**

Assume the state of meditation by first practicing a relaxation exercise. Inhale for four seconds. Hold the breath for four seconds. Exhale for four seconds. Hold the exhalation for four seconds. Repeat the process for as many times as possible.

Count from 100 backwards that is 100, 99, 88, etc, until you reach 1. Now count the normal way from 1 to 100. Concentrate on your counting and see the figures in your mind's eye as you count.

Next have an orange before you. First look at the orange for thirty seconds and note the shape, color and texture. Now put away the orange but see it in your mind's eye for thirty seconds. If your mind wonders bring it back to the image until you could see it continuously for about five minutes or more.

Now share your day with the rest of the family. This is the individual disclosure session. What happened to you, your friends and teachers during the day? What special role did you play in school? What contribution did you make in school? Did you get hurt at work or in school? If you did how did it happen and who was responsible? What have you done to address the issue? What did others do to address the issue? How do you feel?

Next take inventory of your activities today. Where did you go? What did you do? Who did you meet? What did you contribute? How did you affect your environment? How did the environment affect you? Is there any thing you did that you could have done differently? How could you have done it next time?

Now visualize the next day of your life in the family, at work or in school. What do you want to see happen? For the family you might want harmony, understanding and unity. For work you might want to accomplish your work goals and get along with your boss and co-workers. For school you might see that you are getting along with your teachers and fellow students. You are doing your schoolwork and getting good grades as well as participating in school activities and doing well.

**Month 2, Week 1, Day 4**

Assume the state of meditation by first practicing a relaxation exercise. Inhale for four seconds. Hold the breath for four seconds. Exhale for four seconds. Hold the exhalation for four seconds. Repeat the process for as many times as possible.

Count from 100 backwards that is 100, 99, **88**, etc, until you reach 1. Now count the normal way from 1 to 100. Concentrate on your counting and see the figures in your mind's eye as you count.

Visualize that you are in a boat at the middle of a turbulent sea. The waves rise and fall and you feel like being swallowed by the sea. Gradually visualize the turbulent sea calming down. The sea becomes so calm that you could not even imagine there was ever a storm on that sea. Bring calm and peace to your troubled world with this exercise.

Now share your day with the rest of the family. This is the individual disclosure session. What happened to you, your friends and teachers during the day? What special role did you play in school? What contribution did you make in school? Did you get hurt at work or in school? If you did how did it happen and who was responsible? What have you done to address the issue? What did others do to address the issue? How do you feel?

Next take inventory of your activities today. Where did you go? What did you do? Who did you meet? What did you contribute? How did you affect your environment? How did the environment affect you? Is there any thing you did that you could have done differently? How could you have done it next time?

Now visualize the next day of your life in the family, at work or in school. What do you want to see happen? For the family you might want harmony, understanding and unity. For work you might want to accomplish your work goals and get along with your boss and co-workers. For school you might see that you are getting along with your teachers and fellow students. You are doing your schoolwork and getting good grades as well as participating in school activities and doing well.

## Month 2, Week 1, Day 5

Assume the state of meditation by first practicing a relaxation exercise. Inhale for four seconds. Hold the breath for four seconds. Exhale for four seconds. Hold the exhalation for four seconds. Repeat the process for as many times as possible.

Count from 100 backwards that is 100, 99, 88, etc, until you reach 1. Now count the normal way from 1 to 100. Concentrate on your counting and see the figures in your mind's eye as you count.

Next take inventory of your activities today. Where did you go? What did you do? Who did you meet? What did you contribute? How did you affect your environment? How did the environment affect you? Is there any thing you did that you could have done differently? How could you have done it next time?

Now visualize the next day of your life in the family, at work or in school. What do you want to see happen? For the family you might want harmony, understanding and unity. For work you might want to accomplish your work goals and get along with your boss and co-workers. For school you might see that you are getting along with your teachers and fellow students. You are doing your schoolwork and getting good grades as well as participating in school activities and doing well.

Next Reflect on **Success by Theodore Roosevelt:** I wish to preach, not the doctrine of ignoble ease, but the doctrine of the strenuous life. The life of toil and effort, of labor and strife; to preach that highest form of success which comes not to the man who desires mere easy peace, but to the man who does not shrink from danger, from hardship or from bitter toil, and who out of these wins the splendid ultimate triumph.

Now share your day with the rest of the family. This is the individual disclosure session. What happened to you, your friends and teachers during the day? What special role did you play in

school? What contribution did you make in school? Did you get hurt at work or in school? If you did how did it happen and who was responsible? What have you done to address the issue? What did others do to address the issue? How do you feel?

**Month 2, Week 1, Day 6**

Retire to your sacred place and practice a relaxation exercise. Inhale for four seconds. Hold the breath for four seconds. Exhale for four seconds. Hold the exhalation for four seconds. Repeat the process for as many times as possible.

Count from 100 backwards that is 100, 99, 88, etc, until you reach 1. Now count the normal way from 1 to 100. Concentrate on your counting and see the figures in your mind's eye as you count.

Now reflect on the following: Success in marriage does not come merely through finding the right mate, but through being the right mate. **Barnett R. Brickner**

Next take inventory of your activities today. Where did you go? What did you do? Who did you meet? What did you contribute? How did you affect your environment? How did the environment affect you? Is there any thing you did that you could have done differently? How could you have done it next time?

Lastly visualize the next day of your life in the family, at work or in school. What do you want to see happen? For the family you might want harmony, understanding and unity. For work you might want to accomplish your work goals and get along with your boss and co-workers. For school you might see that you are getting along with your teachers and fellow students. You are doing your schoolwork and getting good grades as well as participating in school activities and doing well.

**Month 2, Week 1, Day 7**

Attend a church, a temple, or any other meeting that brings you together with people for a common goal. If you do not have one you may begin today and find one that meets your interest and inclination. If you want you could also organize a group of your own. For instance you could start an Awakened Living Study Program. You may contact UNISM for more information.

Retire to your sacred place and practice a relaxation exercise. Inhale for four seconds. Hold the breath for four seconds. Exhale for four seconds. Hold the exhalation for four seconds. Repeat the process for as many times as possible.

Choose your favorite meditation posture and practice using the posture. For instance, if you use supports for your back during meditation start practicing your favorite posture without any support.

Next take inventory of your activities today. Where did you go? What did you do? Who did you meet? What did you contribute? How did you affect your environment? How did the environment affect you? Is there any thing you did that you could have done differently? How could you have done it next time?

Lastly visualize the next day of your life in the family, at work or in school. What do you want to see happen? For the family you might want harmony, understanding and unity. For work you might want to accomplish your work goals and get along with your boss and co-workers. For school you might see that you are getting along with your teachers and fellow students. You are doing your schoolwork and getting good grades as well as participating in school activities and doing well.

### Month 2, Week 2, Day 1

Assume the state of meditation by first practicing a relaxation exercise. Inhale for four seconds. Hold the breath for four seconds. Exhale for four seconds. Hold the exhalation for four seconds. Repeat the process for as many times as possible.

Count from 100 backwards that is 100, 99, 88, etc, until you reach 1. Now count the normal way from 1 to 100. Concentrate on your counting and see the figures in your mind's eye as you count.

**Next Reflect on What Money can't Buy by Arne Garborg: For money you can have everything it is said. No, that is not true. You can buy food, but not appetite; medicine, but not health; soft beds, but not sleep; knowledge but not intelligence; glitter, but not comfort; fun, but not pleasure; acquaintances, but not friendship; servants, but not faithfulness; gray hair, but not honor; quiet days, but not peace. The shell of all things you can get for money. But not the kernel. That cannot be had for money.**

Now share your day with the rest of the family. This is the individual disclosure session. What happened to you, your friends and teachers during the day? What special role did you play in school? What contribution did you make in school? Did you get hurt at work or in school? If you did how did it happen and who was responsible? What have you done to address the issue? What did others do to address the issue? How do you feel?

Next take inventory of your activities today. Where did you go? What did you do? Who did you meet? What did you contribute? How did you affect your environment? How did the environment affect you? Is there any thing you did that you could have done differently? How could you have done it next time?

Next visualize the next day of your life in the family, at work or in school. What do you want to see happen? For the family

you might want harmony, understanding and unity. For work you might want to accomplish your work goals and get along with your boss and co-workers. For school you might see that you are getting along with your teachers and fellow students. You are doing your schoolwork and getting good grades as well as participating in school activities and doing well.

**Month 2, Week 2, Day 2**

Assume the state of meditation by first practicing a relaxation exercise. Inhale for four seconds. Hold the breath for four seconds. Exhale for four seconds. Hold the exhalation for four seconds. Repeat the process for as many times as possible.

Count from 100 backwards that is 100, 99, 88, etc, until you reach 1. Now count the normal way from 1 to 100. Concentrate on your counting and see the figures in your mind's eye as you count.

**Next Reflect on Right Understanding by Anonymous:** Recognize your direct,
one to one relationship with the Universe. Society has interjected itself so completely into our minds and heart that we have lost sovereignty over our lives. In reality there is a fundamental connection between just you and life and there is nothing whatsoever in between. Get rid of all you have borrowed from outside sources and try to see life with your own eyes. The impact of this understanding gives one a sense of aloneness, not loneliness, and brings with it a sense of power and freedom essential to sustaining your spirit. You have been born into this universe, that is the only license you need in order to live your life according to your terms. Reflecting on death brings home this point. Being able to stand alone gives you immense strength. Having a good sense of humor and a happy frame of mind is also going to play an important role in keeping your

confidence up. The importance of having a sense of humor cannot be overstated, as you will soon realize that it is better to laugh at the antics of your mind than to take it to task or become demoralized.

Now share your day with the rest of the family. This is the individual disclosure session. What happened to you, your friends and teachers during the day? What special role did you play in school? What contribution did you make in school? Did you get hurt at work or in school? If you did how did it happen and who was responsible? What have you done to address the issue? What did others do to address the issue? How do you feel?

Next take inventory of your activities today. Where did you go? What did you do? Who did you meet? What did you contribute? How did you affect your environment? How did the environment affect you? Is there any thing you did that you could have done differently? How could you have done it next time?

Now visualize the next day of your life in the family, at work or in school. What do you want to see happen? For the family you might want harmony, understanding and unity. For work you might want to accomplish your work goals and get along with your boss and co-workers. For school you might see that you are getting along with your teachers and fellow students. You are doing your schoolwork and getting good grades as well as participating in school activities and doing well.

**Month 2, Week 2, Day 3**

Assume the state of meditation by first practicing a relaxation exercise. Inhale for four seconds. Hold the breath for four seconds. Exhale for four seconds. Hold the exhalation for four seconds. Repeat the process for as many times as possible.

Count from 100 backwards that is 100, 99, 88, etc, until you reach 1. Now count the normal way from 1 to 100. Concentrate on your counting and see the figures in your mind's eye as you count.

Next visualize that you are in a wood and playing with squirrels. First a squirrel follows you as you walk in the wood. Then you stop and get some nuts from your bag to feed the squirrel. As you feed the squirrel other squirrels begin to join the feast. You get more nuts from your bag to feed them but finally ran out of nuts. Now count the number of squirrels you fed.

Now share your day with the rest of the family. This is the individual disclosure session. What happened to you, your friends and teachers during the day? What special role did you play in school? What contribution did you make in school? Did you get hurt at work or in school? If you did how did it happen and who was responsible? What have you done to address the issue? What did others do to address the issue? How do you feel?

Next take inventory of your activities today. Where did you go? What did you do? Who did you meet? What did you contribute? How did you affect your environment? How did the environment affect you? Is there any thing you did that you could have done differently? How could you have done it next time?

Next visualize the next day of your life in the family, at work or in school. What do you want to see happen? For the family you might want harmony, understanding and unity. For work you might want to accomplish your work goals and get along with your boss and co-workers. For school you might see that you are getting along with your teachers and fellow students. You are doing your schoolwork and getting good grades as well as participating in school activities and doing well.

### Month 2, Week 2, Day 4

Assume the state of meditation by first practicing a relaxation exercise. Inhale for four seconds. Hold the breath for four seconds. Exhale for four seconds. Hold the exhalation for four seconds. Repeat the process for as many times as possible.

Count from 100 backwards that is 100, 99, 88, etc, until you reach 1. Now count the normal way from 1 to 100. Concentrate on your counting and see the figures in your mind's eye as you count.

Next reflect on **Forgiveness by Anonymous:** Forgiveness loosens the knot of hurt. It lightens your body-mind burden. Feeling guilty for holding negative thoughts? Forgive yourself and let that go too. Enjoy the harmonious feelings that follow.

Now share your day with the rest of the family. This is the individual disclosure session. What happened to you, your friends and teachers during the day? What special role did you play in school? What contribution did you make in school? Did you get hurt at work or in school? If you did how did it happen and who was responsible? What have you done to address the issue? What did others do to address the issue? How do you feel?

Next take inventory of your activities today. Where did you go? What did you do? Who did you meet? What did you contribute? How did you affect your environment? How did the environment affect you? Is there any thing you did that you could have done differently? How could you have done it next time?

Next visualize the next day of your life in the family, at work or in school. What do you want to see happen? For the family you might want harmony, understanding and unity. For work you might want to accomplish your work goals and get along with your boss and co-workers. For school you might see that you are getting along with your teachers and fellow students. You are doing your

schoolwork and getting good grades as well as participating in school activities and doing well.

**Month 2, Week 2, Day 5**

Assume the state of meditation by first practicing a relaxation exercise. Inhale for four seconds. Hold the breath for four seconds. Exhale for four seconds. Hold the exhalation for four seconds. Repeat the process for as many times as possible.

Count from 100 backwards that is 100, 99, 88, etc, until you reach 1. Now count the normal way from 1 to 100. Concentrate on your counting and see the figures in your mind's eye as you count.

Next reflect on a **Prayer by the Dalai Lama:**
May I become at all times, both now and forever
A protector for those without protection
A guide for those who have lost their way
A ship for those with oceans to cross
A sanctuary for those in danger
A lamp for those without light
A place of refuge for those who lack shelter
And a servant to all in need.

Now share your day with the rest of the family. This is the individual disclosure session. What happened to you, your friends and teachers during the day? What special role did you play in school? What contribution did you make in school? Did you get hurt at work or in school? If you did how did it happen and who was responsible? What have you done to address the issue? What did others do to address the issue? How do you feel?

Next take inventory of your activities today. Where did you go? What did you do? Who did you meet? What did you contribute? How did you affect your environment? How did the

environment affect you? Is there any thing you did that you could have done differently? How could you have done it next time?

Now visualize the next day of your life in the family, at work or in school. What do you want to see happen? For the family you might want harmony, understanding and unity. For work you might want to accomplish your work goals and get along with your boss and co-workers. For school you might see that you are getting along with your teachers and fellow students. You are doing your schoolwork and getting good grades as well as participating in school activities and doing well.

### Month 2, Week 2, Day 6

Retire to your sacred place and practice a relaxation exercise. Inhale for four seconds. Hold the breath for four seconds. Exhale for four seconds. Hold the exhalation for four seconds. Repeat the process for as many times as possible.

Count from 100 backwards that is 100, 99, 88, etc, until you reach 1. Now count the normal way from 1 to 100. Concentrate on your counting and see the figures in your mind's eye as you count.

Now reflect on the following: When you make the sacrifice in marriage, you're sacrificing not to each other but to unity in a relationship. - **Joseph Campbell**

Next take inventory of your activities today. Where did you go? What did you do? Who did you meet? What did you contribute? How did you affect your environment? How did the environment affect you? Is there any thing you did that you could have done differently? How could you have done it next time?

Lastly visualize the next day of your life in the family, at work or in school. What do you want to see happen? For the family you might want harmony, understanding and unity. For work you might want to accomplish your work goals and get along with your

boss and co-workers. For school you might see that you are getting along with your teachers and fellow students. You are doing your schoolwork and getting good grades as well as participating in school activities and doing well.

### Month 2, Week 2, Day 7

Attend a church, a temple, or any other meeting that brings you together with people for a common goal. If you do not have one you may begin today and find one that meets your interest and inclination. If you want you could also organize a group of your own. For instance you could start an Awakened Living Study Program. You may contact UNISM for more information.

Retire to your sacred place and practice a relaxation exercise. Inhale for four seconds. Hold the breath for four seconds. Exhale for four seconds. Hold the exhalation for four seconds. Repeat the process for as many times as possible.

Choose your favorite meditation posture and practice using the posture. For instance, if you use supports for your back during meditation start practicing your favorite posture without any support.

Next take inventory of your activities today. Where did you go? What did you do? Who did you meet? What did you contribute? How did you affect your environment? How did the environment affect you? Is there any thing you did that you could have done differently? How could you have done it next time?

Lastly visualize the next day of your life in the family, at work or in school. What do you want to see happen? For the family you might want harmony, understanding and unity. For work you might want to accomplish your work goals and get along with your boss and co-workers. For school you might see that you are getting along with your teachers and fellow students. You are doing your

schoolwork and getting good grades as well as participating in school activities and doing well.

**Month 2, Week 3, Day 1**

Assume the state of meditation by first practicing a relaxation exercise. Inhale for four seconds. Hold the breath for four seconds. Exhale for four seconds. Hold the exhalation for four seconds. Repeat the process for as many times as possible.

Count from 100 backwards that is 100, 99, 88, etc, until you reach 1. Now count the normal way from 1 to 100. Concentrate on your counting and see the figures in your mind's eye as you count.

Next reflect on a **Life by the Buddha:**

Life is short.
Time is fleeting.
Uncover the True Nature.
Purify the mind and heart to attain happiness.
Be kind; be compassionate.
Be generous; do good.
Concentrate.
Understand.
Awaken.
Overcome
   . . . greed with generosity,
   . . . anger with loving kindness,
   . . . ignorance with understanding.

Now share your day with the rest of the family. This is the individual disclosure session. What happened to you, your friends and teachers during the day? What special role did you play in school? What contribution did you make in school? Did you get hurt at work or in school? If you did how did it happen and who

was responsible? What have you done to address the issue? What did others do to address the issue? How do you feel?

Next take inventory of your activities today. Where did you go? What did you do? Who did you meet? What did you contribute? How did you affect your environment? How did the environment affect you? Is there any thing you did that you could have done differently? How could you have done it next time?

Now visualize the next day of your life in the family, at work or in school. What do you want to see happen? For the family you might want harmony, understanding and unity. For work you might want to accomplish your work goals and get along with your boss and co-workers. For school you might see that you are getting along with your teachers and fellow students. You are doing your schoolwork and getting good grades as well as participating in school activities and doing well.

**Month 2, Week 3, Day 2:**

Assume the state of meditation by first practicing a relaxation exercise. Inhale for four seconds. Hold the breath for four seconds. Exhale for four seconds. Hold the exhalation for four seconds. Repeat the process for as many times as possible.

Count from 100 backwards that is 100, 99, 88, etc, until you reach 1. Now count the normal way from 1 to 100. Concentrate on your counting and see the figures in your mind's eye as you count.

Next reflect on **First They Came ------ by Martin Niemoeller:**

They came first for the Communists,
and I didn't speak up because I wasn't a Communist.
Then they came for the Jews,
and I didn't speak up because I wasn't a Jew.

Then they came for the trade unionists,
and I didn't speak up because I wasn't a trade unionist.
Then they came for the Catholics,
and I didn't speak up because I was a Protestant.
Then they came for me,
and by that time no one was left to speak up.

Now share your day with the rest of the family. This is the individual disclosure session. What happened to you, your friends and teachers during the day? What special role did you play in school? What contribution did you make in school? Did you get hurt at work or in school? If you did how did it happen and who was responsible? What have you done to address the issue? What did others do to address the issue? How do you feel?

Next take inventory of your activities today. Where did you go? What did you do? Who did you meet? What did you contribute? How did you affect your environment? How did the environment affect you? Is there any thing you did that you could have done differently? How could you have done it next time?

Next visualize the next day of your life in the family, at work or in school. What do you want to see happen? For the family you might want harmony, understanding and unity. For work you might want to accomplish your work goals and get along with your boss and co-workers. For school you might see that you are getting along with your teachers and fellow students. You are doing your schoolwork and getting good grades as well as participating in school activities and doing well.

**Month 2, Week 3, Day 3**

Assume the state of meditation by first practicing a relaxation exercise. Inhale for four seconds. Hold the breath for four seconds.

Exhale for four seconds. Hold the exhalation for four seconds. Repeat the process for as many times as possible.

Count from 100 backwards that is 100, 99, 88, etc, until you reach 1. Now count the normal way from 1 to 100. Concentrate on your counting and see the figures in your mind's eye as you count.

Next reflect on the following: The real act of marriage takes place in the heart, not in the ballroom or church or synagogue. It's a choice you make - not just on your wedding day, but over and over again -- and that choice is reflected in the way you treat your husband or wife. - **Barbara De Angelis**

Now share your day with the rest of the family. This is the individual disclosure session. What happened to you, your friends and teachers during the day? What special role did you play in school? What contribution did you make in school? Did you get hurt at work or in school? If you did how did it happen and who was responsible? What have you done to address the issue? What did others do to address the issue? How do you feel?

Next take inventory of your activities today. Where did you go? What did you do? Who did you meet? What did you contribute? How did you affect your environment? How did the environment affect you? Is there any thing you did that you could have done differently? How could you have done it next time?

Next visualize the next day of your life in the family, at work or in school. What do you want to see happen? For the family you might want harmony, understanding and unity. For work you might want to accomplish your work goals and get along with your boss and co-workers. For school you might see that you are getting along with your teachers and fellow students. You are doing your schoolwork and getting good grades as well as participating in school activities and doing well.

**Month 2, Week 3, Day 4**:

Assume the state of meditation by first practicing a relaxation exercise. Inhale for four seconds. Hold the breath for four seconds. Exhale for four seconds. Hold the exhalation for four seconds. Repeat the process for as many times as possible.

Count from 100 backwards that is 100, 99, 88, etc, until you reach 1. Now count the normal way from 1 to 100. Concentrate on your counting and see the figures in your mind's eye as you count.

Visualize that you are crabbing at your favorite spot by the ocean. You have 2 crabbing nets. Stick a chicken leg in each of the crabbing nets and throw into the water. Visualize that a number crabs are in each of the nets. Pull the nets after about ten minutes. Throw the nets back after removing the crabs. Do this for about an hour. How many crabs did you catch? Now return all the crabs back to the sea and return home.

Now share your day with the rest of the family. This is the individual disclosure session. What happened to you, your friends and teachers during the day? What special role did you play in school? What contribution did you make in school? Did you get hurt at work or in school? If you did how did it happen and who was responsible? What have you done to address the issue? What did others do to address the issue? How do you feel?

Next take inventory of your activities today. Where did you go? What did you do? Who did you meet? What did you contribute? How did you affect your environment? How did the environment affect you? Is there any thing you did that you could have done differently? How could you have done it next time?

Next visualize the next day of your life in the family, at work or in school. What do you want to see happen? For the family you might want harmony, understanding and unity. For work you

might want to accomplish your work goals and get along with your boss and co-workers. For school you might see that you are getting along with your teachers and fellow students. You are doing your schoolwork and getting good grades as well as participating in school activities and doing well.

**Month 2, Week 3, Day 5**:

Assume the state of meditation by first practicing a relaxation exercise. Inhale for four seconds. Hold the breath for four seconds. Exhale for four seconds. Hold the exhalation for four seconds. Repeat the process for as many times as possible.

Count from 100 backwards that is 100, 99, 88, etc, until you reach 1. Now count the normal way from 1 to 100. Concentrate on your counting and see the figures in your mind's eye as you count.

Next reflect on, **On Science and Reason by Robert Ingersoll**

To love justice, to long for the right,
to love mercy, to pity the suffering, to assist the weak,
to forget wrongs and remember benefits--
to love the truth, to be sincere, to utter honest words,
to love liberty, to wage relentless war against slavery in all its forms,
to love wife and child and friend, to make a happy home,
to love the beautiful; in art, in nature,
to cultivate the mind, to be familiar with the mighty thoughts that genius has expressed, the noble deeds of all the world,
to cultivate courage and cheerfulness, to make others happy,
to fill life with the splendor of generous acts, the warmth of loving words,
to discard error, to destroy prejudice, to receive new truths with gladness,

to cultivate hope, to see the calm beyond the storm, the dawn beyond the night,
to do the best that can be done and then to be resigned---
this is the religion of reason, the creed of science.
This satisfies the brain and heart.

Now share your day with the rest of the family. This is the individual disclosure session. What happened to you, your friends and teachers during the day? What special role did you play in school? What contribution did you make in school? Did you get hurt at work or in school? If you did how did it happen and who was responsible? What have you done to address the issue? What did others do to address the issue? How do you feel?

Next take inventory of your activities today. Where did you go? What did you do? Who did you meet? What did you contribute? How did you affect your environment? How did the environment affect you? Is there any thing you did that you could have done differently? How could you have done it next time?

Now visualize the next day of your life in the family, at work or in school. What do you want to see happen? For the family you might want harmony, understanding and unity. For work you might want to accomplish your work goals and get along with your boss and co-workers. For school you might see that you are getting along with your teachers and fellow students. You are doing your schoolwork and getting good grades as well as participating in school activities and doing well.

**Month 2, Week 3, Day 6**

Retire to your sacred place and practice a relaxation exercise. Inhale for four seconds. Hold the breath for four seconds. Exhale for four seconds. Hold the exhalation for four seconds. Repeat the process for as many times as possible.

Count from 100 backwards that is 100, 99, 88, etc, until you reach 1. Now count the normal way from 1 to 100. Concentrate on your counting and see the figures in your mind's eye as you count.

Reflect on the following: Love is a gift of one's inner most soul to another so both can be whole. **Buddha**

Next take inventory of your activities today. Where did you go? What did you do? Who did you meet? What did you contribute? How did you affect your environment? How did the environment affect you? Is there any thing you did that you could have done differently? How could you have done it next time?

Lastly visualize the next day of your life in the family, at work or in school. What do you want to see happen? For the family you might want harmony, understanding and unity. For work you might want to accomplish your work goals and get along with your boss and co-workers. For school you might see that you are getting along with your teachers and fellow students. You are doing your schoolwork and getting good grades as well as participating in school activities and doing well.

**Month 2, Week 3, Day 7**

Attend a church, a temple, or any other meeting that brings you together with people for a common goal. If you do not have one you may begin today and find one that meets your interest and inclination. If you want you could also organize a group of your own. For instance you could start an Awakened Living Study Program. You may contact UNISM for more information.

Retire to your sacred place and practice a relaxation exercise. Inhale for four seconds. Hold the breath for four seconds. Exhale for four seconds. Hold the exhalation for four seconds. Repeat the process for as many times as possible.

Choose your favorite meditation posture and practice using the posture. For instance, if you use supports for your back during meditation start practicing your favorite posture without any support.

Next take inventory of your activities today. Where did you go? What did you do? Who did you meet? What did you contribute? How did you affect your environment? How did the environment affect you? Is there any thing you did that you could have done differently? How could you have done it next time?

Lastly visualize the next day of your life in the family, at work or in school. What do you want to see happen? For the family you might want harmony, understanding and unity. For work you might want to accomplish your work goals and get along with your boss and co-workers. For school you might see that you are getting along with your teachers and fellow students. You are doing your schoolwork and getting good grades as well as participating in school activities and doing well.

**Month 2, Week 4, Day 1**

Assume the state of meditation by first practicing a relaxation exercise. Inhale for four seconds. Hold the breath for four seconds. Exhale for four seconds. Hold the exhalation for four seconds. Repeat the process for as many times as possible.

Count from 100 backwards that is 100, 99, 88, etc, until you reach 1. Now count the normal way from 1 to 100. Concentrate on your counting and see the figures in your mind's eye as you count.

Next reflect on **Yes, We Can by President Barack Obama:**

When we have faced down impossible odds,
when we've been told we're not ready or that we shouldn't try or that we can't, generations of Americans have responded with

a simple creed that sums up the spirit of a people:
Yes, we can.
Yes, we can.
Yes, we can.
It was a creed written into the founding documents that declared the destiny of a nation:
Yes, we can.
It was whispered by slaves and abolitionists as they blazed a trail towards freedom through the darkest of nights:
Yes, we can.
It was sung by immigrants as they struck out from distant shores and pioneers who pushed westward against an unforgiving wilderness:
Yes, we can.
It was the call of workers who organized,
women who reached for the ballot,
a president who chose the moon as our new frontier,
and a king who took us to the mountaintop and pointed the way to the promised land:
Yes, we can, to justice and equality.
Yes, we can, to opportunity and prosperity.
Yes, we can heal this nation.
Yes, we can repair this world.
Yes, we can.

    Now share your day with the rest of the family. This is the individual disclosure session. What happened to you, your friends and teachers during the day? What special role did you play in school? What contribution did you make in school? Did you get hurt at work or in school? If you did how did it happen and who was responsible? What have you done to address the issue? What did others do to address the issue? How do you feel?

Next take inventory of your activities today. Where did you go? What did you do? Who did you meet? What did you contribute? How did you affect your environment? How did the environment affect you? Is there any thing you did that you could have done differently? How could you have done it next time?

Now visualize the next day of your life in the family, at work or in school. What do you want to see happen? For the family you might want harmony, understanding and unity. For work you might want to accomplish your work goals and get along with your boss and co-workers. For school you might see that you are getting along with your teachers and fellow students. You are doing your schoolwork and getting good grades as well as participating in school activities and doing well.

### Month 2, Week 4, Day 2

Assume the state of meditation by first practicing a relaxation exercise. Inhale for four seconds. Hold the breath for four seconds. Exhale for four seconds. Hold the exhalation for four seconds. Repeat the process for as many times as possible.

Count from 100 backwards that is 100, 99, 88, etc, until you reach 1. Now count the normal way from 1 to 100. Concentrate on your counting and see the figures in your mind's eye as you count.

Next reflect on **Don't Give up by Vicki Silvers:**

There may be times when you feel
as if you have taken a million steps towards
your dreams, and acted on your plans, only to find
yourself in the same place that you began from.
At times like this, you must not give up.

You must continue on. Though you may feel
lost, bewildered, and alone, continue to believe
in yourself. Do not allow discouragement and

doubt to blur your vision and wash away your dreams. Visualize your way beyond the detours, standstills, and obstacles.

... Whatever the hurt of the moment may be, it will pass. Tomorrow is always a new dawn.

Now share your day with the rest of the family. This is the individual disclosure session. What happened to you, your friends and teachers during the day? What special role did you play in school? What contribution did you make in school? Did you get hurt at work or in school? If you did how did it happen and who was responsible? What have you done to address the issue? What did others do to address the issue? How do you feel?

Next take inventory of your activities today. Where did you go? What did you do? Who did you meet? What did you contribute? How did you affect your environment? How did the environment affect you? Is there any thing you did that you could have done differently? How could you have done it next time?

Now visualize the next day of your life in the family, at work or in school. What do you want to see happen? For the family you might want harmony, understanding and unity. For work you might want to accomplish your work goals and get along with your boss and co-workers. For school you might see that you are getting along with your teachers and fellow students. You are doing your schoolwork and getting good grades as well as participating in school activities and doing well.

**Month 2, Week 4, Day 3**

Assume the state of meditation by first practicing a relaxation exercise. Inhale for four seconds. Hold the breath for four seconds.

Exhale for four seconds. Hold the exhalation for four seconds. Repeat the process for as many times as possible.

Count from 100 backwards that is 100, 99, 88, etc, until you reach 1. Now count the normal way from 1 to 100. Concentrate on your counting and see the figures in your mind's eye as you count.

Next have a lemon before you. First look at the lemon for thirty seconds and note the shape, color and texture. Now put away the lemon but see it in your mind's eye for thirty seconds. If your mind wonders bring it back to the image until you could see it continuously for about five minutes or more.

Now share your day with the rest of the family. This is the individual disclosure session. What happened to you, your friends and teachers during the day? What special role did you play in school? What contribution did you make in school? Did you get hurt at work or in school? If you did how did it happen and who was responsible? What have you done to address the issue? What did others do to address the issue? How do you feel?

Next take inventory of your activities today. Where did you go? What did you do? Who did you meet? What did you contribute? How did you affect your environment? How did the environment affect you? Is there any thing you did that you could have done differently? How could you have done it next time?

Next visualize the next day of your life in the family, at work or in school. What do you want to see happen? For the family you might want harmony, understanding and unity. For work you might want to accomplish your work goals and get along with your boss and co-workers. For school you might see that you are getting along with your teachers and fellow students. You are doing your schoolwork and getting good grades as well as participating in school activities and doing well.

## Month 2, Week 4, Day 4

Assume the state of meditation by first practicing a relaxation exercise. Inhale for four seconds. Hold the breath for four seconds. Exhale for four seconds. Hold the exhalation for four seconds. Repeat the process for as many times as possible.

Count from 100 backwards that is 100, 99, 88, etc, until you reach 1. Now count the normal way from 1 to 100. Concentrate on your counting and see the figures in your mind's eye as you count.

Next visualize that you are in a snow-covered meadow. Go to the center and begin to build a snow family including a man, woman, children, and a pet. How tall is your snowman? How tall is your snowwoman? How tall are the children? What is the family pet? How tall is the pet? What are they wearing? Now take down all the snow people and pets. Compare your answers with those of other family members.

Now share your day with the rest of the family. This is the individual disclosure session. What happened to you, your friends and teachers during the day? What special role did you play in school? What contribution did you make in school? Did you get hurt at work or in school? If you did how did it happen and who was responsible? What have you done to address the issue? What did others do to address the issue? How do you feel?

Next take inventory of your activities today. Where did you go? What did you do? Who did you meet? What did you contribute? How did you affect your environment? How did the environment affect you? Is there any thing you did that you could have done differently? How could you have done it next time?

Next visualize the next day of your life in the family, at work or in school. What do you want to see happen? For the family you might want harmony, understanding and unity. For work you might want to accomplish your work goals and get along with your

boss and co-workers. For school you might see that you are getting along with your teachers and fellow students. You are doing your schoolwork and getting good grades as well as participating in school activities and doing well.

### Month 2, Week 4, Day 5

Assume the state of meditation by first practicing a relaxation exercise. Inhale for four seconds. Hold the breath for four seconds. Exhale for four seconds. Hold the exhalation for four seconds. Repeat the process for as many times as possible.

Count from 100 backwards that is 100, 99, 88, etc, until you reach 1. Now count the normal way from 1 to 100. Concentrate on your counting and see the figures in your mind's eye as you count.

Next reflect **on Life by the Buddha:**
*"This existence of ours is as transient as autumn clouds,*
*To watch the birth and death of beings is like looking at the*
*Movements of dance,*
*A lifetime is like a flash of lightning in the sky,*
*Rushing by, like a torrent down a steep mountain."*

Now share your day with the rest of the family. This is the individual disclosure session. What happened to you, your friends and teachers during the day? What special role did you play in school? What contribution did you make in school? Did you get hurt at work or in school? If you did how did it happen and who was responsible? What have you done to address the issue? What did others do to address the issue? How do you feel?

Next take inventory of your activities today. Where did you go? What did you do? Who did you meet? What did you contribute? How did you affect your environment? How did the environment affect you? Is there any thing you did that you could have done differently? How could you have done it next time?

Next visualize the next day of your life in the family, at work or in school. What do you want to see happen? For the family you might want harmony, understanding and unity. For work you might want to accomplish your work goals and get along with your boss and co-workers. For school you might see that you are getting along with your teachers and fellow students. You are doing your schoolwork and getting good grades as well as participating in school activities and doing well.

**Month 2, Week 4, Day 6**

Retire to your sacred place and practice a relaxation exercise. Inhale for four seconds. Hold the breath for four seconds. Exhale for four seconds. Hold the exhalation for four seconds. Repeat the process for as many times as possible.

Count from 100 backwards that is 100, 99, 88, etc, until you reach 1. Now count the normal way from 1 to 100. Concentrate on your counting and see the figures in your mind's eye as you count.

Now reflect on the following: If you raise your children to feel that they can accomplish any goal or task they decide upon, you will have succeeded as a parent and you will have given your children the greatest of all blessings. **Brian Tracy**

Next take inventory of your activities today. Where did you go? What did you do? Who did you meet? What did you contribute? How did you affect your environment? How did the environment affect you? Is there any thing you did that you could have done differently? How could you have done it next time?

Lastly visualize the next day of your life in the family, at work or in school. What do you want to see happen? For the family you might want harmony, understanding and unity. For work you might want to accomplish your work goals and get along with your boss and co-workers. For school you might see that you are getting along with your teachers and fellow students. You are doing your schoolwork and getting good grades as well as participating in school activities and doing well.

**Month 2, Week 4, Day 7**

Attend a church, a temple, or any other meeting that brings you together with people for a common goal. If you do not have one you may begin today and find one that meets your interest and inclination. If you want you could also organize a group of your own. For instance you could start an Awakened Living Study Program. You may contact UNISM for more information.

Retire to your sacred place and practice a relaxation exercise. Inhale for four seconds. Hold the breath for four seconds. Exhale for four seconds. Hold the exhalation for four seconds. Repeat the process for as many times as possible.

Choose your favorite meditation posture and practice using the posture. For instance, if you use supports for your back during meditation start practicing your favorite posture without any support.

Next take inventory of your activities today. Where did you go? What did you do? Who did you meet? What did you contribute? How did you affect your environment? How did the environment affect you? Is there any thing you did that you could have done differently? How could you have done it next time?

Lastly visualize the next day of your life in the family, at work or in school. What do you want to see happen? For the family you might want harmony, understanding and unity. For work you might want to accomplish your work goals and get along with your boss and co-workers. For school you might see that you are getting along with your teachers and fellow students. You are doing your

schoolwork and getting good grades as well as participating in school activities and doing well.

## Family Meditation: Third Month

**Goal**

The goal of the third month of meditation is to manage our emotions. Emotions are a part of our lives. There is no day that goes by without one feeling happy, loving, hopeful, faithful, optimistic, sympathetic, joyful, curious, interested, enthusiastic, inspirational, proud, laughing, contented, accepting, and peaceful. On the other hand there is no day that goes by without someone feeling disappointed, hurt, frustrated, guilty, hopeless, jealous, revengeful, greedy, blaming, regretful, resentful, lustful, angry, hostile, fearful, hateful, grieving, superstitious and proud. There is nothing wrong in feeling these emotions because the emotions are not good or bad in themselves. It is in our reactions that the emotions could result in something good or bad. For instance if you are angry with your parent and you hit her you have done something bad. On the other hand if you are happy and you clean the house you have done something good. The challenge is to find out the link to your emotions and do the things that foster your life and avoid the things that hurt others.

**Month 3, Week 1, Day 1**

Assume the state of meditation by first practicing a relaxation exercise. Inhale for four seconds. Hold the breath for four seconds. Exhale for four seconds. Hold the exhalation for four seconds. Repeat the process for as many times as possible.

Count from 100 backwards that is 100, 99, 88, etc, until you reach 1. Now count the normal way from 1 to 100. Concentrate on your counting and see the figures in your mind's eye as you count.

Next reflect on Being Present with our Children by Nancy Hathaway:

One of the greatest delights in being a parent is being present with our children. When we are truly present, we feel complete, whole and fully alive. The practice of parenting mindfully means being in touch/ aware/ present with what is happening in our lives right now, in this moment with loving, non-judgmental attention. When we use mindfulness to be more in touch with our children, we are able to take delight in the small pleasures of everyday life, as well as being better able to stand in the middle of chaos. As we become more centered and balanced, we can respond to stressful situations with clarity and freshness instead of reacting out of old patterns. Living mindfully with our families, we provide a more loving home, as well as a role model for our children as they explore the world around them.

Now share your day with the rest of the family. This is the individual disclosure session. What happened to you, your friends and teachers during the day? What special role did you play in school? What contribution did you make in school? Did you get hurt at work or in school? If you did how did it happen and who was responsible? What have you done to address the issue? What did others do to address the issue? How do you feel?

Next take inventory of your activities today. Where did you go? What did you do? Who did you meet? What did you contribute? How did you affect your environment? How did the environment affect you? Is there any thing you did that you could have done differently? How could you have done it next time?

Next visualize the next day of your life in the family, at work or in school. What do you want to see happen? For the family you might want harmony, understanding and unity. For work you might want to accomplish your work goals and get along with your boss and co-workers. For school you might see that you are getting along with your teachers and fellow students. You are doing your

schoolwork and getting good grades as well as participating in school activities and doing well.

**Month 3, Week 1, Day 2**

Assume the state of meditation by first practicing a relaxation exercise. Inhale for four seconds. Hold the breath for four seconds. Exhale for four seconds. Hold the exhalation for four seconds. Repeat the process for as many times as possible.

Count from 100 backwards that is 100, 99, 88, etc, until you reach 1. Now count the normal way from 1 to 100. Concentrate on your counting and see the figures in your mind's eye as you count.

Next reflect on Selflessness by the Buddha:

There is nothing more worthy
than the virtue of selflessness.
Selfless unites people.
It is a healing herb that unifies
strangers and brings
families together.
It is the love for others that is
higher than self-love;
It is our only hope.

Now share your day with the rest of the family. This is the individual disclosure session. What happened to you, your friends and teachers during the day? What special role did you play in school? What contribution did you make in school? Did you get hurt at work or in school? If you did how did it happen and who was responsible? What have you done to address the issue? What did others do to address the issue? How do you feel?

Next take inventory of your activities today. Where did you go? What did you do? Who did you meet? What did you contribute? How did you affect your environment? How did the

environment affect you? Is there any thing you did that you could have done differently? How could you have done it next time?

Next visualize the next day of your life in the family, at work or in school. What do you want to see happen? For the family you might want harmony, understanding and unity. For work you might want to accomplish your work goals and get along with your boss and co-workers. For school you might see that you are getting along with your teachers and fellow students. You are doing your schoolwork and getting good grades as well as participating in school activities and doing well.

**Month 3, Week 1, Day 3**

Assume the state of meditation by first practicing a relaxation exercise. Inhale for four seconds. Hold the breath for four seconds. Exhale for four seconds. Hold the exhalation for four seconds. Repeat the process for as many times as possible.

Count from 100 backwards that is 100, 99, 88, etc, until you reach 1. Now count the normal way from 1 to 100. Concentrate on your counting and see the figures in your mind's eye as you count.

Consider a positive emotion that you felt recently. What happened before you started feeling the emotion? Go through the event in your mind's eye including all the people involved. What triggered the emotion? Was it what someone said or what you saw or what you thought? How did you react to the emotion? What did you do after you felt the emotion? Now that you are reliving what happened would you say that your reaction was appropriate? What could you have done differently?

Now share your day with the rest of the family. This is the individual disclosure session. What happened to you, your friends and teachers during the day? What special role did you play in school? What contribution did you make in school? Did you get

hurt at work or in school? If you did how did it happen and who was responsible? What have you done to address the issue? What did others do to address the issue? How do you feel?

Next take inventory of your activities today. Where did you go? What did you do? Who did you meet? What did you contribute? How did you affect your environment? How did the environment affect you? Is there any thing you did that you could have done differently? How could you have done it next time?

Now visualize the next day of your life in the family, at work or in school. What do you want to see happen? For the family you might want harmony, understanding and unity. For work you might want to accomplish your work goals and get along with your boss and co-workers. For school you might see that you are getting along with your teachers and fellow students. You are doing your schoolwork and getting good grades as well as participating in school activities and doing well.

**Month 3, Week 1, Day 4**

Assume the state of meditation by first practicing a relaxation exercise. Inhale for four seconds. Hold the breath for four seconds. Exhale for four seconds. Hold the exhalation for four seconds. Repeat the process for as many times as possible.

Count from 100 backwards that is 100, 99, 88, etc, until you reach 1. Now count the normal way from 1 to 100. Concentrate on your counting and see the figures in your mind's eye as you count.

Consider a negative emotion that you felt recently. What happened before you started feeling the emotion? Go through the event in your mind's eye including all the people involved. What triggered the emotion? Was it what someone said or what you saw or what you thought? How did you react to the emotion? What did you do after you felt the emotion? Now that you are reliving what happened would you say that your reaction was appropriate? What could you have done differently?

Now share your day with the rest of the family. This is the individual disclosure session. What happened to you, your friends and teachers during the day? What special role did you play in school? What contribution did you make in school? Did you get hurt at work or in school? If you did how did it happen and who was responsible? What have you done to address the issue? What did others do to address the issue? How do you feel?

Next take inventory of your activities today. Where did you go? What did you do? Who did you meet? What did you contribute? How did you affect your environment? How did the environment affect you? Is there any thing you did that you could have done differently? How could you have done it next time?

Now visualize the next day of your life in the family, at work or in school. What do you want to see happen? For the family you might want harmony, understanding and unity. For work you might want to accomplish your work goals and get along with your boss and co-workers. For school you might see that you are getting along with your teachers and fellow students. You are doing your schoolwork and getting good grades as well as participating in school activities and doing well.

**Month 3, Week 1, Day 5**

Assume the state of meditation by first practicing a relaxation exercise. Inhale for four seconds. Hold the breath for four seconds. Exhale for four seconds. Hold the exhalation for four seconds. Repeat the process for as many times as possible.

Count from 100 backwards that is 100, 99, 88, etc, until you reach 1. Now count the normal way from 1 to 100. Concentrate on your counting and see the figures in your mind's eye as you count.

Next reflect on Peace by Black Elk: The first peace, which is the most important, is that which comes within the souls of people when they realize their relationship, their oneness, with the universe and all its powers, and when they realize that at the center of the universe dwells Wakan-Tanka, and that this center is really everywhere, it is within each of us. This is the real peace, and the others are but reflections of this. The second peace is that which is made between two individuals, and the third is that which is made between two nations. But above all you should understand that there can never be peace between nations until there is known that true peace, which, as I have often said, is within the souls of men.

Now share your day with the rest of the family. This is the individual disclosure session. What happened to you, your friends and teachers during the day? What special role did you play in school? What contribution did you make in school? Did you get hurt at work or in school? If you did how did it happen and who was responsible? What have you done to address the issue? What did others do to address the issue? How do you feel?

Next take inventory of your activities today. Where did you go? What did you do? Who did you meet? What did you contribute? How did you affect your environment? How did the environment affect you? Is there any thing you did that you could have done differently? How could you have done it next time?

Next visualize the next day of your life in the family, at work or in school. What do you want to see happen? For the family you might want harmony, understanding and unity. For work you might want to accomplish your work goals and get along with your boss and co-workers. For school you might see that you are getting along with your teachers and fellow students. You are doing your schoolwork and getting good grades as well as participating in school activities and doing well.

## Month 3, Week 1, Day 6

Retire to your sacred place and practice a relaxation exercise. Inhale for four seconds. Hold the breath for four seconds. Exhale for four seconds. Hold the exhalation for four seconds. Repeat the process for as many times as possible.

Count from 100 backwards that is 100, 99, 88, etc, until you reach 1. Now count the normal way from 1 to 100. Concentrate on your counting and see the figures in your mind's eye as you count.

Now reflect on the following: Educate your children to <u>self-control</u>, to the habit of holding passion and <u>prejudice</u> and evil tendencies subject to an upright and reasoning will, and you have done much to abolish misery from their future and crimes from society. Benjamin Franklin

Next take inventory of your activities today. Where did you go? What did you do? Who did you meet? What did you contribute? How did you affect your environment? How did the environment affect you? Is there any thing you did that you could have done differently? How could you have done it next time?

Lastly visualize the next day of your life in the family, at work or in school. What do you want to see happen? For the family you might want harmony, understanding and unity. For work you might want to accomplish your work goals and get along with your boss and co-workers. For school you might see that you are getting along with your teachers and fellow students. You are doing your schoolwork and getting good grades as well as participating in school activities and doing well.

### Month 3, Week 1, Day 7

Attend a church, a temple, or any other meeting that brings you together with people for a common goal. If you do not have one you may begin today and find one that meets your interest and inclination. If you want you could also organize a group of your own. For instance you could start an Awakened Living Study Program. You may contact UNISM for more information.

Retire to your sacred place and practice a relaxation exercise. Inhale for four seconds. Hold the breath for four seconds. Exhale for four seconds. Hold the exhalation for four seconds. Repeat the process for as many times as possible.

Choose your favorite meditation posture and practice using the posture. For instance, if you use supports for your back during meditation start practicing your favorite posture without any support.

Next take inventory of your activities today. Where did you go? What did you do? Who did you meet? What did you contribute? How did you affect your environment? How did the environment affect you? Is there any thing you did that you could have done differently? How could you have done it next time?

Lastly visualize the next day of your life in the family, at work or in school. What do you want to see happen? For the family you might want harmony, understanding and unity. For work you might want to accomplish your work goals and get along with your boss and co-workers. For school you might see that you are getting along with your teachers and fellow students. You are doing your schoolwork and getting good grades as well as participating in school activities and doing well.

## Month 3, Week 2, Day 1

Assume the state of meditation by first practicing a relaxation exercise. Inhale for four seconds. Hold the breath for four seconds. Exhale for four seconds. Hold the exhalation for four seconds. Repeat the process for as many times as possible.

Count from 100 backwards that is 100, 99, 88, etc, until you reach 1. Now count the normal way from 1 to 100. Concentrate on your counting and see the figures in your mind's eye as you count.

Next reflect on the Greatest by Atisha:

*The greatest achievement is selflessness.*
*The greatest worth is self-mastery.*
*The greatest quality is seeking to serve others.*
*The greatest precept is continual awareness.*
*The greatest medicine is the emptiness of everything.*
*The greatest action is not conforming with the world's ways.*
*The greatest magic is transmuting the passions.*
*The greatest generosity is non-attachment.*
*The greatest goodness is peace of mind.*
*The greatest practice is humility.*
*The greatest effort is not concerned with results.*
*The greatest meditation is a mind that lets go.*
*The greatest wisdom is seeing through appearances."*

Now share your day with the rest of the family. This is the individual disclosure session. What happened to you, your friends and teachers during the day? What special role did you play in school? What contribution did you make in school? Did you get hurt at work or in school? If you did how did it happen and who was responsible? What have you done to address the issue? What did others do to address the issue? How do you feel?

Next take inventory of your activities today. Where did you go? What did you do? Who did you meet? What did you

contribute? How did you affect your environment? How did the environment affect you? Is there any thing you did that you could have done differently? How could you have done it next time?

Now visualize the next day of your life in the family, at work or in school. What do you want to see happen? For the family you might want harmony, understanding and unity. For work you might want to accomplish your work goals and get along with your boss and co-workers. For school you might see that you are getting along with your teachers and fellow students. You are doing your schoolwork and getting good grades as well as participating in school activities and doing well.

**Month 3, Week 2, Day 2**

Assume the state of meditation by first practicing a relaxation exercise. Inhale for four seconds. Hold the breath for four seconds. Exhale for four seconds. Hold the exhalation for four seconds. Repeat the process for as many times as possible.

Count from 100 backwards that is 100, 99, 88, etc, until you reach 1. Now count the normal way from 1 to 100. Concentrate on your counting and see the figures in your mind's eye as you count.

Next reflect on Donkey in the Well by Anonymous

One day a farmer's donkey fell down into a well. The animal cried piteously for hours as the farmer tried to figure out what to do. Finally he decided the animal was old, that the well needed to be covered anyway and that it just wasn't worth retrieving the donkey.

So he invited all his neighbors to come over and help him. They all grabbed a shovel and began to shovel dirt into the well. At first, the donkey realized what was happening and cried horribly. Then, to everyone's amazement, he quieted down. A few shovel loads later, the farmer finally looked down the well and was astonished at what he saw. With every shovel of dirt that hit his back, the donkey was doing something amazing. He would shake it off and take a step up. As the farmer's neighbors continued to shovel dirt on top of the animal, he would shake it off and take a step up. Pretty soon, everyone was amazed as the donkey stepped up over the edge of the well and trotted off! Life is going to shovel dirt on you, all kinds of dirt. The trick to getting out of the well is to shake it off and take a step up.

Now share your day with the rest of the family. This is the individual disclosure session. What happened to you, your friends and teachers during the day? What special role did you play in school? What contribution did you make in school? Did you get hurt at work or in school? If you did how did it happen and who was responsible? What have you done to address the issue? What did others do to address the issue? How do you feel?

Next take inventory of your activities today. Where did you go? What did you do? Who did you meet? What did you contribute? How did you affect your environment? How did the environment affect you? Is there any thing you did that you could have done differently? How could you have done it next time?

Now visualize the next day of your life in the family, at work or in school. What do you want to see happen? For the family you might want harmony, understanding and unity. For work you might want to accomplish your work goals and get along with your boss and co-workers. For school you might see that you are getting along with your teachers and fellow students. You are doing your schoolwork and getting good grades as well as participating in school activities and doing well.

**Month 3, Week 2, Day 3**

Assume the state of meditation by first practicing a relaxation exercise. Inhale for four seconds. Hold the breath for four seconds. Exhale for four seconds. Hold the exhalation for four seconds. Repeat the process for as many times as possible.

Count from 100 backwards that is 100, 99, 88, etc, until you reach 1. Now count the normal way from 1 to 100. Concentrate on your counting and see the figures in your mind's eye as you count.

Next reflect on Initiative by Shanon Hughes

*As daylight fades and twilight approaches,*
*Swift and steady night soon encroaches,*
*So seize this moment and contemplate your next,*
*What will you do with the moments you have left?*
*For no gravestone could ever eulogize,*
*The death of great dreams unrealized.*

Now share your day with the rest of the family. This is the individual disclosure session. What happened to you, your friends and teachers during the day? What special role did you play in school? What contribution did you make in school? Did you get hurt at work or in school? If you did how did it happen and who was responsible? What have you done to address the issue? What did others do to address the issue? How do you feel?

Next take inventory of your activities today. Where did you go? What did you do? Who did you meet? What did you contribute? How did you affect your environment? How did the environment affect you? Is there any thing you did that you could have done differently? How could you have done it next time?

Next visualize the next day of your life in the family, at work or in school. What do you want to see happen? For the family you might want harmony, understanding and unity. For work you might want to accomplish your work goals and get along with your

boss and co-workers. For school you might see that you are getting along with your teachers and fellow students. You are doing your schoolwork and getting good grades as well as participating in school activities and doing well.

**Month 3, Week 2, Day 4**

Assume the state of meditation by first practicing a relaxation exercise. Inhale for four seconds. Hold the breath for four seconds. Exhale for four seconds. Hold the exhalation for four seconds. Repeat the process for as many times as possible.

Count from 100 backwards that is 100, 99, 88, etc, until you reach 1. Now count the normal way from 1 to 100. Concentrate on your counting and see the figures in your mind's eye as you count.

Next reflect on Mindfulness by the Buddha

**Do not dwell in the past.**
**Do not dream of the future.**
**Concentrate the mind on the**
**present moment.**

Now share your day with the rest of the family. This is the individual disclosure session. What happened to you, your friends and teachers during the day? What special role did you play in school? What contribution did you make in school? Did you get hurt at work or in school? If you did how did it happen and who was responsible? What have you done to address the issue? What did others do to address the issue? How do you feel?

Next take inventory of your activities today. Where did you go? What did you do? Who did you meet? What did you contribute? How did you affect your environment? How did the environment affect you? Is there any thing you did that you could have done differently? How could you have done it next time?

Next visualize the next day of your life in the family, at work or in school. What do you want to see happen? For the family you might want harmony, understanding and unity. For work you might want to accomplish your work goals and get along with your boss and co-workers. For school you might see that you are getting along with your teachers and fellow students. You are doing your schoolwork and getting good grades as well as participating in school activities and doing well.

**Month 3, Week 2, Day 5**

Assume the state of meditation by first practicing a relaxation exercise. Inhale for four seconds. Hold the breath for four seconds. Exhale for four seconds. Hold the exhalation for four seconds. Repeat the process for as many times as possible.

Count from 100 backwards that is 100, 99, 88, etc, until you reach 1. Now count the normal way from 1 to 100. Concentrate on your counting and see the figures in your mind's eye as you count.

Next reflect on the Family by the Buddha:

A family is a place where minds come in contact with one another. If these minds love one another the home will be as beautiful as a flower garden. But if these minds get out of harmony with one another it is like a storm that plays havoc with the garden.

Now share your day with the rest of the family. This is the individual disclosure session. What happened to you, your friends and teachers during the day? What special role did you play in school? What contribution did you make in school? Did you get hurt at work or in school? If you did how did it happen and who was responsible? What have you done to address the issue? What did others do to address the issue? How do you feel?

Next take inventory of your activities today. Where did you go? What did you do? Who did you meet? What did you

contribute? How did you affect your environment? How did the environment affect you? Is there any thing you did that you could have done differently? How could you have done it next time?

Next visualize the next day of your life in the family, at work or in school. What do you want to see happen? For the family you might want harmony, understanding and unity. For work you might want to accomplish your work goals and get along with your boss and co-workers. For school you might see that you are getting along with your teachers and fellow students. You are doing your schoolwork and getting good grades as well as participating in school activities and doing well.

**Month 3, Week 2, Day 6**

Retire to your sacred place and practice a relaxation exercise. Inhale for four seconds. Hold the breath for four seconds. Exhale for four seconds. Hold the exhalation for four seconds. Repeat the process for as many times as possible.

Count from 100 backwards that is 100, 99, 88, etc, until you reach 1. Now count the normal way from 1 to 100. Concentrate on your counting and see the figures in your mind's eye as you count.

Now reflect on the following: 4 Children need love, especially when they do not deserve it. Harold Hulbert

Next take inventory of your activities today. Where did you go? What did you do? Who did you meet? What did you contribute? How did you affect your environment? How did the environment affect you? Is there any thing you did that you could have done differently? How could you have done it next time?

Lastly visualize the next day of your life in the family, at work or in school. What do you want to see happen? For the family you might want harmony, understanding and unity. For work you might want to accomplish your work goals and get along with your

boss and co-workers. For school you might see that you are getting along with your teachers and fellow students. You are doing your schoolwork and getting good grades as well as participating in school activities and doing well.

### Month 3, Week 2, Day 7

Attend a church, a temple, or any other meeting that brings you together with people for a common goal. If you do not have one you may begin today and find one that meets your interest and inclination. If you want you could also organize a group of your own. For instance you could start an Awakened Living Study Program. You may contact UNISM for more information.

Retire to your sacred place and practice a relaxation exercise. Inhale for four seconds. Hold the breath for four seconds. Exhale for four seconds. Hold the exhalation for four seconds. Repeat the process for as many times as possible.

Choose your favorite meditation posture and practice using the posture. For instance, if you use supports for your back during meditation start practicing your favorite posture without any support.

Next take inventory of your activities today. Where did you go? What did you do? Who did you meet? What did you contribute? How did you affect your environment? How did the environment affect you? Is there any thing you did that you could have done differently? How could you have done it next time?

Lastly visualize the next day of your life in the family, at work or in school. What do you want to see happen? For the family you might want harmony, understanding and unity. For work you might want to accomplish your work goals and get along with your boss and co-workers. For school you might see that you are getting along with your teachers and fellow students. You are doing your

schoolwork and getting good grades as well as participating in school activities and doing well.

### Month 3, Week 3, Day 1

Assume the state of meditation by first practicing a relaxation exercise. Inhale for four seconds. Hold the breath for four seconds. Exhale for four seconds. Hold the exhalation for four seconds. Repeat the process for as many times as possible.

Count from 100 backwards that is 100, 99, 88, etc, until you reach 1. Now count the normal way from 1 to 100. Concentrate on your counting and see the figures in your mind's eye as you count.

Next reflect on the Belief by the Buddha:

Do not believe in anything simply because you have heard it. Do not believe in anything simply because it is spoken and rumored by many. Do not believe in anything simply because it is found written in your religious books. Do not believe in anything merely on the authority of your teachers and elders. Do not believe in traditions because they have been handed down for many generations. But after observation and analysis, when you find that anything agrees with reason and is conducive to the good and benefit of one and all, then accept it and live up to it.

Now share your day with the rest of the family. This is the individual disclosure session. What happened to you, your friends and teachers during the day? What special role did you play in school? What contribution did you make in school? Did you get hurt at work or in school? If you did how did it happen and who was responsible? What have you done to address the issue? What did others do to address the issue? How do you feel?

Next take inventory of your activities today. Where did you go? What did you do? Who did you meet? What did you contribute? How did you affect your environment? How did the

environment affect you? Is there any thing you did that you could have done differently? How could you have done it next time?

Next visualize the next day of your life in the family, at work or in school. What do you want to see happen? For the family you might want harmony, understanding and unity. For work you might want to accomplish your work goals and get along with your boss and co-workers. For school you might see that you are getting along with your teachers and fellow students. You are doing your schoolwork and getting good grades as well as participating in school activities and doing well.

**Month 3, Week 3, Day 2**

Assume the state of meditation by first practicing a relaxation exercise. Inhale for four seconds. Hold the breath for four seconds. Exhale for four seconds. Hold the exhalation for four seconds. Repeat the process for as many times as possible.

Count from 100 backwards that is 100, 99, 88, etc, until you reach 1. Now count the normal way from 1 to 100. Concentrate on your counting and see the figures in your mind's eye as you count.

Next take inventory of your activities today. Where did you go? What did you do? Who did you meet? What did you contribute? How did you affect your environment? How did the environment affect you? Is there any thing you did that you could have done differently? How could you have done it next time?

Next visualize the next day of your life in the family, at work or in school. What do you want to see happen? For the family you might want harmony, understanding and unity. For work you might want to accomplish your work goals and get along with your boss and co-workers. For school you might see that you are getting along with your teachers and fellow students. You are doing your

schoolwork and getting good grades as well as participating in school activities and doing well.

Next reflect on the following: Learn to enjoy every minute of your life. Be happy now. Don't wait for something outside of yourself to make you happy in the future. Think how really precious is the time you have to spend, whether it's at work or with your family. Every minute should be enjoyed and savored. Earl Nightingale

**Month 3, Week 3, Day 3**

Assume the state of meditation by first practicing a relaxation exercise. Inhale for four seconds. Hold the breath for four seconds. Exhale for four seconds. Hold the exhalation for four seconds. Repeat the process for as many times as possible.

Count from 100 backwards that is 100, 99, 88, etc, until you reach 1. Now count the normal way from 1 to 100. Concentrate on your counting and see the figures in your mind's eye as you count.

Next reflect on the Earth by the Native American Wisdom:

You must teach your children that the ground beneath their feet is the ashes of your grandfathers. So that they will respect the land, tell your children that the earth is rich with the lives of our kin. Teach your children what we have taught our children, that the earth is our mother. Whatever befalls the earth befalls the sons of the earth. If men spit upon the ground, they spit upon themselves.

Now share your day with the rest of the family. This is the individual disclosure session. What happened to you, your friends and teachers during the day? What special role did you play in school? What contribution did you make in school? Did you get hurt at work or in school? If you did how did it happen and who was responsible? What have you done to address the issue? What did others do to address the issue? How do you feel?

Next take inventory of your activities today. Where did you go? What did you do? Who did you meet? What did you contribute? How did you affect your environment? How did the environment affect you? Is there any thing you did that you could have done differently? How could you have done it next time?

Next visualize the next day of your life in the family, at work or in school. What do you want to see happen? For the family you might want harmony, understanding and unity. For work you might want to accomplish your work goals and get along with your boss and co-workers. For school you might see that you are getting along with your teachers and fellow students. You are doing your schoolwork and getting good grades as well as participating in school activities and doing well.

**Month 3, Week 3, Day 4**

Assume the state of meditation by first practicing a relaxation exercise. Inhale for four seconds. Hold the breath for four seconds. Exhale for four seconds. Hold the exhalation for four seconds. Repeat the process for as many times as possible.

Count from 100 backwards that is 100, 99, 88, etc, until you reach 1. Now count the normal way from 1 to 100. Concentrate on your counting and see the figures in your mind's eye as you count.

Next reflect on the Body by Thirukural

The body requires no medicine if you eat only after the food you have already eaten is digested. Once digestion is complete, eat with moderation; that is the way to prolong the life of the body. Life remains unharmed when one eats with restraint, refraining from foods that have proven disagreeable. The pleasures of health abide in the man who eats moderately. The pains of disease dwell with him who eats excessively. The thoughtless glutton who gorges himself beyond the limits of his digestive fires will be consumed by limitless ills.

Now share your day with the rest of the family. This is the individual disclosure session. What happened to you, your friends and teachers during the day? What special role did you play in school? What contribution did you make in school? Did you get hurt at work or in school? If you did how did it happen and who was responsible? What have you done to address the issue? What did others do to address the issue? How do you feel?

Next take inventory of your activities today. Where did you go? What did you do? Who did you meet? What did you contribute? How did you affect your environment? How did the environment affect you? Is there any thing you did that you could have done differently? How could you have done it next time?

Next visualize the next day of your life in the family, at work or in school. What do you want to see happen? For the family you might want harmony, understanding and unity. For work you might want to accomplish your work goals and get along with your boss and co-workers. For school you might see that you are getting along with your teachers and fellow students. You are doing your schoolwork and getting good grades as well as participating in school activities and doing well.

**Month 3, Week 3, Day 5**

Assume the state of meditation by first practicing a relaxation exercise. Inhale for four seconds. Hold the breath for four seconds. Exhale for four seconds. Hold the exhalation for four seconds. Repeat the process for as many times as possible.

Count from 100 backwards that is 100, 99, 88, etc, until you reach 1. Now count the normal way from 1 to 100. Concentrate on your counting and see the figures in your mind's eye as you count.

Next reflect on the Lion and the Mouse by Aesop

Once when a Lion was asleep a little Mouse began running up and down upon him; this soon wakened the Lion, who placed his huge paw upon him, and opened his big jaws to swallow him. "Pardon, O King," cried the little Mouse: "forgive me this time, I shall never forget it: who knows but what I may be able to do you a turn some of these days?" The Lion was so tickled at the idea of the Mouse being able to help him that he lifted up his paw and let him go. Some time after the Lion was caught in a trap, and the hunters who desired to carry him alive to the King, tied him to a tree while they went in search of a wagon to carry him on. Just then the little Mouse happened to pass by, and seeing the sad plight in which the Lion was, went up to him and soon gnawed away the ropes that bound the King of the Beasts. "Was I not right?" said the little Mouse.

Now share your day with the rest of the family. This is the individual disclosure session. What happened to you, your friends and teachers during the day? What special role did you play in school? What contribution did you make in school? Did you get hurt at work or in school? If you did how did it happen and who was responsible? What have you done to address the issue? What did others do to address the issue? How do you feel?

Next take inventory of your activities today. Where did you go? What did you do? Who did you meet? What did you contribute? How did you affect your environment? How did the environment affect you? Is there any thing you did that you could have done differently? How could you have done it next time?

Next visualize the next day of your life in the family, at work or in school. What do you want to see happen? For the family you might want harmony, understanding and unity. For work you might want to accomplish your work goals and get along with your

boss and co-workers. For school you might see that you are getting along with your teachers and fellow students. You are doing your schoolwork and getting good grades as well as participating in school activities and doing well.

**Month 3, Week 3, Day 6**

Retire to your sacred place and practice a relaxation exercise. Inhale for four seconds. Hold the breath for four seconds. Exhale for four seconds. Hold the exhalation for four seconds. Repeat the process for as many times as possible.

Count from 100 backwards that is 100, 99, 88, etc, until you reach 1. Now count the normal way from 1 to 100. Concentrate on your counting and see the figures in your mind's eye as you count.

Now reflect on the following: No matter what you've done for yourself or for humanity, if you can't look back on having given love and attention to your own family, what have you really accomplished? Lee Iacocca

Next take inventory of your activities today. Where did you go? What did you do? Who did you meet? What did you contribute? How did you affect your environment? How did the environment affect you? Is there any thing you did that you could have done differently? How could you have done it next time?

Lastly visualize the next day of your life in the family, at work or in school. What do you want to see happen? For the family you might want harmony, understanding and unity. For work you might want to accomplish your work goals and get along with your boss and co-workers. For school you might see that you are getting along with your teachers and fellow students. You are doing your schoolwork and getting good grades as well as participating in school activities and doing well.

### Month 3, Week 3, Day 7

Attend a church, a temple, or any other meeting that brings you together with people for a common goal. If you do not have one you may begin today and find one that meets your interest and inclination. If you want you could also organize a group of your own. For instance you could start an Awakened Living Study Program. You may contact UNISM for more information.

Retire to your sacred place and practice a relaxation exercise. Inhale for four seconds. Hold the breath for four seconds. Exhale for four seconds. Hold the exhalation for four seconds. Repeat the process for as many times as possible.

Choose your favorite meditation posture and practice using the posture. For instance, if you use supports for your back during meditation start practicing your favorite posture without any support.

Next take inventory of your activities today. Where did you go? What did you do? Who did you meet? What did you contribute? How did you affect your environment? How did the environment affect you? Is there any thing you did that you could have done differently? How could you have done it next time?

Lastly visualize the next day of your life in the family, at work or in school. What do you want to see happen? For the family you might want harmony, understanding and unity. For work you might want to accomplish your work goals and get along with your boss and co-workers. For school you might see that you are getting along with your teachers and fellow students. You are doing your schoolwork and getting good grades as well as participating in school activities and doing well.

## Month 3, Week 4, Day 1

Assume the state of meditation by first practicing a relaxation exercise. Inhale for four seconds. Hold the breath for four seconds. Exhale for four seconds. Hold the exhalation for four seconds. Repeat the process for as many times as possible.

Count from 100 backwards that is 100, 99, 88, etc, until you reach 1. Now count the normal way from 1 to 100. Concentrate on your counting and see the figures in your mind's eye as you count.

Next reflect on A Fable by **Robert Ingersoll**

A devout clergyman sought every opportunity to impress upon the mind of his son the fact that God takes care of all his creatures. Happening, one day, to see a crane wading in quest of food, the good man pointed out to his son the perfect adaptation of the crane to get his living in that manner. "See," said he, "how his legs are formed for wading! What a long slender bill he has! Observe how nicely he folds his feet when putting them in or drawing them out of the water! He does not cause the slightest ripple. He is thus enabled to approach the fish without giving them any notice of his arrival." . . . "Yes," replied the boy. "I think I see the goodness of God, at least so far as the crane is concerned. But after all, father, don't you think the arrangement a little tough on the fish?"

Now share your day with the rest of the family. This is the individual disclosure session. What happened to you, your friends and teachers during the day? What special role did you play in school? What contribution did you make in school? Did you get hurt at work or in school? If you did how did it happen and who was responsible? What have you done to address the issue? What did others do to address the issue? How do you feel?

Next take inventory of your activities today. Where did you go? What did you do? Who did you meet? What did you contribute? How did you affect your environment? How did the

environment affect you? Is there any thing you did that you could have done differently? How could you have done it next time?

Next visualize the next day of your life in the family, at work or in school. What do you want to see happen? For the family you might want harmony, understanding and unity. For work you might want to accomplish your work goals and get along with your boss and co-workers. For school you might see that you are getting along with your teachers and fellow students. You are doing your schoolwork and getting good grades as well as participating in school activities and doing well.

### Month 3, Week 4, Day 2

Assume the state of meditation by first practicing a relaxation exercise. Inhale for four seconds. Hold the breath for four seconds. Exhale for four seconds. Hold the exhalation for four seconds. Repeat the process for as many times as possible.

Count from 100 backwards that is 100, 99, 88, etc, until you reach 1. Now count the normal way from 1 to 100. Concentrate on your counting and see the figures in your mind's eye as you count.

Next reflect on the following: Knowledge is power. Information is liberating. Education is the premise of progress, in every society, in every family. Kofi Annan

Now share your day with the rest of the family. This is the individual disclosure session. What happened to you, your friends and teachers during the day? What special role did you play in school? What contribution did you make in school? Did you get hurt at work or in school? If you did how did it happen and who was responsible? What have you done to address the issue? What did others do to address the issue? How do you feel?

Next take inventory of your activities today. Where did you go? What did you do? Who did you meet? What did you

contribute? How did you affect your environment? How did the environment affect you? Is there any thing you did that you could have done differently? How could you have done it next time?

Next visualize the next day of your life in the family, at work or in school. What do you want to see happen? For the family you might want harmony, understanding and unity. For work you might want to accomplish your work goals and get along with your boss and co-workers. For school you might see that you are getting along with your teachers and fellow students. You are doing your schoolwork and getting good grades as well as participating in school activities and doing well.

**Month 3, Week 4, Day 3**

Assume the state of meditation by first practicing a relaxation exercise. Inhale for four seconds. Hold the breath for four seconds. Exhale for four seconds. Hold the exhalation for four seconds. Repeat the process for as many times as possible.

Count from 100 backwards that is 100, 99, 88, etc, until you reach 1. Now count the normal way from 1 to 100. Concentrate on your counting and see the figures in your mind's eye as you count.

Next reflect on Think Like a Tree by **Karen I. Shragg**

Soak up the sun
Affirm life's magic
Be graceful in the wind
Stand tall after a storm
Feel refreshed after it rains
Grow strong without notice
Be prepared for each season
Provide shelter to strangers
Hang tough through a cold spell
Emerge renewed at the first signs of spring

Stay deeply rooted while reaching for the sky
Be still long enough to
hear your own leaves rustling

Now share your day with the rest of the family. This is the individual disclosure session. What happened to you, your friends and teachers during the day? What special role did you play in school? What contribution did you make in school? Did you get hurt at work or in school? If you did how did it happen and who was responsible? What have you done to address the issue? What did others do to address the issue? How do you feel?

Next take inventory of your activities today. Where did you go? What did you do? Who did you meet? What did you contribute? How did you affect your environment? How did the environment affect you? Is there any thing you did that you could have done differently? How could you have done it next time?

Next visualize the next day of your life in the family, at work or in school. What do you want to see happen? For the family you might want harmony, understanding and unity. For work you might want to accomplish your work goals and get along with your boss and co-workers. For school you might see that you are getting along with your teachers and fellow students. You are doing your schoolwork and getting good grades as well as participating in school activities and doing well.

**Month 3, Week 4, Day 4**

Assume the state of meditation by first practicing a relaxation exercise. Inhale for four seconds. Hold the breath for four seconds. Exhale for four seconds. Hold the exhalation for four seconds. Repeat the process for as many times as possible.

Count from 100 backwards that is 100, 99, 88, etc, until you reach 1. Now count the normal way from 1 to 100. Concentrate on your counting and see the figures in your mind's eye as you count.

Next reflect on The Two Travelers and the Farmer by **Ashliman D.L**

A traveler came upon an old farmer hoeing in his field beside the road. Eager to rest his feet, the wanderer hailed the countryman, who seemed happy enough to straighten his back and talk for a moment. "What sort of people live in the next town?" asked the stranger. "What were the people like where you've come from?" replied the farmer, answering the question with another question. "They were a bad lot. Troublemakers all, and lazy too. The most selfish people in the world, and not a one of them to be trusted. I'm happy to be leaving the scoundrels." "Is that so?" replied the old farmer. "Well, I'm afraid that you'll find the same sort in the next town. Disappointed, the traveler trudged on his way, and the farmer returned to his work. Some time later another stranger, coming from the same direction, hailed the farmer, and they stopped to talk. "What sort of people live in the next town?" he asked. "What were the people like where you've come from?" replied the farmer once again. "They were the best people in the world. Hard working, honest, and friendly. I'm sorry to be leaving them." "Fear not," said the farmer. "You'll find the same sort in the next town."

Now share your day with the rest of the family. This is the individual disclosure session. What happened to you, your friends and teachers during the day? What special role did you play in school? What contribution did you make in school? Did you get hurt at work or in school? If you did how did it happen and who was responsible? What have you done to address the issue? What did others do to address the issue? How do you feel?

Next take inventory of your activities today. Where did you go? What did you do? Who did you meet? What did you contribute? How did you affect your environment? How did the environment affect you? Is there any thing you did that you could have done differently? How could you have done it next time?

Next visualize the next day of your life in the family, at work or in school. What do you want to see happen? For the family you might want harmony, understanding and unity. For work you might want to accomplish your work goals and get along with your boss and co-workers. For school you might see that you are getting along with your teachers and fellow students. You are doing your schoolwork and getting good grades as well as participating in school activities and doing well.

**Month 3, Week 4, Day 5**

Assume the state of meditation by first practicing a relaxation exercise. Inhale for four seconds. Hold the breath for four seconds. Exhale for four seconds. Hold the exhalation for four seconds. Repeat the process for as many times as possible.

Count from 100 backwards that is 100, 99, 88, etc, until you reach 1. Now count the normal way from 1 to 100. Concentrate on your counting and see the figures in your mind's eye as you count.

Next reflect on Failure by **GABRIEL OKPE**

I believe a failure is that man that remains on the ground when he falls because he fears if he raises he might fall again, or that man that accept what people think of or call him, better still he is that man that thinks "that task is too big for me", " I can't Possibly do that", "It is not yet my time/turn". Because all these elude a man of the prize that awaits the activist.

Now share your day with the rest of the family. This is the individual disclosure session. What happened to you, your friends

and teachers during the day? What special role did you play in school? What contribution did you make in school? Did you get hurt at work or in school? If you did how did it happen and who was responsible? What have you done to address the issue? What did others do to address the issue? How do you feel?

Next take inventory of your activities today. Where did you go? What did you do? Who did you meet? What did you contribute? How did you affect your environment? How did the environment affect you? Is there any thing you did that you could have done differently? How could you have done it next time?

Next visualize the next day of your life in the family, at work or in school. What do you want to see happen? For the family you might want harmony, understanding and unity. For work you might want to accomplish your work goals and get along with your boss and co-workers. For school you might see that you are getting along with your teachers and fellow students. You are doing your schoolwork and getting good grades as well as participating in school activities and doing well.

**Month 3, Week 4, Day 6**

Retire to your sacred place and practice a relaxation exercise. Inhale for four seconds. Hold the breath for four seconds. Exhale for four seconds. Hold the exhalation for four seconds. Repeat the process for as many times as possible.

Count from 100 backwards that is 100, 99, 88, etc, until you reach 1. Now count the normal way from 1 to 100. Concentrate on your counting and see the figures in your mind's eye as you count.

Now reflect on the following: Love is patient, love is kind. It does not envy, it does not boast, it is not proud. It is not rude, it is not self-seeking, it is not easily angered, it keeps no record of wrongs. Love does not delight in evil but rejoices with the truth.

It always protects, always trusts, always hopes, always perseveres. Love never fails. But where there are prophecies, they will cease; where there are tongues, they will be stilled; where there is knowledge, it will pass away. New Testament:1 Corinthians 13:4-8

Next take inventory of your activities today. Where did you go? What did you do? Who did you meet? What did you contribute? How did you affect your environment? How did the environment affect you? Is there any thing you did that you could have done differently? How could you have done it next time?

Lastly visualize the next day of your life in the family, at work or in school. What do you want to see happen? For the family you might want harmony, understanding and unity. For work you might want to accomplish your work goals and get along with your boss and co-workers. For school you might see that you are getting along with your teachers and fellow students. You are doing your schoolwork and getting good grades as well as participating in school activities and doing well.

**Month 3, Week 4, Day 7**

Attend a church, a temple, or any other meeting that brings you together with people for a common goal. If you do not have one you may begin today and find one that meets your interest and inclination. If you want you could also organize a group of your own. For instance you could start an Awakened Living Study Program. You may contact UNISM for more information.

Retire to your sacred place and practice a relaxation exercise. Inhale for four seconds. Hold the breath for four seconds. Exhale for four seconds. Hold the exhalation for four seconds. Repeat the process for as many times as possible.

Choose your favorite meditation posture and practice using the posture. For instance, if you use supports for your back during

meditation start practicing your favorite posture without any support.

Next take inventory of your activities today. Where did you go? What did you do? Who did you meet? What did you contribute? How did you affect your environment? How did the environment affect you? Is there any thing you did that you could have done differently? How could you have done it next time?

Lastly visualize the next day of your life in the family, at work or in school. What do you want to see happen? For the family you might want harmony, understanding and unity. For work you might want to accomplish your work goals and get along with your boss and co-workers. For school you might see that you are getting along with your teachers and fellow students. You are doing your schoolwork and getting good grades as well as participating in school activities and doing well.

## Family Meditation: Fourth Month

### Goal

The goal of the fourth month of meditation is to improve our health. Overweight, fast food, stress, anger, fear, superstition, inactivity, bullies, pollution, immunization, injury, violence, drugs, alcohol, and tobacco are a few areas that could be a source of problems to our health. The focus of this month is to take an inventory of our lives at home, work and school in order to determine our risk areas.

### Month 4, Week 1, Day 1

Assume the state of meditation by first practicing a relaxation exercise. Inhale for four seconds. Hold the breath for four seconds. Exhale for four seconds. Hold the exhalation for four seconds. Repeat the process for as many times as possible.

Count from 100 backwards that is 100, 99, 88, etc, until you reach 1. Now count the normal way from 1 to 100. Concentrate on your counting and see the figures in your mind's eye as you count.

Next reflect on Persistence by **Calvin Coolidge**

Nothing in the world can take the place of persistence.
Talent will not... nothing is more common than unsuccessful people will talent.
Genius will not... unrewarded genius is almost legendary.
Education will not.... the world is full of educated derelicts.
Persistence and determination alone are omnipotent.

Now share your day with the rest of the family. This is the individual disclosure session. What happened to you, your friends and teachers during the day? What special role did you play in school? What contribution did you make in school? Did you get hurt at work or in school? If you did how did it happen and who

was responsible? What have you done to address the issue? What did others do to address the issue? How do you feel?

Next take inventory of your activities today. Where did you go? What did you do? Who did you meet? What did you contribute? How did you affect your environment? How did the environment affect you? Is there any thing you did that you could have done differently? How could you have done it next time?

Next visualize the next day of your life in the family, at work or in school. What do you want to see happen? For the family you might want harmony, understanding and unity. For work you might want to accomplish your work goals and get along with your boss and co-workers. For school you might see that you are getting along with your teachers and fellow students. You are doing your schoolwork and getting good grades as well as participating in school activities and doing well.

**Month 4, Week 1, Day 2**

Assume the state of meditation by first practicing a relaxation exercise. Inhale for four seconds. Hold the breath for four seconds. Exhale for four seconds. Hold the exhalation for four seconds. Repeat the process for as many times as possible.

Count from 100 backwards that is 100, 99, 88, etc, until you reach 1. Now count the normal way from 1 to 100. Concentrate on your counting and see the figures in your mind's eye as you count.

Next read the USDA Dietary guideline for your age group and discuss the recommended servings and food groups with the rest of the family. You may download the USDA Dietary Guideline from their website or write to the Department for free printed copies.

Now share your day with the rest of the family. This is the individual disclosure session. What happened to you, your friends

and teachers during the day? What special role did you play in school? What contribution did you make in school? Did you get hurt at work or in school? If you did how did it happen and who was responsible? What have you done to address the issue? What did others do to address the issue? How do you feel?

Next take inventory of your activities today. Where did you go? What did you do? Who did you meet? What did you contribute? How did you affect your environment? How did the environment affect you? Is there any thing you did that you could have done differently? How could you have done it next time?

Next visualize the next day of your life in the family, at work or in school. What do you want to see happen? For the family you might want harmony, understanding and unity. For work you might want to accomplish your work goals and get along with your boss and co-workers. For school you might see that you are getting along with your teachers and fellow students. You are doing your schoolwork and getting good grades as well as participating in school activities and doing well.

**Month 4, Week 1, Day 3**

Assume the state of meditation by first practicing a relaxation exercise. Inhale for four seconds. Hold the breath for four seconds. Exhale for four seconds. Hold the exhalation for four seconds. Repeat the process for as many times as possible.

Count from 100 backwards that is 100, 99, 88, etc, until you reach 1. Now count the normal way from 1 to 100. Concentrate on your counting and see the figures in your mind's eye as you count.

Consider the food you eat daily. Do you eat a balanced meal? How many servings of milk or dairy products; meats, fish, poultry, eggs, nuts or legumes; vegetables; fruit; bread, cereal, grains or pasta do you eat daily? How often do you use fats and oils in your food? According to the Food Guide Pyramid a balanced meal contains food from 6 groups including fats and oils; bread, cereal, grains or pasta; fruits; vegetables; meats, fish, poultry, eggs, nuts or legumes; and milk or dairy products. A serving is a recommended amount of food to be consumed at a time or in one sitting. For more information please check out the USDA website for your dietary guideline.

Now share your day with the rest of the family. This is the individual disclosure session. What happened to you, your friends and teachers during the day? What special role did you play in school? What contribution did you make in school? Did you get hurt at work or in school? If you did how did it happen and who was responsible? What have you done to address the issue? What did others do to address the issue? How do you feel?

Next take inventory of your activities today. Where did you go? What did you do? Who did you meet? What did you contribute? How did you affect your environment? How did the environment affect you? Is there any thing you did that you could have done differently? How could you have done it next time?

Next visualize the next day of your life in the family, at work or in school. What do you want to see happen? For the family you might want harmony, understanding and unity. For work you might want to accomplish your work goals and get along with your boss and co-workers. For school you might see that you are getting along with your teachers and fellow students. You are doing your schoolwork and getting good grades as well as participating in school activities and doing well.

**Month 4, Week 1, Day 4**

Assume the state of meditation by first practicing a relaxation exercise. Inhale for four seconds. Hold the breath for four seconds.

Exhale for four seconds. Hold the exhalation for four seconds. Repeat the process for as many times as possible.

Count from 100 backwards that is 100, 99, 88, etc, until you reach 1. Now count the normal way from 1 to 100. Concentrate on your counting and see the figures in your mind's eye as you count.

Next reflect on Natural Interconnection by **Hannah Dresner**

It is a natural aspect of the world's design that life forms are interdependent. If compassion means empathic awareness of that natural interconnection, then compassion is a law of nature we cannot deny. If we want to live in harmony with the logic of our world, we can't ignore the parts of us that are custodians of the earth and our brothers' and sisters' keepers. We're responsible for one another's well being whether we choose to act in accordance with that responsibility or not, because our well being is inescapably collective.

Now share your day with the rest of the family. This is the individual disclosure session. What happened to you, your friends and teachers during the day? What special role did you play in school? What contribution did you make in school? Did you get hurt at work or in school? If you did how did it happen and who was responsible? What have you done to address the issue? What did others do to address the issue? How do you feel?

Next take inventory of your activities today. Where did you go? What did you do? Who did you meet? What did you contribute? How did you affect your environment? How did the environment affect you? Is there any thing you did that you could have done differently? How could you have done it next time?

Next visualize the next day of your life in the family, at work or in school. What do you want to see happen? For the family you might want harmony, understanding and unity. For work you

might want to accomplish your work goals and get along with your boss and co-workers. For school you might see that you are getting along with your teachers and fellow students. You are doing your schoolwork and getting good grades as well as participating in school activities and doing well.

### Month 4, Week 1, Day 5

Assume the state of meditation by first practicing a relaxation exercise. Inhale for four seconds. Hold the breath for four seconds. Exhale for four seconds. Hold the exhalation for four seconds. Repeat the process for as many times as possible.

Count from 100 backwards that is 100, 99, 88, etc, until you reach 1. Now count the normal way from 1 to 100. Concentrate on your counting and see the figures in your mind's eye as you count.

Next reflect on History and Responsibility by **Gerda Lerner**

We can learn from history how past generations thought and acted, how they responded to the demands of their time and how they solved their problems. We can learn by analogy, not by example, for our circumstances will always be different than theirs were. The main thing history can teach us is that human actions have consequences and that certain choices, once made, cannot be undone. They foreclose the possibility of making other choices and thus they determine future events.

Now share your day with the rest of the family. This is the individual disclosure session. What happened to you, your friends and teachers during the day? What special role did you play in school? What contribution did you make in school? Did you get hurt at work or in school? If you did how did it happen and who was responsible? What have you done to address the issue? What did others do to address the issue? How do you feel?

Next take inventory of your activities today. Where did you go? What did you do? Who did you meet? What did you contribute? How did you affect your environment? How did the environment affect you? Is there any thing you did that you could have done differently? How could you have done it next time?

Next visualize the next day of your life in the family, at work or in school. What do you want to see happen? For the family you might want harmony, understanding and unity. For work you might want to accomplish your work goals and get along with your boss and co-workers. For school you might see that you are getting along with your teachers and fellow students. You are doing your schoolwork and getting good grades as well as participating in school activities and doing well.

### Month 4, Week 1, Day 6

Retire to your sacred place and practice a relaxation exercise. Inhale for four seconds. Hold the breath for four seconds. Exhale for four seconds. Hold the exhalation for four seconds. Repeat the process for as many times as possible.

Count from 100 backwards that is 100, 99, 88, etc, until you reach 1. Now count the normal way from 1 to 100. Concentrate on your counting and see the figures in your mind's eye as you count.

Now reflect on the following: The creative individual has the capacity to free himself from the web of social pressures in which the rest of us are caught. He is capable of questioning the assumptions that the rest of us accept. John W. Gardner

Next take inventory of your activities today. Where did you go? What did you do? Who did you meet? What did you contribute? How did you affect your environment? How did the environment affect you? Is there any thing you did that you could have done differently? How could you have done it next time?

Lastly visualize the next day of your life in the family, at work or in school. What do you want to see happen? For the family you might want harmony, understanding and unity. For work you might want to accomplish your work goals and get along with your boss and co-workers. For school you might see that you are getting along with your teachers and fellow students. You are doing your schoolwork and getting good grades as well as participating in school activities and doing well.

**Month 4, Week 1, Day 7**

Attend a church, a temple, or any other meeting that brings you together with people for a common goal. If you do not have one you may begin today and find one that meets your interest and inclination. If you want you could also organize a group of your own. For instance you could start an Awakened Living Study Program. You may contact UNISM for more information.

Retire to your sacred place and practice a relaxation exercise. Inhale for four seconds. Hold the breath for four seconds. Exhale for four seconds. Hold the exhalation for four seconds. Repeat the process for as many times as possible.

Choose your favorite meditation posture and practice using the posture. For instance, if you use supports for your back during meditation start practicing your favorite posture without any support.

Next take inventory of your activities today. Where did you go? What did you do? Who did you meet? What did you contribute? How did you affect your environment? How did the environment affect you? Is there any thing you did that you could have done differently? How could you have done it next time?

Lastly visualize the next day of your life in the family, at work or in school. What do you want to see happen? For the family

you might want harmony, understanding and unity. For work you might want to accomplish your work goals and get along with your boss and co-workers. For school you might see that you are getting along with your teachers and fellow students. You are doing your schoolwork and getting good grades as well as participating in school activities and doing well.

**Month 4, Week 2, Day 1**

Assume the state of meditation by first practicing a relaxation exercise. Inhale for four seconds. Hold the breath for four seconds. Exhale for four seconds. Hold the exhalation for four seconds. Repeat the process for as many times as possible.

Count from 100 backwards that is 100, 99, 88, etc, until you reach 1. Now count the normal way from 1 to 100. Concentrate on your counting and see the figures in your mind's eye as you count.

Next reflect on Peace by the Dalai Lama

Peace . . . starts within each one of us. When we have inner peace, we can be at peace with those around us. When our community is in a state of peace, it can share that peace with neighboring communities, and so on. When we feel love and kindness towards others, it not only makes others feel loved and cared for, but it helps us also to develop inner happiness and peace. And there are ways in which we can consciously work to develop feelings of love and kindness. For some of us, the most effective way to do so is through religious practice. For others it may be non-religious practices. What is important is that we each make a sincere effort to take our responsibility for each other and for the natural environment we live in seriously.

Now share your day with the rest of the family. This is the individual disclosure session. What happened to you, your friends and teachers during the day? What special role did you play in

school? What contribution did you make in school? Did you get hurt at work or in school? If you did how did it happen and who was responsible? What have you done to address the issue? What did others do to address the issue? How do you feel?

Next take inventory of your activities today. Where did you go? What did you do? Who did you meet? What did you contribute? How did you affect your environment? How did the environment affect you? Is there any thing you did that you could have done differently? How could you have done it next time?

Next visualize the next day of your life in the family, at work or in school. What do you want to see happen? For the family you might want harmony, understanding and unity. For work you might want to accomplish your work goals and get along with your boss and co-workers. For school you might see that you are getting along with your teachers and fellow students. You are doing your schoolwork and getting good grades as well as participating in school activities and doing well.

**Month 4, Week 2, Day 2**

Assume the state of meditation by first practicing a relaxation exercise. Inhale for four seconds. Hold the breath for four seconds. Exhale for four seconds. Hold the exhalation for four seconds. Repeat the process for as many times as possible.

Count from 100 backwards that is 100, 99, 88, etc, until you reach 1. Now count the normal way from 1 to 100. Concentrate on your counting and see the figures in your mind's eye as you count.

Next consider a health problem that you experience and reflect on it. For instance if you are afraid of something what is it that makes you afraid and why are you afraid of it. Is it lack of knowledge or superstition? Some people are afraid of snakes or spiders. Confront the agent or reconcile with the person and try to achieve balance. Share your meditation with the rest of the family.

Now share your day with the rest of the family. This is the individual disclosure session. What happened to you, your friends and teachers during the day? What special role did you play in school? What contribution did you make in school? Did you get hurt at work or in school? If you did how did it happen and who was responsible? What have you done to address the issue? What did others do to address the issue? How do you feel?

Next take inventory of your activities today. Where did you go? What did you do? Who did you meet? What did you contribute? How did you affect your environment? How did the environment affect you? Is there any thing you did that you could have done differently? How could you have done it next time?

Next visualize the next day of your life in the family, at work or in school. What do you want to see happen? For the family you might want harmony, understanding and unity. For work you might want to accomplish your work goals and get along with your boss and co-workers. For school you might see that you are getting along with your teachers and fellow students. You are doing your schoolwork and getting good grades as well as participating in school activities and doing well.

### Month 4, Week 2, Day 3

Assume the state of meditation by first practicing a relaxation exercise. Inhale for four seconds. Hold the breath for four seconds. Exhale for four seconds. Hold the exhalation for four seconds. Repeat the process for as many times as possible.

Count from 100 backwards that is 100, 99, 88, etc, until you reach 1. Now count the normal way from 1 to 100. Concentrate on your counting and see the figures in your mind's eye as you count.

Next reflect on The True Test of the American Ideal by Barack Obama

The true test of the American ideal is whether we're able to recognize our failings and then rise together to meet the challenges of our time. Whether we allow ourselves to be shaped by events and history, or whether we act to shape them. Whether chance of birth or circumstance decides life's big winners and losers, or whether we build a community where, at the very least, everyone has a chance to work hard, get ahead, and reach their dreams.

Now share your day with the rest of the family. This is the individual disclosure session. What happened to you, your friends and teachers during the day? What special role did you play in school? What contribution did you make in school? Did you get hurt at work or in school? If you did how did it happen and who was responsible? What have you done to address the issue? What did others do to address the issue? How do you feel?

Next take inventory of your activities today. Where did you go? What did you do? Who did you meet? What did you contribute? How did you affect your environment? How did the environment affect you? Is there any thing you did that you could have done differently? How could you have done it next time?

Next visualize the next day of your life in the family, at work or in school. What do you want to see happen? For the family you might want harmony, understanding and unity. For work you might want to accomplish your work goals and get along with your boss and co-workers. For school you might see that you are getting along with your teachers and fellow students. You are doing your schoolwork and getting good grades as well as participating in school activities and doing well.

**Month 4, Week 2, Day 4**

Assume the state of meditation by first practicing a relaxation exercise. Inhale for four seconds. Hold the breath for four seconds. Exhale for four seconds. Hold the exhalation for four seconds. Repeat the process for as many times as possible.

Count from 100 backwards that is 100, 99, 88, etc, until you reach 1. Now count the normal way from 1 to 100. Concentrate on your counting and see the figures in your mind's eye as you count.

Next consider what you think of most of the time. Is the thought a distraction or does it add to your present well being and future good? If it is a distraction have you considered replacing it with a progressive thought? For instance thinking about money or your bills does not help you to get money to pay your bills. But looking for a part time job to make extra income to pay off your bills will help. Alternatively, reducing your financial commitments on certain things like cable TV, eating out and even selling your big home for a smaller one or moving to a less expensive apartment could help. In this meditation begin to confront your unprogressive thoughts and replace them with uplifting ones.

Now share your day with the rest of the family. This is the individual disclosure session. What happened to you, your friends and teachers during the day? What special role did you play in school? What contribution did you make in school? Did you get hurt at work or in school? If you did how did it happen and who was responsible? What have you done to address the issue? What did others do to address the issue? How do you feel?

Next take inventory of your activities today. Where did you go? What did you do? Who did you meet? What did you contribute? How did you affect your environment? How did the environment affect you? Is there any thing you did that you could have done differently? How could you have done it next time?

Next visualize the next day of your life in the family, at work or in school. What do you want to see happen? For the family you might want harmony, understanding and unity. For work you might want to accomplish your work goals and get along with your boss and co-workers. For school you might see that you are getting along with your teachers and fellow students. You are doing your schoolwork and getting good grades as well as participating in school activities and doing well.

**Month 4, Week 2, Day 5**

Assume the state of meditation by first practicing a relaxation exercise. Inhale for four seconds. Hold the breath for four seconds. Exhale for four seconds. Hold the exhalation for four seconds. Repeat the process for as many times as possible.

Count from 100 backwards that is 100, 99, 88, etc, until you reach 1. Now count the normal way from 1 to 100. Concentrate on your counting and see the figures in your mind's eye as you count.

Next reflect on The Intelligent and Good man by **Robert Ingersoll**

The intelligent and good man holds in his affections the good and true of every land--the boundaries of countries are not the limitations of his sympathies. Caring nothing for race, or color, he loves those who speak other languages and worship other gods. Between him and those who suffer, there is no impassable gulf. He salutes the world, and extends the hand of friendship to the human race. He does not bow before a provincial and patriotic god--one who protects his tribe or nation, and abhors the rest of mankind.

Now share your day with the rest of the family. This is the individual disclosure session. What happened to you, your friends and teachers during the day? What special role did you play in school? What contribution did you make in school? Did you get

hurt at work or in school? If you did how did it happen and who was responsible? What have you done to address the issue? What did others do to address the issue? How do you feel?

Next take inventory of your activities today. Where did you go? What did you do? Who did you meet? What did you contribute? How did you affect your environment? How did the environment affect you? Is there any thing you did that you could have done differently? How could you have done it next time?

Next visualize the next day of your life in the family, at work or in school. What do you want to see happen? For the family you might want harmony, understanding and unity. For work you might want to accomplish your work goals and get along with your boss and co-workers. For school you might see that you are getting along with your teachers and fellow students. You are doing your schoolwork and getting good grades as well as participating in school activities and doing well.

**Month 4, Week 2, Day 6**

Retire to your sacred place and practice a relaxation exercise. Inhale for four seconds. Hold the breath for four seconds. Exhale for four seconds. Hold the exhalation for four seconds. Repeat the process for as many times as possible.

Count from 100 backwards that is 100, 99, 88, etc, until you reach 1. Now count the normal way from 1 to 100. Concentrate on your counting and see the figures in your mind's eye as you count.

Now reflect on the following: Do not follow where the path may lead. Go, instead, where there is no path and leave a trail." Ralph Waldo Emerson

Next take inventory of your activities today. Where did you go? What did you do? Who did you meet? What did you contribute? How did you affect your environment? How did the

environment affect you? Is there any thing you did that you could have done differently? How could you have done it next time?

Lastly visualize the next day of your life in the family, at work or in school. What do you want to see happen? For the family you might want harmony, understanding and unity. For work you might want to accomplish your work goals and get along with your boss and co-workers. For school you might see that you are getting along with your teachers and fellow students. You are doing your schoolwork and getting good grades as well as participating in school activities and doing well.

**Month 4, Week 2, Day 7**

Attend a church, a temple, or any other meeting that brings you together with people for a common goal. If you do not have one you may begin today and find one that meets your interest and inclination. If you want you could also organize a group of your own. For instance you could start an Awakened Living Study Program. You may contact UNISM for more information.

Retire to your sacred place and practice a relaxation exercise. Inhale for four seconds. Hold the breath for four seconds. Exhale for four seconds. Hold the exhalation for four seconds. Repeat the process for as many times as possible.

Choose your favorite meditation posture and practice using the posture. For instance, if you use supports for your back during meditation start practicing your favorite posture without any support.

Next take inventory of your activities today. Where did you go? What did you do? Who did you meet? What did you contribute? How did you affect your environment? How did the environment affect you? Is there any thing you did that you could have done differently? How could you have done it next time?

Lastly visualize the next day of your life in the family, at work or in school. What do you want to see happen? For the family you might want harmony, understanding and unity. For work you might want to accomplish your work goals and get along with your boss and co-workers. For school you might see that you are getting along with your teachers and fellow students. You are doing your schoolwork and getting good grades as well as participating in school activities and doing well.

**Month 4, Week 3, Day 1**

Assume the state of meditation by first practicing a relaxation exercise. Inhale for four seconds. Hold the breath for four seconds. Exhale for four seconds. Hold the exhalation for four seconds. Repeat the process for as many times as possible.

Count from 100 backwards that is 100, 99, 88, etc, until you reach 1. Now count the normal way from 1 to 100. Concentrate on your counting and see the figures in your mind's eye as you count.

Next consider how you spend your time each day. Would you say that you spend your time well for your good and the good of the Earth? Knowing that your time on Earth is limited what can you do now to improve yourself or the Earth? You may consider a hobby that contributes to the general good. Do you have a hobby? What are your interests? Meditate on your interests and discuss with the rest of the family.

Now share your day with the rest of the family. This is the individual disclosure session. What happened to you, your friends and teachers during the day? What special role did you play in school? What contribution did you make in school? Did you get hurt at work or in school? If you did how did it happen and who was responsible? What have you done to address the issue? What did others do to address the issue? How do you feel?

Next take inventory of your activities today. Where did you go? What did you do? Who did you meet? What did you contribute? How did you affect your environment? How did the environment affect you? Is there any thing you did that you could have done differently? How could you have done it next time?

Next visualize the next day of your life in the family, at work or in school. What do you want to see happen? For the family you might want harmony, understanding and unity. For work you might want to accomplish your work goals and get along with your boss and co-workers. For school you might see that you are getting along with your teachers and fellow students. You are doing your schoolwork and getting good grades as well as participating in school activities and doing well.

**Month 4, Week 3, Day 2**

Assume the state of meditation by first practicing a relaxation exercise. Inhale for four seconds. Hold the breath for four seconds. Exhale for four seconds. Hold the exhalation for four seconds. Repeat the process for as many times as possible.

Count from 100 backwards that is 100, 99, 88, etc, until you reach 1. Now count the normal way from 1 to 100. Concentrate on your counting and see the figures in your mind's eye as you count.

Next reflect on the Roots of Violence by Mohandas Gandhi
The Roots of Violence:
Wealth without work,
Pleasure without conscience,
Knowledge without character,
Commerce without morality,
Science without humanity,
Worship without sacrifice,
Politics without principles.

Now share your day with the rest of the family. This is the individual disclosure session. What happened to you, your friends and teachers during the day? What special role did you play in school? What contribution did you make in school? Did you get hurt at work or in school? If you did how did it happen and who was responsible? What have you done to address the issue? What did others do to address the issue? How do you feel?

Next take inventory of your activities today. Where did you go? What did you do? Who did you meet? What did you contribute? How did you affect your environment? How did the environment affect you? Is there any thing you did that you could have done differently? How could you have done it next time?

Next visualize the next day of your life in the family, at work or in school. What do you want to see happen? For the family you might want harmony, understanding and unity. For work you might want to accomplish your work goals and get along with your boss and co-workers. For school you might see that you are getting along with your teachers and fellow students. You are doing your schoolwork and getting good grades as well as participating in school activities and doing well.

**Month 4, Week 3, Day 3**

Assume the state of meditation by first practicing a relaxation exercise. Inhale for four seconds. Hold the breath for four seconds. Exhale for four seconds. Hold the exhalation for four seconds. Repeat the process for as many times as possible.

Count from 100 backwards that is 100, 99, 88, etc, until you reach 1. Now count the normal way from 1 to 100. Concentrate on your counting and see the figures in your mind's eye as you count.

Next reflect on the place you call home; the place where you live. Is your home clean? Does your home bring out the best in you? Are you happy in your home? Do you appreciate your home? Are you satisfied with your home? If you are not happy with your home why are you not happy? What could you do to achieve balance? Meditate on these things and share with the rest of the family.

Now share your day with the rest of the family. This is the individual disclosure session. What happened to you, your friends and teachers during the day? What special role did you play in school? What contribution did you make in school? Did you get hurt at work or in school? If you did how did it happen and who was responsible? What have you done to address the issue? What did others do to address the issue? How do you feel?

Next take inventory of your activities today. Where did you go? What did you do? Who did you meet? What did you contribute? How did you affect your environment? How did the environment affect you? Is there any thing you did that you could have done differently? How could you have done it next time?

Now visualize the next day of your life in the family, at work or in school. What do you want to see happen? For the family you might want harmony, understanding and unity. For work you might want to accomplish your work goals and get along with your boss and co-workers. For school you might see that you are getting along with your teachers and fellow students. You are doing your schoolwork and getting good grades as well as participating in school activities and doing well.

**Month 4, Week 3, Day 4**

Assume the state of meditation by first practicing a relaxation exercise. Inhale for four seconds. Hold the breath for four seconds. Exhale for four seconds. Hold the exhalation for four seconds. Repeat the process for as many times as possible.

Count from 100 backwards that is 100, 99, 88, etc, until you reach 1. Now count the normal way from 1 to 100. Concentrate on your counting and see the figures in your mind's eye as you count.

Next reflect on Live a Good Life by **Marcus Aurelius:**

Live a good life. If there are gods and they are just, they will not care how devout you have been, but will welcome you based on the virtues you have lived by. If there are gods, but unjust, then you should not want to worship them. If there are no gods, then you will be gone, but will have lived a noble life that will live on in the memories of your loved ones.

Now share your day with the rest of the family. This is the individual disclosure session. What happened to you, your friends and teachers during the day? What special role did you play in school? What contribution did you make in school? Did you get hurt at work or in school? If you did how did it happen and who was responsible? What have you done to address the issue? What did others do to address the issue? How do you feel?

Next take inventory of your activities today. Where did you go? What did you do? Who did you meet? What did you contribute? How did you affect your environment? How did the environment affect you? Is there any thing you did that you could have done differently? How could you have done it next time?

Next visualize the next day of your life in the family, at work or in school. What do you want to see happen? For the family you might want harmony, understanding and unity. For work you might want to accomplish your work goals and get along with your boss and co-workers. For school you might see that you are getting along with your teachers and fellow students. You are doing your schoolwork and getting good grades as well as participating in school activities and doing well.

## Month 4, Week 3, Day 5

Assume the state of meditation by first practicing a relaxation exercise. Inhale for four seconds. Hold the breath for four seconds. Exhale for four seconds. Hold the exhalation for four seconds. Repeat the process for as many times as possible.

Count from 100 backwards that is 100, 99, 88, etc, until you reach 1. Now count the normal way from 1 to 100. Concentrate on your counting and see the figures in your mind's eye as you count.

Next reflect on your neighborhood; that is the environment surrounding your home. Is your neighborhood safe? Are you happy with your neighbors? Is the environment clean? Is the air clean? Are you happy in the neighborhood? If you are not happy in your neighborhood why are you not happy? What could you do to achieve balance? Meditate on these things and share with the rest of the family.

Now share your day with the rest of the family. This is the individual disclosure session. What happened to you, your friends and teachers during the day? What special role did you play in school? What contribution did you make in school? Did you get hurt at work or in school? If you did how did it happen and who was responsible? What have you done to address the issue? What did others do to address the issue? How do you feel?

Next take inventory of your activities today. Where did you go? What did you do? Who did you meet? What did you contribute? How did you affect your environment? How did the environment affect you? Is there any thing you did that you could have done differently? How could you have done it next time?

Next visualize the next day of your life in the family, at work or in school. What do you want to see happen? For the family you might want harmony, understanding and unity. For work you might want to accomplish your work goals and get along with your

boss and co-workers. For school you might see that you are getting along with your teachers and fellow students. You are doing your schoolwork and getting good grades as well as participating in school activities and doing well.

**Month 4, Week 3, Day 6**

Retire to your sacred place and practice a relaxation exercise. Inhale for four seconds. Hold the breath for four seconds. Exhale for four seconds. Hold the exhalation for four seconds. Repeat the process for as many times as possible.

Count from 100 backwards that is 100, 99, 88, etc, until you reach 1. Now count the normal way from 1 to 100. Concentrate on your counting and see the figures in your mind's eye as you count.

Now reflect on the following: "Whenever you find yourself on the side of the majority, it is time to pause and reflect." Mark Twain

Next take inventory of your activities today. Where did you go? What did you do? Who did you meet? What did you contribute? How did you affect your environment? How did the environment affect you? Is there any thing you did that you could have done differently? How could you have done it next time?

Lastly visualize the next day of your life in the family, at work or in school. What do you want to see happen? For the family you might want harmony, understanding and unity. For work you might want to accomplish your work goals and get along with your boss and co-workers. For school you might see that you are getting along with your teachers and fellow students. You are doing your schoolwork and getting good grades as well as participating in school activities and doing well.

**Month 4, Week 3, Day 7**

Attend a church, a temple, or any other meeting that brings you together with people for a common goal. If you do not have one you may begin today and find one that meets your interest and inclination. If you want you could also organize a group of your own. For instance you could start an Awakened Living Study Program. You may contact UNISM for more information.

Retire to your sacred place and practice a relaxation exercise. Inhale for four seconds. Hold the breath for four seconds. Exhale for four seconds. Hold the exhalation for four seconds. Repeat the process for as many times as possible.

Choose your favorite meditation posture and practice using the posture. For instance, if you use supports for your back during meditation start practicing your favorite posture without any support.

Next take inventory of your activities today. Where did you go? What did you do? Who did you meet? What did you contribute? How did you affect your environment? How did the environment affect you? Is there any thing you did that you could have done differently? How could you have done it next time?

Lastly visualize the next day of your life in the family, at work or in school. What do you want to see happen? For the family you might want harmony, understanding and unity. For work you might want to accomplish your work goals and get along with your boss and co-workers. For school you might see that you are getting along with your teachers and fellow students. You are doing your schoolwork and getting good grades as well as participating in school activities and doing well.

**Month 4, Week 4, Day 1**

Assume the state of meditation by first practicing a relaxation exercise. Inhale for four seconds. Hold the breath for four seconds. Exhale for four seconds. Hold the exhalation for four seconds. Repeat the process for as many times as possible.

Count from 100 backwards that is 100, 99, 88, etc, until you reach 1. Now count the normal way from 1 to 100. Concentrate on your counting and see the figures in your mind's eye as you count.

Next reflect on Before it is too late by Frank Herbert Sweet:
If you have a tender message,
Or a loving word to say,
Do not wait till you forget it,
But whisper it today;
The tender word unspoken,
The letter never sent,
The long forgotten messages,
The wealth of love unspent-
For these some hearts are breaking,
For these some loved ones wait;
So show them that you care for them
Before it is too late.

Now share your day with the rest of the family. This is the individual disclosure session. What happened to you, your friends and teachers during the day? What special role did you play in school? What contribution did you make in school? Did you get hurt at work or in school? If you did how did it happen and who was responsible? What have you done to address the issue? What did others do to address the issue? How do you feel?

Next take inventory of your activities today. Where did you go? What did you do? Who did you meet? What did you contribute? How did you affect your environment? How did the

environment affect you? Is there any thing you did that you could have done differently? How could you have done it next time?

Next visualize the next day of your life in the family, at work or in school. What do you want to see happen? For the family you might want harmony, understanding and unity. For work you might want to accomplish your work goals and get along with your boss and co-workers. For school you might see that you are getting along with your teachers and fellow students. You are doing your schoolwork and getting good grades as well as participating in school activities and doing well.

**Month 4, Week 4, Day 2**

Assume the state of meditation by first practicing a relaxation exercise. Inhale for four seconds. Hold the breath for four seconds. Exhale for four seconds. Hold the exhalation for four seconds. Repeat the process for as many times as possible.

Count from 100 backwards that is 100, 99, 88, etc, until you reach 1. Now count the normal way from 1 to 100. Concentrate on your counting and see the figures in your mind's eye as you count.

Next reflect on What do you worship by Gangaji

"The meaning of your life depends on which ideas you permit to use you. Who you think you are determines where you put your attention. Where you direct your attention creates your life experiences, and brings a new course of events into being. Where you habitually put your attention is what you worship. What do you worship in this mindstream called your life?"

Now share your day with the rest of the family. This is the individual disclosure session. What happened to you, your friends and teachers during the day? What special role did you play in school? What contribution did you make in school? Did you get hurt at work or in school? If you did how did it happen and who

was responsible? What have you done to address the issue? What did others do to address the issue? How do you feel?

Next take inventory of your activities today. Where did you go? What did you do? Who did you meet? What did you contribute? How did you affect your environment? How did the environment affect you? Is there any thing you did that you could have done differently? How could you have done it next time?

Next visualize the next day of your life in the family, at work or in school. What do you want to see happen? For the family you might want harmony, understanding and unity. For work you might want to accomplish your work goals and get along with your boss and co-workers. For school you might see that you are getting along with your teachers and fellow students. You are doing your schoolwork and getting good grades as well as participating in school activities and doing well.

**Month 4, Week 4, Day**

Assume the state of meditation by first practicing a relaxation exercise. Inhale for four seconds. Hold the breath for four seconds. Exhale for four seconds. Hold the exhalation for four seconds. Repeat the process for as many times as possible.

Count from 100 backwards that is 100, 99, 88, etc, until you reach 1. Now count the normal way from 1 to 100. Concentrate on your counting and see the figures in your mind's eye as you count.

Next consider your school or work environment. Are you comfortable at work? Are you comfortable at school? Are there issues at work that you need to address? Are these issues at school that you need to address? What are these issues? Meditate on them and discuss them with the rest of the family.

Now share your day with the rest of the family. This is the individual disclosure session. What happened to you, your friends

and teachers during the day? What special role did you play in school? What contribution did you make in school? Did you get hurt at work or in school? If you did how did it happen and who was responsible? What have you done to address the issue? What did others do to address the issue? How do you feel?

Next take inventory of your activities today. Where did you go? What did you do? Who did you meet? What did you contribute? How did you affect your environment? How did the environment affect you? Is there any thing you did that you could have done differently? How could you have done it next time?

Next visualize the next day of your life in the family, at work or in school. What do you want to see happen? For the family you might want harmony, understanding and unity. For work you might want to accomplish your work goals and get along with your boss and co-workers. For school you might see that you are getting along with your teachers and fellow students. You are doing your schoolwork and getting good grades as well as participating in school activities and doing well.

**Month 4, Week 4, Day 4**

Assume the state of meditation by first practicing a relaxation exercise. Inhale for four seconds. Hold the breath for four seconds. Exhale for four seconds. Hold the exhalation for four seconds. Repeat the process for as many times as possible.

Count from 100 backwards that is 100, 99, 88, etc, until you reach 1. Now count the normal way from 1 to 100. Concentrate on your counting and see the figures in your mind's eye as you count.

Next reflect on Relationship by Stephen R. Covey:

The most important ingredient we put into any relationship is not what we say or what we do, but what we are. And if our words and our actions come from superficial human relations techniques (the Personality Ethic) rather than from our own inner core (the Character Ethic), others will sense that duplicity. We simply won't be able to create and sustain the foundation necessary for effective interdependence.

Now share your day with the rest of the family. This is the individual disclosure session. What happened to you, your friends and teachers during the day? What special role did you play in school? What contribution did you make in school? Did you get hurt at work or in school? If you did how did it happen and who was responsible? What have you done to address the issue? What did others do to address the issue? How do you feel?

Next take inventory of your activities today. Where did you go? What did you do? Who did you meet? What did you contribute? How did you affect your environment? How did the environment affect you? Is there any thing you did that you could have done differently? How could you have done it next time?

Next visualize the next day of your life in the family, at work or in school. What do you want to see happen? For the family you might want harmony, understanding and unity. For work you might want to accomplish your work goals and get along with your boss and co-workers. For school you might see that you are getting along with your teachers and fellow students. You are doing your schoolwork and getting good grades as well as participating in school activities and doing well.

**Month 4, Week 4, Day 5**

Assume the state of meditation by first practicing a relaxation exercise. Inhale for four seconds. Hold the breath for four seconds. Exhale for four seconds. Hold the exhalation for four seconds. Repeat the process for as many times as possible.

Count from 100 backwards that is 100, 99, 88, etc, until you reach 1. Now count the normal way from 1 to 100. Concentrate on your counting and see the figures in your mind's eye as you count.

Next reflect on Understanding Drug Addiction by HELPGUIDE. Addiction is a complex disorder characterized by compulsive drug use. People who are addicted feel an overwhelming, uncontrollable need for drugs or alcohol, even in the face of negative consequences. This self-destructive behavior can be hard to understand. Why continue doing something that's hurting you? Why is it so hard to stop? The answer lies in the brain. Repeated drug use alters the brain—causing long-lasting changes to the way it looks and functions. These brain changes interfere with your ability to think clearly, exercise good judgment, control your behavior, and feel normal without drugs. These changes are also responsible, in large part, for the drug cravings and compulsion to use that make addiction so powerful.

Now share your day with the rest of the family. This is the individual disclosure session. What happened to you, your friends and teachers during the day? What special role did you play in school? What contribution did you make in school? Did you get hurt at work or in school? If you did how did it happen and who was responsible? What have you done to address the issue? What did others do to address the issue? How do you feel?

Next take inventory of your activities today. Where did you go? What did you do? Who did you meet? What did you contribute? How did you affect your environment? How did the environment affect you? Is there any thing you did that you could have done differently? How could you have done it next time?

Next visualize the next day of your life in the family, at work or in school. What do you want to see happen? For the family you might want harmony, understanding and unity. For work you

might want to accomplish your work goals and get along with your boss and co-workers. For school you might see that you are getting along with your teachers and fellow students. You are doing your schoolwork and getting good grades as well as participating in school activities and doing well.

### Month 4, Week 4, Day 6

Retire to your sacred place and practice a relaxation exercise. Inhale for four seconds. Hold the breath for four seconds. Exhale for four seconds. Hold the exhalation for four seconds. Repeat the process for as many times as possible.

Count from 100 backwards that is 100, 99, 88, etc, until you reach 1. Now count the normal way from 1 to 100. Concentrate on your counting and see the figures in your mind's eye as you count.

Now reflect on the following: *If you take responsibility for yourself you will develop a hunger to accomplish your dreams."*
**Les Brown**

Next take inventory of your activities today. Where did you go? What did you do? Who did you meet? What did you contribute? How did you affect your environment? How did the environment affect you? Is there any thing you did that you could have done differently? How could you have done it next time?

Lastly visualize the next day of your life in the family, at work or in school. What do you want to see happen? For the family you might want harmony, understanding and unity. For work you might want to accomplish your work goals and get along with your boss and co-workers. For school you might see that you are getting along with your teachers and fellow students. You are doing your schoolwork and getting good grades as well as participating in school activities and doing well.

## Month 4, Week 4, Day 7

Attend a church, a temple, or any other meeting that brings you together with people for a common goal. If you do not have one you may begin today and find one that meets your interest and inclination. If you want you could also organize a group of your own. For instance you could start an Awakened Living Study Program. You may contact UNISM for more information.

Retire to your sacred place and practice a relaxation exercise. Inhale for four seconds. Hold the breath for four seconds. Exhale for four seconds. Hold the exhalation for four seconds. Repeat the process for as many times as possible.

Choose your favorite meditation posture and practice using the posture. For instance, if you use supports for your back during meditation start practicing your favorite posture without any support.

Next take inventory of your activities today. Where did you go? What did you do? Who did you meet? What did you contribute? How did you affect your environment? How did the environment affect you? Is there any thing you did that you could have done differently? How could you have done it next time?

Lastly visualize the next day of your life in the family, at work or in school. What do you want to see happen? For the family you might want harmony, understanding and unity. For work you might want to accomplish your work goals and get along with your boss and co-workers. For school you might see that you are getting along with your teachers and fellow students. You are doing your schoolwork and getting good grades as well as participating in school activities and doing well.

## Family Meditation: Fifth Month

**Goal**

The goal of the fifth month of meditation is to enhance the LOVE within us. If I speak in the tongues of men and of angels, but have not love, I am a noisy gong or a clanging cymbal. And if I have prophetic powers, and understand all mysteries and all knowledge, and if I have all faith, so as to remove mountains, but have not love, I am nothing. If I give away all I have, and if I deliver my body to be burned, but have not love, I gain nothing. Love is patient and kind; love is not jealous or boastful; it is not arrogant or rude. Love does not insist on its own way; it is not irritable or resentful; it does not rejoice at wrong, but rejoices in the right. Love bears all things, believes all things, hopes all things, endures all things. Love never ends; as for prophecies, they will pass away; as for tongues, they will cease; as for knowledge, it will pass away. For our knowledge is imperfect and our prophecy is imperfect; but when the perfect comes, the imperfect will pass away. When I was a child, I spoke like a child, I thought like a child, I reasoned like a child; when I became a man, I gave up childish ways. For now we see in a mirror dimly, but then face to face. Now I know in part; then I shall understand fully, even as I have been fully understood. So faith, hope, love abide, these three; but the greatest of these is love. (Bible:1 Corinthians 13:1-13).

**Month 5, Week 1, Day 1**

Assume the state of meditation by first practicing a relaxation exercise. Inhale for four seconds. Hold the breath for four seconds. Exhale for four seconds. Hold the exhalation for four seconds. Repeat the process for as many times as possible.

Count from 100 backwards that is 100, 99, 88, etc, until you reach 1. Now count the normal way from 1 to 100. Concentrate on your counting and see the figures in your mind's eye as you count.

Next reflect on Persistence by Orison Sweet Marden:

There is genius and power in persistence. It conquers all opposers; it gives confidence; it annihilates obstacles. Everybody believes in the determined man. People know that when he undertakes a thing, the battle is half won, for his rule is to accomplish whatever he sets out to do.

Now share your day with the rest of the family. This is the individual disclosure session. What happened to you, your friends and teachers during the day? What special role did you play in school? What contribution did you make in school? Did you get hurt at work or in school? If you did how did it happen and who was responsible? What have you done to address the issue? What did others do to address the issue? How do you feel?

Next take inventory of your activities today. Where did you go? What did you do? Who did you meet? What did you contribute? How did you affect your environment? How did the environment affect you? Is there any thing you did that you could have done differently? How could you have done it next time?

Now visualize the next day of your life in the family, at work or in school. What do you want to see happen? For the family you might want harmony, understanding and unity. For work you might want to accomplish your work goals and get along with your boss and co-workers. For school you might see that you are getting along with your teachers and fellow students. You are doing your schoolwork and getting good grades as well as participating in school activities and doing well.

### Month 5, Week 1, Day 2

Assume the state of meditation by first practicing a relaxation exercise. Inhale for four seconds. Hold the breath for four seconds. Exhale for four seconds. Hold the exhalation for four seconds. Repeat the process for as many times as possible.

Count from 100 backwards that is 100, 99, 88, etc, until you reach 1. Now count the normal way from 1 to 100. Concentrate on your counting and see the figures in your mind's eye as you count.

Next reflect on Iroquois Thanksgiving:

We return thanks to our mother, the earth, which sustains us.
We return thanks to the rivers and streams, which supply us with water.
We return thanks to all herbs, which furnish medicines for the cure of our diseases.
We return thanks to the moon and stars, which have given to us their light when the sun was gone. We return thanks to the sun, that has looked upon the earth with a beneficent eye. Lastly, we return thanks to the Great Spirit, in Whom is embodied all goodness, and Who directs all things for the good of Her children.

Now share your day with the rest of the family. This is the individual disclosure session. What happened to you, your friends and teachers during the day? What special role did you play in school? What contribution did you make in school? Did you get hurt at work or in school? If you did how did it happen and who was responsible? What have you done to address the issue? What did others do to address the issue? How do you feel?

Next make a presentation on the Earth. Why is the Earth important to all living things? What can we do help the Earth?

Next take inventory of your activities today. Where did you go? What did you do? Who did you meet? What did you contribute? How did you affect your environment? How did the

environment affect you? Is there any thing you did that you could have done differently? How could you have done it next time?

Next visualize the next day of your life in the family, at work or in school. What do you want to see happen? For the family you might want harmony, understanding and unity. For work you might want to accomplish your work goals and get along with your boss and co-workers. For school you might see that you are getting along with your teachers and fellow students. You are doing your schoolwork and getting good grades as well as participating in school activities and doing well.

**Month 5, Week 1, Day 3**

Assume the state of meditation by first practicing a relaxation exercise. Inhale for four seconds. Hold the breath for four seconds. Exhale for four seconds. Hold the exhalation for four seconds. Repeat the process for as many times as possible.

Count from 100 backwards that is 100, 99, 88, etc, until you reach 1. Now count the normal way from 1 to 100. Concentrate on your counting and see the figures in your mind's eye as you count.

Next consider all the aspects of Universal Love including the LOVE the Universe has for all creatures, LOVE as the underlying mystery within the Universe and the Love we aught to have for all creatures. Reflect on each aspect of Universal Love. What does each mean to you? Be a channel of Universal Love; receive it and give it away. You can do that by opening yourself to the love of the Universe. You may visualize it as a WHITE LIGHT flowing from the Universe into your being. Let it cleanse all parts of your body and heal you and as soon as you feel healed send the same LIGHT to heal your family, your co-workers, friends, teachers and anyone that comes to mind.

Now share your day with the rest of the family. This is the individual disclosure session. What happened to you, your friends and teachers during the day? What special role did you play in school? What contribution did you make in school? Did you get hurt at work or in school? If you did how did it happen and who was responsible? What have you done to address the issue? What did others do to address the issue? How do you feel?

Next take inventory of your activities today. Where did you go? What did you do? Who did you meet? What did you contribute? How did you affect your environment? How did the environment affect you? Is there any thing you did that you could have done differently? How could you have done it next time?

Next visualize the next day of your life in the family, at work or in school. What do you want to see happen? For the family you might want harmony, understanding and unity. For work you might want to accomplish your work goals and get along with your boss and co-workers. For school you might see that you are getting along with your teachers and fellow students. You are doing your schoolwork and getting good grades as well as participating in school activities and doing well.

**Month 5, Week 1, Day 4**

Assume the state of meditation by first practicing a relaxation exercise. Inhale for four seconds. Hold the breath for four seconds. Exhale for four seconds. Hold the exhalation for four seconds. Repeat the process for as many times as possible.

Count from 100 backwards that is 100, 99, 88, etc, until you reach 1. Now count the normal way from 1 to 100. Concentrate on your counting and see the figures in your mind's eye as you count.

Next consider the word Love. What does it mean to you? Meditate on the following passage from the New Testament: But to you who are listening I say: Love your enemies, do good to those who hate you, bless those who curse you, pray for those who mistreat you. If someone slaps you on one cheek, turn to them the other also. If someone takes your coat, do not withhold your shirt from them. Give to everyone who asks you, and if anyone takes what belongs to you, do not demand it back. Do to others as you would have them do to you. "If you love those who love you, what credit is that to you? Even sinners love those who love them. And if you do good to those who are good to you, what credit is that to you? Even sinners do that. And if you lend to those from whom you expect repayment, what credit is that to you? Even sinners lend to sinners, expecting to be repaid in full. But love your enemies, do good to them, and lend to them without expecting to get anything back. Then your reward will be great, and you will be children of the Most High, because he is kind to the ungrateful and wicked. Be merciful, just as Father is merciful.(New Testament: Luke 6:27-36). Discuss these teachings with respect to your life and the life of your family.

Now share your day with the rest of the family. This is the individual disclosure session. What happened to you, your friends and teachers during the day? What special role did you play in school? What contribution did you make in school? Did you get hurt at work or in school? If you did how did it happen and who was responsible? What have you done to address the issue? What did others do to address the issue? How do you feel?

Next take inventory of your activities today. Where did you go? What did you do? Who did you meet? What did you contribute? How did you affect your environment? How did the environment affect you? Is there any thing you did that you could have done differently? How could you have done it next time?

Next visualize the next day of your life in the family, at work or in school. What do you want to see happen? For the family you might want harmony, understanding and unity. For work you might want to accomplish your work goals and get along with your boss and co-workers. For school you might see that you are getting along with your teachers and fellow students. You are doing your schoolwork and getting good grades as well as participating in school activities and doing well.

**Month 5, Week 1, Day 5**

Assume the state of meditation by first practicing a relaxation exercise. Inhale for four seconds. Hold the breath for four seconds. Exhale for four seconds. Hold the exhalation for four seconds. Repeat the process for as many times as possible.

Count from 100 backwards that is 100, 99, 88, etc, until you reach 1. Now count the normal way from 1 to 100. Concentrate on your counting and see the figures in your mind's eye as you count.

Next reflect on I am the only One by Edward Everett Hale

I am only one,
But still I am one.
I cannot do everything,
But still I can do something.
And because I cannot do everything
I will not refuse to do something that I can do.

Now share your day with the rest of the family. This is the individual disclosure session. What happened to you, your friends and teachers during the day? What special role did you play in school? What contribution did you make in school? Did you get hurt at work or in school? If you did how did it happen and who was responsible? What have you done to address the issue? What did others do to address the issue? How do you feel?

Next take inventory of your activities today. Where did you go? What did you do? Who did you meet? What did you contribute? How did you affect your environment? How did the environment affect you? Is there any thing you did that you could have done differently? How could you have done it next time?

Next visualize the next day of your life in the family, at work or in school. What do you want to see happen? For the family you might want harmony, understanding and unity. For work you might want to accomplish your work goals and get along with your boss and co-workers. For school you might see that you are getting along with your teachers and fellow students. You are doing your schoolwork and getting good grades as well as participating in school activities and doing well.

## Month 5, Week 1, Day 6

Retire to your sacred place and practice a relaxation exercise. Inhale for four seconds. Hold the breath for four seconds. Exhale for four seconds. Hold the exhalation for four seconds. Repeat the process for as many times as possible.

Count from 100 backwards that is 100, 99, 88, etc, until you reach 1. Now count the normal way from 1 to 100. Concentrate on your counting and see the figures in your mind's eye as you count.

Now reflect on the following: *Though I am not always responsible for what happens to me, I am responsible for how I handle what happens to me.* ***Zig Ziglar***

Next take inventory of your activities today. Where did you go? What did you do? Who did you meet? What did you contribute? How did you affect your environment? How did the environment affect you? Is there any thing you did that you could have done differently? How could you have done it next time?

Lastly visualize the next day of your life in the family, at work or in school. What do you want to see happen? For the family you might want harmony, understanding and unity. For work you might want to accomplish your work goals and get along with your boss and co-workers. For school you might see that you are getting along with your teachers and fellow students. You are doing your schoolwork and getting good grades as well as participating in school activities and doing well.

**Month 5, Week 1, Day 7**

Attend a church, a temple, or any other meeting that brings you together with people for a common goal. If you do not have one you may begin today and find one that meets your interest and inclination. If you want you could also organize a group of your own. For instance you could start an Awakened Living Study Program. You may contact UNISM for more information.

Retire to your sacred place and practice a relaxation exercise. Inhale for four seconds. Hold the breath for four seconds. Exhale for four seconds. Hold the exhalation for four seconds. Repeat the process for as many times as possible.

Choose your favorite meditation posture and practice using the posture. For instance, if you use supports for your back during meditation start practicing your favorite posture without any support.

Next take inventory of your activities today. Where did you go? What did you do? Who did you meet? What did you contribute? How did you affect your environment? How did the environment affect you? Is there any thing you did that you could have done differently? How could you have done it next time?

Lastly visualize the next day of your life in the family, at work or in school. What do you want to see happen? For the family

you might want harmony, understanding and unity. For work you might want to accomplish your work goals and get along with your boss and co-workers. For school you might see that you are getting along with your teachers and fellow students. You are doing your schoolwork and getting good grades as well as participating in school activities and doing well.

**Month 5, Week 2, Day 1**

Assume the state of meditation by first practicing a relaxation exercise. Inhale for four seconds. Hold the breath for four seconds. Exhale for four seconds. Hold the exhalation for four seconds. Repeat the process for as many times as possible.

Count from 100 backwards that is 100, 99, 88, etc, until you reach 1. Now count the normal way from 1 to 100. Concentrate on your counting and see the figures in your mind's eye as you count.

Next reflect on Compassion by Stephen R. Covey

Look at the weaknesses of others with compassion, not accusation. It's not what they're not doing or should be doing that's the issue. The issue is your own chosen response to the situation and what you should be doing. If you start to think the problem is "out there," stop yourself. That thought is the problem.

Now share your day with the rest of the family. This is the individual disclosure session. What happened to you, your friends and teachers during the day? What special role did you play in school? What contribution did you make in school? Did you get hurt at work or in school? If you did how did it happen and who was responsible? What have you done to address the issue? What did others do to address the issue? How do you feel?

Next take inventory of your activities today. Where did you go? What did you do? Who did you meet? What did you contribute? How did you affect your environment? How did the

environment affect you? Is there any thing you did that you could have done differently? How could you have done it next time?

Next visualize the next day of your life in the family, at work or in school. What do you want to see happen? For the family you might want harmony, understanding and unity. For work you might want to accomplish your work goals and get along with your boss and co-workers. For school you might see that you are getting along with your teachers and fellow students. You are doing your schoolwork and getting good grades as well as participating in school activities and doing well.

**Month 5, Week 2, Day 2**

Assume the state of meditation by first practicing a relaxation exercise. Inhale for four seconds. Hold the breath for four seconds. Exhale for four seconds. Hold the exhalation for four seconds. Repeat the process for as many times as possible.

Count from 100 backwards that is 100, 99, 88, etc, until you reach 1. Now count the normal way from 1 to 100. Concentrate on your counting and see the figures in your mind's eye as you count.

Next reflect on Love and Kindness by the Dalai Lama:

When we feel love and kindness toward others, it not only makes others feel loved and cared for, but it helps us also to develop inner happiness and peace.

Now share your day with the rest of the family. This is the individual disclosure session. What happened to you, your friends and teachers during the day? What special role did you play in school? What contribution did you make in school? Did you get hurt at work or in school? If you did how did it happen and who was responsible? What have you done to address the issue? What did others do to address the issue? How do you feel?

Next take inventory of your activities today. Where did you go? What did you do? Who did you meet? What did you contribute? How did you affect your environment? How did the environment affect you? Is there any thing you did that you could have done differently? How could you have done it next time?

Next visualize the next day of your life in the family, at work or in school. What do you want to see happen? For the family you might want harmony, understanding and unity. For work you might want to accomplish your work goals and get along with your boss and co-workers. For school you might see that you are getting along with your teachers and fellow students. You are doing your schoolwork and getting good grades as well as participating in school activities and doing well.

**Month 5, Week 2, Day 3**

Assume the state of meditation by first practicing a relaxation exercise. Inhale for four seconds. Hold the breath for four seconds. Exhale for four seconds. Hold the exhalation for four seconds. Repeat the process for as many times as possible.

Count from 100 backwards that is 100, 99, 88, etc, until you reach 1. Now count the normal way from 1 to 100. Concentrate on your counting and see the figures in your mind's eye as you count.

Next take inventory of your activities today. Where did you go? What did you do? Who did you meet? What did you contribute? How did you affect your environment? How did the environment affect you? Is there any thing you did that you could have done differently? How could you have done it next time?

Next visualize the next day of your life in the family, at work or in school. What do you want to see happen? For the family you might want harmony, understanding and unity. For work you might want to accomplish your work goals and get along with your

boss and co-workers. For school you might see that you are getting along with your teachers and fellow students. You are doing your schoolwork and getting good grades as well as participating in school activities and doing well.

Next meditate on the following: Whenever you're in conflict with someone, there is one factor that can make the difference between damaging your relationship and deepening it. That factor is attitude. William James

Now share your day with the rest of the family. This is the individual disclosure session. What happened to you, your friends and teachers during the day? What special role did you play in school? What contribution did you make in school? Did you get hurt at work or in school? If you did how did it happen and who was responsible? What have you done to address the issue? What did others do to address the issue? How do you feel?

Next make a presentation on Adolescence. When does adolescence begin? What are the physical signs of adolescence? What are the emotional signs of adolescence? What are the challenges of Adolescence? How could one deal with adolescence?

### Month 5, Week 2, Day 4

Assume the state of meditation by first practicing a relaxation exercise. Inhale for four seconds. Hold the breath for four seconds. Exhale for four seconds. Hold the exhalation for four seconds. Repeat the process for as many times as possible.

Count from 100 backwards that is 100, 99, 88, etc, until you reach 1. Now count the normal way from 1 to 100. Concentrate on your counting and see the figures in your mind's eye as you count.

Next Reflect on the following Jain teaching: Have benevolence towards all living beings, joy at the sight of the virtuous, compassion and sympathy for the afflicted, and tolerance towards the indolent and ill-behaved. Tattvarthasutra 7.11.

Now share your day with the rest of the family. This is the individual disclosure session. What happened to you, your friends and teachers during the day? What special role did you play in school? What contribution did you make in school? Did you get hurt at work or in school? If you did how did it happen and who was responsible? What have you done to address the issue? What did others do to address the issue? How do you feel?

Next take inventory of your activities today. Where did you go? What did you do? Who did you meet? What did you contribute? How did you affect your environment? How did the environment affect you? Is there any thing you did that you could have done differently? How could you have done it next time?

Next visualize the next day of your life in the family, at work or in school. What do you want to see happen? For the family you might want harmony, understanding and unity. For work you might want to accomplish your work goals and get along with your boss and co-workers. For school you might see that you are getting along with your teachers and fellow students. You are doing your schoolwork and getting good grades as well as participating in school activities and doing well.

**Month 5, Week 2, Day 5**

Assume the state of meditation by first practicing a relaxation exercise. Inhale for four seconds. Hold the breath for four seconds. Exhale for four seconds. Hold the exhalation for four seconds. Repeat the process for as many times as possible.

Count from 100 backwards that is 100, 99, 88, etc, until you reach 1. Now count the normal way from 1 to 100. Concentrate on your counting and see the figures in your mind's eye as you count.

Next Reflect on the following Family is about giving 100% of what you have to the family. Dr. Sonari

Now share your day with the rest of the family. This is the individual disclosure session. What happened to you, your friends and teachers during the day? What special role did you play in school? What contribution did you make in school? Did you get hurt at work or in school? If you did how did it happen and who was responsible? What have you done to address the issue? What did others do to address the issue? How do you feel?

Next take inventory of your activities today. Where did you go? What did you do? Who did you meet? What did you contribute? How did you affect your environment? How did the environment affect you? Is there any thing you did that you could have done differently? How could you have done it next time?

Next visualize the next day of your life in the family, at work or in school. What do you want to see happen? For the family you might want harmony, understanding and unity. For work you might want to accomplish your work goals and get along with your boss and co-workers. For school you might see that you are getting along with your teachers and fellow students. You are doing your schoolwork and getting good grades as well as participating in school activities and doing well.

**Month 5, Week 2, Day 6**

Retire to your sacred place and practice a relaxation exercise. Inhale for four seconds. Hold the breath for four seconds. Exhale for four seconds. Hold the exhalation for four seconds. Repeat the process for as many times as possible.

Count from 100 backwards that is 100, 99, 88, etc, until you reach 1. Now count the normal way from 1 to 100. Concentrate on your counting and see the figures in your mind's eye as you count.

Now reflect on the following: The practice of patience toward one another, the overlooking of one another's defects, and the bearing of one another's burdens is the most elementary condition of all human and social activity in the family, in the professions, and in society. Lawrence G Lovasi

Next take inventory of your activities today. Where did you go? What did you do? Who did you meet? What did you contribute? How did you affect your environment? How did the environment affect you? Is there any thing you did that you could have done differently? How could you have done it next time?

Lastly visualize the next day of your life in the family, at work or in school. What do you want to see happen? For the family you might want harmony, understanding and unity. For work you might want to accomplish your work goals and get along with your boss and co-workers. For school you might see that you are getting along with your teachers and fellow students. You are doing your schoolwork and getting good grades as well as participating in school activities and doing well.

## Month 5, Week 2, Day 7

Attend a church, a temple, or any other meeting that brings you together with people for a common goal. If you do not have one you may begin today and find one that meets your interest and inclination. If you want you could also organize a group of your own. For instance you could start an Awakened Living Study Program. You may contact UNISM for more information.

Retire to your sacred place and practice a relaxation exercise. Inhale for four seconds. Hold the breath for four seconds. Exhale for four seconds. Hold the exhalation for four seconds. Repeat the process for as many times as possible.

Choose your favorite meditation posture and practice using the posture. For instance, if you use supports for your back during meditation start practicing your favorite posture without any support.

Next take inventory of your activities today. Where did you go? What did you do? Who did you meet? What did you contribute? How did you affect your environment? How did the environment affect you? Is there any thing you did that you could have done differently? How could you have done it next time?

Lastly visualize the next day of your life in the family, at work or in school. What do you want to see happen? For the family you might want harmony, understanding and unity. For work you might want to accomplish your work goals and get along with your boss and co-workers. For school you might see that you are getting along with your teachers and fellow students. You are doing your schoolwork and getting good grades as well as participating in school activities and doing well.

**Month 5, Week 3, Day 1**

Assume the state of meditation by first practicing a relaxation exercise. Inhale for four seconds. Hold the breath for four seconds. Exhale for four seconds. Hold the exhalation for four seconds. Repeat the process for as many times as possible.

Count from 100 backwards that is 100, 99, 88, etc, until you reach 1. Now count the normal way from 1 to 100. Concentrate on your counting and see the figures in your mind's eye as you count.

Next reflect on Interconnectedness by the Dalai Lama:

There is no self-interest completely unrelated to others' interests. Due to the fundamental interconnectedness which lies at the heart of reality, your interest is also my interest. From this it becomes clear that "my" interest and "your" interest are intimately connected. In a deep sense, they converge.

Now share your day with the rest of the family. This is the individual disclosure session. What happened to you, your friends and teachers during the day? What special role did you play in school? What contribution did you make in school? Did you get hurt at work or in school? If you did how did it happen and who was responsible? What have you done to address the issue? What did others do to address the issue? How do you feel?

Next take inventory of your activities today. Where did you go? What did you do? Who did you meet? What did you contribute? How did you affect your environment? How did the environment affect you? Is there any thing you did that you could have done differently? How could you have done it next time?

Next visualize the next day of your life in the family, at work or in school. What do you want to see happen? For the family you might want harmony, understanding and unity. For work you might want to accomplish your work goals and get along with your boss and co-workers. For school you might see that you are getting along with your teachers and fellow students. You are doing your schoolwork and getting good grades as well as participating in school activities and doing well.

**Month 5, Week 3, Day 2**

Assume the state of meditation by first practicing a relaxation exercise. Inhale for four seconds. Hold the breath for four seconds. Exhale for four seconds. Hold the exhalation for four seconds. Repeat the process for as many times as possible.

Count from 100 backwards that is 100, 99, 88, etc, until you reach 1. Now count the normal way from 1 to 100. Concentrate on your counting and see the figures in your mind's eye as you count.

Next reflect on a Spiritual Revolution by the Dalai Lama:

My call for a spiritual revolution is thus not a call for a religious revolution. Nor is it a reference to a way of life that is somehow other-worldly, still less to something magical or mysterious. Rather, it is a call for a radical re-orientation away from our habitual preoccupation with self towards concern for the wider community of beings with whom we are connected, and for conduct which recognizes others interests alongside our own.

Now share your day with the rest of the family. This is the individual disclosure session. What happened to you, your friends and teachers during the day? What special role did you play in school? What contribution did you make in school? Did you get hurt at work or in school? If you did how did it happen and who was responsible? What have you done to address the issue? What did others do to address the issue? How do you feel?

Next take inventory of your activities today. Where did you go? What did you do? Who did you meet? What did you contribute? How did you affect your environment? How did the environment affect you? Is there any thing you did that you could have done differently? How could you have done it next time?

Next visualize the next day of your life in the family, at work or in school. What do you want to see happen? For the family you might want harmony, understanding and unity. For work you might want to accomplish your work goals and get along with your boss and co-workers. For school you might see that you are getting along with your teachers and fellow students. You are doing your schoolwork and getting good grades as well as participating in school activities and doing well.

Month 5, Week 3, Day 3

Assume the state of meditation by first practicing a relaxation exercise. Inhale for four seconds. Hold the breath for four seconds. Exhale for four seconds. Hold the exhalation for four seconds. Repeat the process for as many times as possible.

Count from 100 backwards that is 100, 99, 88, etc, until you reach 1. Now count the normal way from 1 to 100. Concentrate on your counting and see the figures in your mind's eye as you count.

Next take inventory of your activities today. Where did you go? What did you do? Who did you meet? What did you contribute? How did you affect your environment? How did the environment affect you? Is there any thing you did that you could have done differently? How could you have done it next time?

Next visualize the next day of your life in the family, at work or in school. What do you want to see happen? For the family you might want harmony, understanding and unity. For work you might want to accomplish your work goals and get along with your boss and co-workers. For school you might see that you are getting along with your teachers and fellow students. You are doing your schoolwork and getting good grades as well as participating in school activities and doing well.

Next meditate on the following: Every person has both a bad heart and a good heart. No matter how good a man seems, he has some evil. No matter how bad a man seems, there is some good about him. No man is perfect. Native American Religions. Mohawk Tradition

Now share your day with the rest of the family. This is the individual disclosure session. What happened to you, your friends and teachers during the day? What special role did you play in school? What contribution did you make in school? Did you get hurt at work or in school? If you did how did it happen and who

was responsible? What have you done to address the issue? What did others do to address the issue? How do you feel?

**Month 5, Week 3, Day 4**

Assume the state of meditation by first practicing a relaxation exercise. Inhale for four seconds. Hold the breath for four seconds. Exhale for four seconds. Hold the exhalation for four seconds. Repeat the process for as many times as possible.

Count from 100 backwards that is 100, 99, 88, etc, until you reach 1. Now count the normal way from 1 to 100. Concentrate on your counting and see the figures in your mind's eye as you count.

Next reflect on a the Relationship between Spirituality and Ethical Practice by the Dalai Lama: What is the relationship between spirituality and ethical practice? Since love and compassion and similar qualities all, by definition, presume some level of concern for others' well-being, they presume ethical restraint. We cannot be loving and compassionate unless at the same time we curb our own harmful impulses and desires.

Now share your day with the rest of the family. This is the individual disclosure session. What happened to you, your friends and teachers during the day? What special role did you play in school? What contribution did you make in school? Did you get hurt at work or in school? If you did how did it happen and who was responsible? What have you done to address the issue? What did others do to address the issue? How do you feel?

Next take inventory of your activities today. Where did you go? What did you do? Who did you meet? What did you contribute? How did you affect your environment? How did the environment affect you? Is there any thing you did that you could have done differently? How could you have done it next time?

Now visualize the next day of your life in the family, at work or in school. What do you want to see happen? For the family you might want harmony, understanding and unity. For work you might want to accomplish your work goals and get along with your boss and co-workers. For school you might see that you are getting along with your teachers and fellow students. You are doing your schoolwork and getting good grades as well as participating in school activities and doing well.

**Month 5, Week 3, Day 5**

Assume the state of meditation by first practicing a relaxation exercise. Inhale for four seconds. Hold the breath for four seconds. Exhale for four seconds. Hold the exhalation for four seconds. Repeat the process for as many times as possible.

Count from 100 backwards that is 100, 99, 88, etc, until you reach 1. Now count the normal way from 1 to 100. Concentrate on your counting and see the figures in your mind's eye as you count.

Next meditate on the following teaching from the Bhagavad Gita: Constantly disciplining himself, free from sin, the man of discipline easily achieves perfect joy in harmony with the infinite spirit. Arming himself with discipline, seeing everything with an equal eye, he sees the self in all creatures and all creatures in the self. He who sees me everywhere and sees everything in me will not be lost to me, and I will not be lost to him. I exist in all creatures, so the disciplined man devoted to me grasps the oneness of life; wherever he is, he is in me. When he sees identity in everything, whether joy or suffering, through analogy with the self, he is deemed a man of pure discipline. Bhagavad Gita 6.28-32.

Now share your day with the rest of the family. This is the individual disclosure session. What happened to you, your friends and teachers during the day? What special role did you play in

school? What contribution did you make in school? Did you get hurt at work or in school? If you did how did it happen and who was responsible? What have you done to address the issue? What did others do to address the issue? How do you feel?

Next take inventory of your activities today. Where did you go? What did you do? Who did you meet? What did you contribute? How did you affect your environment? How did the environment affect you? Is there any thing you did that you could have done differently? How could you have done it next time?

Now visualize the next day of your life in the family, at work or in school. What do you want to see happen? For the family you might want harmony, understanding and unity. For work you might want to accomplish your work goals and get along with your boss and co-workers. For school you might see that you are getting along with your teachers and fellow students. You are doing your schoolwork and getting good grades as well as participating in school activities and doing well.

**Month 5, Week 3, Day 6**

Retire to your sacred place and practice a relaxation exercise. Inhale for four seconds. Hold the breath for four seconds. Exhale for four seconds. Hold the exhalation for four seconds. Repeat the process for as many times as possible.

Count from 100 backwards that is 100, 99, 88, etc, until you reach 1. Now count the normal way from 1 to 100. Concentrate on your counting and see the figures in your mind's eye as you count.

Now reflect on the following: The mind is said to be twofold: The pure and also the impure; Impure--by union with desire; Pure--from desire completely free. Maitri Upanishad 6.34

Next take inventory of your activities today. Where did you go? What did you do? Who did you meet? What did you

contribute? How did you affect your environment? How did the environment affect you? Is there any thing you did that you could have done differently? How could you have done it next time?

Lastly visualize the next day of your life in the family, at work or in school. What do you want to see happen? For the family you might want harmony, understanding and unity. For work you might want to accomplish your work goals and get along with your boss and co-workers. For school you might see that you are getting along with your teachers and fellow students. You are doing your schoolwork and getting good grades as well as participating in school activities and doing well.

**Month 5, Week 3, Day 7**

Attend a church, a temple, or any other meeting that brings you together with people for a common goal. If you do not have one you may begin today and find one that meets your interest and inclination. If you want you could also organize a group of your own. For instance you could start an Awakened Living Study Program. You may contact UNISM for more information.

Retire to your sacred place and practice a relaxation exercise. Inhale for four seconds. Hold the breath for four seconds. Exhale for four seconds. Hold the exhalation for four seconds. Repeat the process for as many times as possible.

Choose your favorite meditation posture and practice using the posture. For instance, if you use supports for your back during meditation start practicing your favorite posture without any support.

Next take inventory of your activities today. Where did you go? What did you do? Who did you meet? What did you contribute? How did you affect your environment? How did the

environment affect you? Is there any thing you did that you could have done differently? How could you have done it next time?

Lastly visualize the next day of your life in the family, at work or in school. What do you want to see happen? For the family you might want harmony, understanding and unity. For work you might want to accomplish your work goals and get along with your boss and co-workers. For school you might see that you are getting along with your teachers and fellow students. You are doing your schoolwork and getting good grades as well as participating in school activities and doing well.

**Month 5, Week 4, Day 1**

Assume the state of meditation by first practicing a relaxation exercise. Inhale for four seconds. Hold the breath for four seconds. Exhale for four seconds. Hold the exhalation for four seconds. Repeat the process for as many times as possible.

Count from 100 backwards that is 100, 99, 88, etc, until you reach 1. Now count the normal way from 1 to 100. Concentrate on your counting and see the figures in your mind's eye as you count.

Next reflect on Ethical Conduct by the Dalai Lama: (Because) the notion of absolute truth is difficult to sustain outside the context of religion, ethical conduct is not something we engage in because it is somehow right in itself but because, like ourselves, all others desire to be happy and to avoid suffering. Given that this is a natural disposition, shared by all, it follows that each individual has a right to pursue this goal. Accordingly, I suggest that one of the things which determines whether an act is ethical or not is its effect on others' experience or expectation of happiness.

Now share your day with the rest of the family. This is the individual disclosure session. What happened to you, your friends and teachers during the day? What special role did you play in

school? What contribution did you make in school? Did you get hurt at work or in school? If you did how did it happen and who was responsible? What have you done to address the issue? What did others do to address the issue? How do you feel?

Next take inventory of your activities today. Where did you go? What did you do? Who did you meet? What did you contribute? How did you affect your environment? How did the environment affect you? Is there any thing you did that you could have done differently? How could you have done it next time?

Now visualize the next day of your life in the family, at work or in school. What do you want to see happen? For the family you might want harmony, understanding and unity. For work you might want to accomplish your work goals and get along with your boss and co-workers. For school you might see that you are getting along with your teachers and fellow students. You are doing your schoolwork and getting good grades as well as participating in school activities and doing well.

### Month 5, Week 4, Day 2

Assume the state of meditation by first practicing a relaxation exercise. Inhale for four seconds. Hold the breath for four seconds. Exhale for four seconds. Hold the exhalation for four seconds. Repeat the process for as many times as possible.

Count from 100 backwards that is 100, 99, 88, etc, until you reach 1. Now count the normal way from 1 to 100. Concentrate on your counting and see the figures in your mind's eye as you count.

Next reflect on Responsibility by the Dalai Lama:

Responsibility . . . lies with each of us individually. Peace, for example, starts within each one of us. When we have inner peace, we can be at peace with those around us. When our community is in a state of peace, it can share that peace with neighboring communities, and so on. When we feel love and kindness towards others, it not only makes others feel loved and cared for, but it helps us also to develop inner happiness and peace. And there are ways in which we can consciously work to develop feelings of love and kindness. For some of us, the most effective way to do so is through religious practice. For others it may be non-religious practices. What is important is that we each make a sincere effort to take our responsibility for each other and for the natural environment we live in seriously.

Now share your day with the rest of the family. This is the individual disclosure session. What happened to you, your friends and teachers during the day? What special role did you play in school? What contribution did you make in school? Did you get hurt at work or in school? If you did how did it happen and who was responsible? What have you done to address the issue? What did others do to address the issue? How do you feel?

Next take inventory of your activities today. Where did you go? What did you do? Who did you meet? What did you contribute? How did you affect your environment? How did the environment affect you? Is there any thing you did that you could have done differently? How could you have done it next time?

Next visualize the next day of your life in the family, at work or in school. What do you want to see happen? For the family you might want harmony, understanding and unity. For work you might want to accomplish your work goals and get along with your boss and co-workers. For school you might see that you are getting along with your teachers and fellow students. You are doing your schoolwork and getting good grades as well as participating in school activities and doing well.

## Month 5, Week 4, Day 3

Assume the state of meditation by first practicing a relaxation exercise. Inhale for four seconds. Hold the breath for four seconds. Exhale for four seconds. Hold the exhalation for four seconds. Repeat the process for as many times as possible.

Count from 100 backwards that is 100, 99, 88, etc, until you reach 1. Now count the normal way from 1 to 100. Concentrate on your counting and see the figures in your mind's eye as you count.

Next take inventory of your activities today. Where did you go? What did you do? Who did you meet? What did you contribute? How did you affect your environment? How did the environment affect you? Is there any thing you did that you could have done differently? How could you have done it next time?

Next visualize the next day of your life in the family, at work or in school. What do you want to see happen? For the family you might want harmony, understanding and unity. For work you might want to accomplish your work goals and get along with your boss and co-workers. For school you might see that you are getting along with your teachers and fellow students. You are doing your schoolwork and getting good grades as well as participating in school activities and doing well.

Next meditate on the following: Love your family. Spend time, be kind & serve one another. Make no room for regrets. Tomorrow is not promised & today is short. Anonymous

Now share your day with the rest of the family. This is the individual disclosure session. What happened to you, your friends and teachers during the day? What special role did you play in school? What contribution did you make in school? Did you get hurt at work or in school? If you did how did it happen and who was responsible? What have you done to address the issue? What did others do to address the issue? How do you feel?

Next make a presentation on your life dream. What is it? What will it take to realize it? What are you doing to bring it about?

**Month 5, Week 4, Day 4**

Assume the state of meditation by first practicing a relaxation exercise. Inhale for four seconds. Hold the breath for four seconds. Exhale for four seconds. Hold the exhalation for four seconds. Repeat the process for as many times as possible.

Count from 100 backwards that is 100, 99, 88, etc, until you reach 1. Now count the normal way from 1 to 100. Concentrate on your counting and see the figures in your mind's eye as you count.

Next reflect on the Purpose of Life by the Dalai Lama:

We can reject everything else: religion, ideology, all received wisdom. But we cannot escape the necessity of love and compassion. This, then, is my true religion, my simple faith. In this sense, there is no need for temple or church, for mosque or synagogue, no need for complicated philosophy, doctrine, or dogma. Our own heart, our own mind, is the temple. The doctrine is compassion. Love for others and respect for their rights and dignity, no matter who or what they are: ultimately these are all we need.

Now share your day with the rest of the family. This is the individual disclosure session. What happened to you, your friends and teachers during the day? What special role did you play in school? What contribution did you make in school? Did you get hurt at work or in school? If you did how did it happen and who was responsible? What have you done to address the issue? What did others do to address the issue? How do you feel?

Next take inventory of your activities today. Where did you go? What did you do? Who did you meet? What did you

contribute? How did you affect your environment? How did the environment affect you? Is there any thing you did that you could have done differently? How could you have done it next time?

Now visualize the next day of your life in the family, at work or in school. What do you want to see happen? For the family you might want harmony, understanding and unity. For work you might want to accomplish your work goals and get along with your boss and co-workers. For school you might see that you are getting along with your teachers and fellow students. You are doing your schoolwork and getting good grades as well as participating in school activities and doing well.

**Month 5, Week 4, Day 5**

Assume the state of meditation by first practicing a relaxation exercise. Inhale for four seconds. Hold the breath for four seconds. Exhale for four seconds. Hold the exhalation for four seconds. Repeat the process for as many times as possible.

Count from 100 backwards that is 100, 99, 88, etc, until you reach 1. Now count the normal way from 1 to 100. Concentrate on your counting and see the figures in your mind's eye as you count.

Next reflect on the True Nature of happiness by the Dalai Lama:

Lack of understanding of the true nature of happiness, it seems to me, is the principal reason why people inflict sufferings on others. They think either that the other's pain may somehow be a cause of happiness for themselves or that their own happiness is more important, regardless of what pain it may cause. But this is shortsighted. No one truly benefits from causing harm to another sentient being. . . . . In the long run causing others misery and infringing their rights to peace and happiness result in anxiety, fear, and suspicion within oneself.

Now share your day with the rest of the family. This is the individual disclosure session. What happened to you, your friends and teachers during the day? What special role did you play in school? What contribution did you make in school? Did you get hurt at work or in school? If you did how did it happen and who was responsible? What have you done to address the issue? What did others do to address the issue? How do you feel?

Next make a presentation on your one-year goal. What is it? What will it take to realize your goal? What are you doing to realize your goal?

Next take inventory of your activities today. Where did you go? What did you do? Who did you meet? What did you contribute? How did you affect your environment? How did the environment affect you? Is there any thing you did that you could have done differently? How could you have done it next time?

Now visualize the next day of your life in the family, at work or in school. What do you want to see happen? For the family you might want harmony, understanding and unity. For work you might want to accomplish your work goals and get along with your boss and co-workers. For school you might see that you are getting along with your teachers and fellow students. You are doing your schoolwork and getting good grades as well as participating in school activities and doing well.

**Month 5, Week 4, Day 6**

Retire to your sacred place and practice a relaxation exercise. Inhale for four seconds. Hold the breath for four seconds. Exhale for four seconds. Hold the exhalation for four seconds. Repeat the process for as many times as possible.

Count from 100 backwards that is 100, 99, 88, etc, until you reach 1. Now count the normal way from 1 to 100. Concentrate on your counting and see the figures in your mind's eye as you count.

Now reflect on the following: The way you help heal the world is you start with your own family. "What can you do to promote world peace? Go home and love your family." ***Mother Theresa***

Next take inventory of your activities today. Where did you go? What did you do? Who did you meet? What did you contribute? How did you affect your environment? How did the environment affect you? Is there any thing you did that you could have done differently? How could you have done it next time?

Lastly visualize the next day of your life in the family, at work or in school. What do you want to see happen? For the family you might want harmony, understanding and unity. For work you might want to accomplish your work goals and get along with your boss and co-workers. For school you might see that you are getting along with your teachers and fellow students. You are doing your schoolwork and getting good grades as well as participating in school activities and doing well.

**Month 5, Week 4, Day 7**

Attend a church, a temple, or any other meeting that brings you together with people for a common goal. If you do not have one you may begin today and find one that meets your interest and inclination. If you want you could also organize a group of your own. For instance you could start an Awakened Living Study Program. You may contact UNISM for more information.

Retire to your sacred place and practice a relaxation exercise. Inhale for four seconds. Hold the breath for four seconds.

Exhale for four seconds. Hold the exhalation for four seconds. Repeat the process for as many times as possible.

Choose your favorite meditation posture and practice using the posture. For instance, if you use supports for your back during meditation start practicing your favorite posture without any support.

Next take inventory of your activities today. Where did you go? What did you do? Who did you meet? What did you contribute? How did you affect your environment? How did the environment affect you? Is there any thing you did that you could have done differently? How could you have done it next time?

Lastly visualize the next day of your life in the family, at work or in school. What do you want to see happen? For the family you might want harmony, understanding and unity. For work you might want to accomplish your work goals and get along with your boss and co-workers. For school you might see that you are getting along with your teachers and fellow students. You are doing your schoolwork and getting good grades as well as participating in school activities and doing well.

# Family Meditation: Sixth Month

The goal of the sixth month of meditation is to develop compassion, health, kindness, generosity, patience, temperance and similar spiritual qualities for our good.

**Month 6, Week 1, Day 1**

Assume the state of meditation by first practicing a relaxation exercise. Inhale for four seconds. Hold the breath for four seconds. Exhale for four seconds. Hold the exhalation for four seconds. Repeat the process for as many times as possible.

Count from 100 backwards that is 100, 99, 88, etc, until you reach 1. Now count the normal way from 1 to 100. Concentrate on your counting and see the figures in your mind's eye as you count.

Now reflect on Unity by Martin Luther King:

An individual has not started living until he can rise above the narrow confines of his individualistic concerns to the broader concerns of all humanity.

Now share your day with the rest of the family. This is the individual disclosure session. What happened to you, your friends and teachers during the day? What special role did you play in school? What contribution did you make in school? Did you get hurt at work or in school? If you did how did it happen and who was responsible? What have you done to address the issue? What did others do to address the issue? How do you feel?

Next take inventory of your activities today. Where did you go? What did you do? Who did you meet? What did you contribute? How did you affect your environment? How did the environment affect you? Is there any thing you did that you could have done differently? How could you have done it next time?

Next visualize the next day of your life in the family, at work or in school. What do you want to see happen? For the family you might want harmony, understanding and unity. For work you might want to accomplish your work goals and get along with your boss and co-workers. For school you might see that you are getting along with your teachers and fellow students. You are doing your schoolwork and getting good grades as well as participating in school activities and doing well.

**Month 6, Week 1, Day 2**

Assume the state of meditation by first practicing a relaxation exercise. Inhale for four seconds. Hold the breath for four seconds. Exhale for four seconds. Hold the exhalation for four seconds. Repeat the process for as many times as possible.

Count from 100 backwards that is 100, 99, 88, etc, until you reach 1. Now count the normal way from 1 to 100. Concentrate on your counting and see the figures in your mind's eye as you count.

Now reflect on Service and Greatness by Martin Luther King:

Everybody can be great . . . because anybody can serve. You don't have to have a college degree to serve. . . . You only need a heart full of grace. A soul generated by love.

Now share your day with the rest of the family. This is the individual disclosure session. What happened to you, your friends and teachers during the day? What special role did you play in school? What contribution did you make in school? Did you get hurt at work or in school? If you did how did it happen and who was responsible? What have you done to address the issue? What did others do to address the issue? How do you feel?

Next take inventory of your activities today. Where did you go? What did you do? Who did you meet? What did you

contribute? How did you affect your environment? How did the environment affect you? Is there any thing you did that you could have done differently? How could you have done it next time?

Next visualize the next day of your life in the family, at work or in school. What do you want to see happen? For the family you might want harmony, understanding and unity. For work you might want to accomplish your work goals and get along with your boss and co-workers. For school you might see that you are getting along with your teachers and fellow students. You are doing your schoolwork and getting good grades as well as participating in school activities and doing well.

### Month 6, Week 1, Day 3

Assume the state of meditation by first practicing a relaxation exercise. Inhale for four seconds. Hold the breath for four seconds. Exhale for four seconds. Hold the exhalation for four seconds. Repeat the process for as many times as possible.

Count from 100 backwards that is 100, 99, 88, etc, until you reach 1. Now count the normal way from 1 to 100. Concentrate on your counting and see the figures in your mind's eye as you count.

Next meditate on compassion. What is compassion? It is feeling or understanding the suffering of another being or creature and doing something to help. According to **Albert Schweitzer** "the purpose of human life is to serve, and to show compassion and the will to help others.

Now share your day with the rest of the family. This is the individual disclosure session. What happened to you, your friends and teachers during the day? What special role did you play in school? What contribution did you make in school? Did you get hurt at work or in school? If you did how did it happen and who

was responsible? What have you done to address the issue? What did others do to address the issue? How do you feel?

Next take inventory of your activities today. Where did you go? What did you do? Who did you meet? What did you contribute? How did you affect your environment? How did the environment affect you? Is there any thing you did that you could have done differently? How could you have done it next time?

Next visualize the next day of your life in the family, at work or in school. What do you want to see happen? For the family you might want harmony, understanding and unity. For work you might want to accomplish your work goals and get along with your boss and co-workers. For school you might see that you are getting along with your teachers and fellow students. You are doing your schoolwork and getting good grades as well as participating in school activities and doing well.

**Month 6, Week 1, Day 4**

Assume the state of meditation by first practicing a relaxation exercise. Inhale for four seconds. Hold the breath for four seconds. Exhale for four seconds. Hold the exhalation for four seconds. Repeat the process for as many times as possible.

Count from 100 backwards that is 100, 99, 88, etc, until you reach 1. Now count the normal way from 1 to 100. Concentrate on your counting and see the figures in your mind's eye as you count.

Now meditate on the following passage: Both the good and the pleasant approach a man. The wise man, pondering over them, discriminates. The wise chooses the good in preference to the pleasant. The simple-minded, for the sake of worldly well-being, prefers the pleasant. Katha Upanishad 1:2:2. What is the good? What is the pleasant? What would you use as a guide to your life?

Now share your day with the rest of the family. This is the individual disclosure session. What happened to you, your friends and teachers during the day? What special role did you play in school? What contribution did you make in school? Did you get hurt at work or in school? If you did how did it happen and who was responsible? What have you done to address the issue? What did others do to address the issue? How do you feel?

Next take inventory of your activities today. Where did you go? What did you do? Who did you meet? What did you contribute? How did you affect your environment? How did the environment affect you? Is there any thing you did that you could have done differently? How could you have done it next time?

Next visualize the next day of your life in the family, at work or in school. What do you want to see happen? For the family you might want harmony, understanding and unity. For work you might want to accomplish your work goals and get along with your boss and co-workers. For school you might see that you are getting along with your teachers and fellow students. You are doing your schoolwork and getting good grades as well as participating in school activities and doing well.

**Month 6, Week 1, Day 5**

Assume the state of meditation by first practicing a relaxation exercise. Inhale for four seconds. Hold the breath for four seconds. Exhale for four seconds. Hold the exhalation for four seconds. Repeat the process for as many times as possible.

Count from 100 backwards that is 100, 99, 88, etc, until you reach 1. Now count the normal way from 1 to 100. Concentrate on your counting and see the figures in your mind's eye as you count.

Now reflect on Responsibility by **Marian Wright Edelman**:

A lot of people are waiting for Martin Luther King or Mahatma Gandhi to come back -- but they are gone. We are it. It is up to us. It is up to you.

Now share your day with the rest of the family. This is the individual disclosure session. What happened to you, your friends and teachers during the day? What special role did you play in school? What contribution did you make in school? Did you get hurt at work or in school? If you did how did it happen and who was responsible? What have you done to address the issue? What did others do to address the issue? How do you feel?

Next take inventory of your activities today. Where did you go? What did you do? Who did you meet? What did you contribute? How did you affect your environment? How did the environment affect you? Is there any thing you did that you could have done differently? How could you have done it next time?

Next visualize the next day of your life in the family, at work or in school. What do you want to see happen? For the family you might want harmony, understanding and unity. For work you might want to accomplish your work goals and get along with your boss and co-workers. For school you might see that you are getting along with your teachers and fellow students. You are doing your schoolwork and getting good grades as well as participating in school activities and doing well.

**Month 6, Week 1, Day 6**

Retire to your sacred place and practice a relaxation exercise. Inhale for four seconds. Hold the breath for four seconds. Exhale for four seconds. Hold the exhalation for four seconds. Repeat the process for as many times as possible.

Count from 100 backwards that is 100, 99, 88, etc, until you reach 1. Now count the normal way from 1 to 100. Concentrate on your counting and see the figures in your mind's eye as you count.

Now reflect on the following: However painful the process of leaving home, for parents and for children, the really frightening thing for both would be the prospect of the child never leaving home. Robert Nelly Bellah

Next take inventory of your activities today. Where did you go? What did you do? Who did you meet? What did you contribute? How did you affect your environment? How did the environment affect you? Is there any thing you did that you could have done differently? How could you have done it next time?

Lastly visualize the next day of your life in the family, at work or in school. What do you want to see happen? For the family you might want harmony, understanding and unity. For work you might want to accomplish your work goals and get along with your boss and co-workers. For school you might see that you are getting along with your teachers and fellow students. You are doing your schoolwork and getting good grades as well as participating in school activities and doing well.

**Month 6, Week 1, Day 7**

Attend a church, a temple, or any other meeting that brings you together with people for a common goal. If you do not have one you may begin today and find one that meets your interest and inclination. If you want you could also organize a group of your own. For instance you could start an Awakened Living Study Program. You may contact UNISM for more information.

Retire to your sacred place and practice a relaxation exercise. Inhale for four seconds. Hold the breath for four seconds.

Exhale for four seconds. Hold the exhalation for four seconds. Repeat the process for as many times as possible.

Choose your favorite meditation posture and practice using the posture. For instance, if you use supports for your back during meditation start practicing your favorite posture without any support.

Next take inventory of your activities today. Where did you go? What did you do? Who did you meet? What did you contribute? How did you affect your environment? How did the environment affect you? Is there any thing you did that you could have done differently? How could you have done it next time?

Lastly visualize the next day of your life in the family, at work or in school. What do you want to see happen? For the family you might want harmony, understanding and unity. For work you might want to accomplish your work goals and get along with your boss and co-workers. For school you might see that you are getting along with your teachers and fellow students. You are doing your schoolwork and getting good grades as well as participating in school activities and doing well.

**Month 6, Week 2, Day 1**

Assume the state of meditation by first practicing a relaxation exercise. Inhale for four seconds. Hold the breath for four seconds. Exhale for four seconds. Hold the exhalation for four seconds. Repeat the process for as many times as possible.

Count from 100 backwards that is 100, 99, 88, etc, until you reach 1. Now count the normal way from 1 to 100. Concentrate on your counting and see the figures in your mind's eye as you count.

Now reflect on the Real American Dream by Martin Luther King:

I look forward confidently to the day when all who work for a living will be one with no thought to their separateness as Negroes, Jews, Italians or any other distinctions. This will be the day when we bring into full realization the American dream -- a dream yet unfulfilled. A dream of equality of opportunity, of privilege and property widely distributed; a dream of a land where men will not take necessities from the many to give luxuries to the few; a dream of a land where men will not argue that the color of a man's skin determines the content of his character; a dream of a nation where all our gifts and resources are held not for ourselves alone, but as instruments of service for the rest of humanity; the dream of country where every man will respect the dignity and worth of the human personality.

Now share your day with the rest of the family. This is the individual disclosure session. What happened to you, your friends and teachers during the day? What special role did you play in school? What contribution did you make in school? Did you get hurt at work or in school? If you did how did it happen and who was responsible? What have you done to address the issue? What did others do to address the issue? How do you feel?

Next take inventory of your activities today. Where did you go? What did you do? Who did you meet? What did you contribute? How did you affect your environment? How did the environment affect you? Is there any thing you did that you could have done differently? How could you have done it next time?

Next visualize the next day of your life in the family, at work or in school. What do you want to see happen? For the family you might want harmony, understanding and unity. For work you might want to accomplish your work goals and get along with your boss and co-workers. For school you might see that you are getting along with your teachers and fellow students. You are doing your

schoolwork and getting good grades as well as participating in school activities and doing well.

**Month 6, Week 2, Day 2**

Assume the state of meditation by first practicing a relaxation exercise. Inhale for four seconds. Hold the breath for four seconds. Exhale for four seconds. Hold the exhalation for four seconds. Repeat the process for as many times as possible.

Count from 100 backwards that is 100, 99, 88, etc, until you reach 1. Now count the normal way from 1 to 100. Concentrate on your counting and see the figures in your mind's eye as you count.

Now reflect on the Interrelated Structure of Reality by Martin Luther King:

Whatever affects one directly, affects all indirectly. I can never be what I ought to be until you are what you ought to be. This is the interrelated structure of reality.

Now share your day with the rest of the family. This is the individual disclosure session. What happened to you, your friends and teachers during the day? What special role did you play in school? What contribution did you make in school? Did you get hurt at work or in school? If you did how did it happen and who was responsible? What have you done to address the issue? What did others do to address the issue? How do you feel?

Next make a presentation on the book you read last week. In your presentation summarize the book and highlight the main message. What did you learn from the book?

Next take inventory of your activities today. Where did you go? What did you do? Who did you meet? What did you contribute? How did you affect your environment? How did the environment affect you? Is there any thing you did that you could have done differently? How could you have done it next time?

Next visualize the next day of your life in the family, at work or in school. What do you want to see happen? For the family you might want harmony, understanding and unity. For work you might want to accomplish your work goals and get along with your boss and co-workers. For school you might see that you are getting along with your teachers and fellow students. You are doing your schoolwork and getting good grades as well as participating in school activities and doing well.

**Month 6, Week 2, Day 3**

Assume the state of meditation by first practicing a relaxation exercise. Inhale for four seconds. Hold the breath for four seconds. Exhale for four seconds. Hold the exhalation for four seconds. Repeat the process for as many times as possible.

Count from 100 backwards that is 100, 99, 88, etc, until you reach 1. Now count the normal way from 1 to 100. Concentrate on your counting and see the figures in your mind's eye as you count.

Meditate on the following passage from the Bhagavad Gita: A man able to endure the force of desire and anger before giving up his body is disciplined and joyful. Bhagavad Gita 5.23. In your meditation consider your desires and discuss with the rest of the family.

Now share your day with the rest of the family. This is the individual disclosure session. What happened to you, your friends and teachers during the day? What special role did you play in school? What contribution did you make in school? Did you get hurt at work or in school? If you did how did it happen and who was responsible? What have you done to address the issue? What did others do to address the issue? How do you feel?

Next take inventory of your activities today. Where did you go? What did you do? Who did you meet? What did you

contribute? How did you affect your environment? How did the environment affect you? Is there any thing you did that you could have done differently? How could you have done it next time?

Now visualize the next day of your life in the family, at work or in school. What do you want to see happen? For the family you might want harmony, understanding and unity. For work you might want to accomplish your work goals and get along with your boss and co-workers. For school you might see that you are getting along with your teachers and fellow students. You are doing your schoolwork and getting good grades as well as participating in school activities and doing well.

**Month 6 Week 2, Day 4**

Assume the state of meditation by first practicing a relaxation exercise. Inhale for four seconds. Hold the breath for four seconds. Exhale for four seconds. Hold the exhalation for four seconds. Repeat the process for as many times as possible.

Count from 100 backwards that is 100, 99, 88, etc, until you reach 1. Now count the normal way from 1 to 100. Concentrate on your counting and see the figures in your mind's eye as you count.

Meditate on the following passage: "Therefore, the kingdom of heaven is like a king who wanted to settle accounts with his servants. As he began the settlement, a man who owed him ten thousand bags of gold was brought to him. Since he was not able to pay, the master ordered that he and his wife and his children and all that he had be sold to repay the debt. "At this the servant fell on his knees before him. 'Be patient with me,' he begged, 'and I will pay back everything.' [27] The servant's master took pity on him, canceled the debt and let him go. "But when that servant went out, he found one of his fellow servants who owed him a hundred silver coins. He grabbed him and began to choke him. 'Pay back what you owe me!' he demanded. "His fellow servant fell to his knees and begged him, 'Be patient with me, and I will pay it back.' "But he refused. Instead, he went off and had the man thrown into prison until he could pay the debt. When the other servants saw what had happened, they were outraged and went and told their master everything that had happened. "Then the master called the servant in. 'You wicked servant,' he said, 'I canceled all that debt of yours because you begged me to. Shouldn't you have had mercy on your fellow servant just as I had on you?' In anger his master handed him over to the jailers to be tortured, until he should pay back all he owed. New Testament: Matthew 18:23-35. Discuss it with the rest of the family.

Now share your day with the rest of the family. This is the individual disclosure session. What happened to you, your friends and teachers during the day? What special role did you play in school? What contribution did you make in school? Did you get hurt at work or in school? If you did how did it happen and who was responsible? What have you done to address the issue? What did others do to address the issue? How do you feel?

Next take inventory of your activities today. Where did you go? What did you do? Who did you meet? What did you contribute? How did you affect your environment? How did the environment affect you? Is there any thing you did that you could have done differently? How could you have done it next time?

Next visualize the next day of your life in the family, at work or in school. What do you want to see happen? For the family you might want harmony, understanding and unity. For work you might want to accomplish your work goals and get along with your boss and co-workers. For school you might see that you are getting along with your teachers and fellow students. You are doing your

schoolwork and getting good grades as well as participating in school activities and doing well.

### Month 6, Week 2, Day 5

Assume the state of meditation by first practicing a relaxation exercise. Inhale for four seconds. Hold the breath for four seconds. Exhale for four seconds. Hold the exhalation for four seconds. Repeat the process for as many times as possible.

Count from 100 backwards that is 100, 99, 88, etc, until you reach 1. Now count the normal way from 1 to 100. Concentrate on your counting and see the figures in your mind's eye as you count.

Now reflect on Forgiveness by Martin Luther King:

We must develop and maintain the capacity to forgive. He who is devoid of the power to forgive is devoid of the power to love. There is some good in the worst of us and some evil in the best of us. When we discover this, we are less prone to hate our enemies.

Now share your day with the rest of the family. This is the individual disclosure session. What happened to you, your friends and teachers during the day? What special role did you play in school? What contribution did you make in school? Did you get hurt at work or in school? If you did how did it happen and who was responsible? What have you done to address the issue? What did others do to address the issue? How do you feel?

Next take inventory of your activities today. Where did you go? What did you do? Who did you meet? What did you contribute? How did you affect your environment? How did the environment affect you? Is there any thing you did that you could have done differently? How could you have done it next time?

Next visualize the next day of your life in the family, at work or in school. What do you want to see happen? For the family you might want harmony, understanding and unity. For work you

might want to accomplish your work goals and get along with your boss and co-workers. For school you might see that you are getting along with your teachers and fellow students. You are doing your schoolwork and getting good grades as well as participating in school activities and doing well.

### Month 6, Week 2, Day 6

Retire to your sacred place and practice a relaxation exercise. Inhale for four seconds. Hold the breath for four seconds. Exhale for four seconds. Hold the exhalation for four seconds. Repeat the process for as many times as possible.

Count from 100 backwards that is 100, 99, 88, etc, until you reach 1. Now count the normal way from 1 to 100. Concentrate on your counting and see the figures in your mind's eye as you count.

Now reflect on the following: The greatest gifts you can give your children are the roots of responsibility and the wings of independence. Denis Waitley

Next take inventory of your activities today. Where did you go? What did you do? Who did you meet? What did you contribute? How did you affect your environment? How did the environment affect you? Is there any thing you did that you could have done differently? How could you have done it next time?

Lastly visualize the next day of your life in the family, at work or in school. What do you want to see happen? For the family you might want harmony, understanding and unity. For work you might want to accomplish your work goals and get along with your boss and co-workers. For school you might see that you are getting along with your teachers and fellow students. You are doing your schoolwork and getting good grades as well as participating in school activities and doing well.

### Month 6, Week 2, Day 7

Attend a church, a temple, or any other meeting that brings you together with people for a common goal. If you do not have one you may begin today and find one that meets your interest and inclination. If you want you could also organize a group of your own. For instance you could start an Awakened Living Study Program. You may contact UNISM for more information.

Retire to your sacred place and practice a relaxation exercise. Inhale for four seconds. Hold the breath for four seconds. Exhale for four seconds. Hold the exhalation for four seconds. Repeat the process for as many times as possible.

Choose your favorite meditation posture and practice using the posture. For instance, if you use supports for your back during meditation start practicing your favorite posture without any support.

Next take inventory of your activities today. Where did you go? What did you do? Who did you meet? What did you contribute? How did you affect your environment? How did the environment affect you? Is there any thing you did that you could have done differently? How could you have done it next time?

Lastly visualize the next day of your life in the family, at work or in school. What do you want to see happen? For the family you might want harmony, understanding and unity. For work you might want to accomplish your work goals and get along with your boss and co-workers. For school you might see that you are getting along with your teachers and fellow students. You are doing your schoolwork and getting good grades as well as participating in school activities and doing well.

### Month 6, Week 3, Day 1

Assume the state of meditation by first practicing a relaxation exercise. Inhale for four seconds. Hold the breath for four seconds. Exhale for four seconds. Hold the exhalation for four seconds. Repeat the process for as many times as possible.

Count from 100 backwards that is 100, 99, 88, etc, until you reach 1. Now count the normal way from 1 to 100. Concentrate on your counting and see the figures in your mind's eye as you count.

Now reflect on Courage by Martin Luther King:

Never, never be afraid to do what's right, especially if the well-being of a person or animal is at stake. Society's punishments are small compared to the wounds we inflict on our soul when we look the other way.

Now share your day with the rest of the family. This is the individual disclosure session. What happened to you, your friends and teachers during the day? What special role did you play in school? What contribution did you make in school? Did you get hurt at work or in school? If you did how did it happen and who was responsible? What have you done to address the issue? What did others do to address the issue? How do you feel?

Next take inventory of your activities today. Where did you go? What did you do? Who did you meet? What did you contribute? How did you affect your environment? How did the environment affect you? Is there any thing you did that you could have done differently? How could you have done it next time?

Next visualize the next day of your life in the family, at work or in school. What do you want to see happen? For the family you might want harmony, understanding and unity. For work you might want to accomplish your work goals and get along with your boss and co-workers. For school you might see that you are getting along with your teachers and fellow students. You are doing your

schoolwork and getting good grades as well as participating in school activities and doing well.

### Month 6, Week 3, Day 2

Assume the state of meditation by first practicing a relaxation exercise. Inhale for four seconds. Hold the breath for four seconds. Exhale for four seconds. Hold the exhalation for four seconds. Repeat the process for as many times as possible.

Count from 100 backwards that is 100, 99, 88, etc, until you reach 1. Now count the normal way from 1 to 100. Concentrate on your counting and see the figures in your mind's eye as you count.

Now reflect on I have a Dream by Martin Luther King:

I have a dream that one day every valley shall be exalted, every hill and mountain shall be made low, the rough places will be made straight and the glory of the Lord shall be revealed and all flesh shall see it together.

Now share your day with the rest of the family. This is the individual disclosure session. What happened to you, your friends and teachers during the day? What special role did you play in school? What contribution did you make in school? Did you get hurt at work or in school? If you did how did it happen and who was responsible? What have you done to address the issue? What did others do to address the issue? How do you feel?

Next take inventory of your activities today. Where did you go? What did you do? Who did you meet? What did you contribute? How did you affect your environment? How did the environment affect you? Is there any thing you did that you could have done differently? How could you have done it next time?

Next visualize the next day of your life in the family, at work or in school. What do you want to see happen? For the family you might want harmony, understanding and unity. For work you

might want to accomplish your work goals and get along with your boss and co-workers. For school you might see that you are getting along with your teachers and fellow students. You are doing your schoolwork and getting good grades as well as participating in school activities and doing well.

### Month 6, Week 3, Day 3

Assume the state of meditation by first practicing a relaxation exercise. Inhale for four seconds. Hold the breath for four seconds. Exhale for four seconds. Hold the exhalation for four seconds. Repeat the process for as many times as possible.

Count from 100 backwards that is 100, 99, 88, etc, until you reach 1. Now count the normal way from 1 to 100. Concentrate on your counting and see the figures in your mind's eye as you count.

Meditate on the following passage: The Buddha said, "When you see someone practicing the Way of giving, aid him joyously, and you will obtain vast and great blessings." A shramana asked: "Is there an end to those blessings?" The Buddha said, "Consider the flame of a single lamp. Though a hundred thousand people come and light their own lamps from it so that they can cook their food and ward off the darkness, the first lamp remains the same as before. Blessings are like this, too" Sutra of Forty-two Sections 10.

Now share your day with the rest of the family. This is the individual disclosure session. What happened to you, your friends and teachers during the day? What special role did you play in school? What contribution did you make in school? Did you get hurt at work or in school? If you did how did it happen and who was responsible? What have you done to address the issue? What did others do to address the issue? How do you feel?

Next take inventory of your activities today. Where did you go? What did you do? Who did you meet? What did you contribute? How did you affect your environment? How did the environment affect you? Is there any thing you did that you could have done differently? How could you have done it next time?

Next visualize the next day of your life in the family, at work or in school. What do you want to see happen? For the family you might want harmony, understanding and unity. For work you might want to accomplish your work goals and get along with your boss and co-workers. For school you might see that you are getting along with your teachers and fellow students. You are doing your schoolwork and getting good grades as well as participating in school activities and doing well.

**Month 6, Week 3, Day 4**

Assume the state of meditation by first practicing a relaxation exercise. Inhale for four seconds. Hold the breath for four seconds. Exhale for four seconds. Hold the exhalation for four seconds. Repeat the process for as many times as possible.

Count from 100 backwards that is 100, 99, 88, etc, until you reach 1. Now count the normal way from 1 to 100. Concentrate on your counting and see the figures in your mind's eye as you count.

Meditate on the following passage: In reply Jesus said: "A man was going down from Jerusalem to Jericho, when he was attacked by robbers. They stripped him of his clothes, beat him and went away, leaving him half dead. [31] A priest happened to be going down the same road, and when he saw the man, he passed by on the other side. [32] So too, a Levite, when he came to the place and saw him, passed by on the other side. [33] But a Samaritan, as he traveled, came where the man was; and when he saw him, he took pity on him. [34] He went to him and bandaged his wounds, pouring on oil and wine. Then he put the man on his own donkey, brought him to an inn and took care of him. [35] The next day he took out two denarii and gave them to the innkeeper. 'Look after him,' he said, 'and when I return, I will reimburse you for any extra expense you may have.' New Testament: Luke10:30-35. Read and meditate on this passage. Discuss it with the rest of the family.

Now share your day with the rest of the family. This is the individual disclosure session. What happened to you, your friends and teachers during the day? What special role did you play in school? What contribution did you make in school? Did you get hurt at work or in school? If you did how did it happen and who was responsible? What have you done to address the issue? What did others do to address the issue? How do you feel?

Next take inventory of your activities today. Where did you go? What did you do? Who did you meet? What did you contribute? How did you affect your environment? How did the environment affect you? Is there any thing you did that you could have done differently? How could you have done it next time?

Next visualize the next day of your life in the family, at work or in school. What do you want to see happen? For the family you might want harmony, understanding and unity. For work you might want to accomplish your work goals and get along with your boss and co-workers. For school you might see that you are getting along with your teachers and fellow students. You are doing your schoolwork and getting good grades as well as participating in school activities and doing well.

**Month 6, Week 3, Day 5**

Assume the state of meditation by first practicing a relaxation exercise. Inhale for four seconds. Hold the breath for four seconds. Exhale for four seconds. Hold the exhalation for four seconds. Repeat the process for as many times as possible.

Count from 100 backwards that is 100, 99, 88, etc, until you reach 1. Now count the normal way from 1 to 100. Concentrate on your counting and see the figures in your mind's eye as you count.

Now reflect on Leadership by Martin Luther King:

May I stress the need for courageous, intelligent, and dedicated leadership... Leaders of sound integrity. Leaders not in love with publicity, but in love with justice. Leaders not in love with money, but in love with humanity. Leaders who can subject their particular egos to the greatness of the cause.

Now share your day with the rest of the family. This is the individual disclosure session. What happened to you, your friends and teachers during the day? What special role did you play in school? What contribution did you make in school? Did you get hurt at work or in school? If you did how did it happen and who was responsible? What have you done to address the issue? What did others do to address the issue? How do you feel?

Next take inventory of your activities today. Where did you go? What did you do? Who did you meet? What did you contribute? How did you affect your environment? How did the environment affect you? Is there any thing you did that you could have done differently? How could you have done it next time?

Next visualize the next day of your life in the family, at work or in school. What do you want to see happen? For the family you might want harmony, understanding and unity. For work you might want to accomplish your work goals and get along with your boss and co-workers. For school you might see that you are getting along with your teachers and fellow students. You are doing your schoolwork and getting good grades as well as participating in school activities and doing well.

**Month 6, Week 3, Day 6**

Retire to your sacred place and practice a relaxation exercise. Inhale for four seconds. Hold the breath for four seconds. Exhale for four seconds. Hold the exhalation for four seconds. Repeat the process for as many times as possible.

Count from 100 backwards that is 100, 99, 88, etc, until you reach 1. Now count the normal way from 1 to 100. Concentrate on your counting and see the figures in your mind's eye as you count.

Now reflect on the following: Holding onto anger is like grasping a hot coal with the intent of throwing it at someone else; you are the one who gets burned. **Buddha**

Next take inventory of your activities today. Where did you go? What did you do? Who did you meet? What did you contribute? How did you affect your environment? How did the environment affect you? Is there any thing you did that you could have done differently? How could you have done it next time?

Lastly visualize the next day of your life in the family, at work or in school. What do you want to see happen? For the family you might want harmony, understanding and unity. For work you might want to accomplish your work goals and get along with your boss and co-workers. For school you might see that you are getting along with your teachers and fellow students. You are doing your schoolwork and getting good grades as well as participating in school activities and doing well.

**Month 6, Week 3, Day 7**

Attend a church, a temple, or any other meeting that brings you together with people for a common goal. If you do not have one you may begin today and find one that meets your interest and inclination. If you want you could also organize a group of your

own. For instance you could start an Awakened Living Study Program. You may contact UNISM for more information.

Retire to your sacred place and practice a relaxation exercise. Inhale for four seconds. Hold the breath for four seconds. Exhale for four seconds. Hold the exhalation for four seconds. Repeat the process for as many times as possible.

Count from 100 backwards that is 100, 99, 88, etc, until you reach 1. Now count the normal way from 1 to 100. Concentrate on your counting and see the figures in your mind's eye as you count.

Choose your favorite meditation posture and practice using the posture. For instance, if you use supports for your back during meditation start practicing your favorite posture without any support.

Next take inventory of your activities today. Where did you go? What did you do? Who did you meet? What did you contribute? How did you affect your environment? How did the environment affect you? Is there any thing you did that you could have done differently? How could you have done it next time?

Lastly visualize the next day of your life in the family, at work or in school. What do you want to see happen? For the family you might want harmony, understanding and unity. For work you might want to accomplish your work goals and get along with your boss and co-workers. For school you might see that you are getting along with your teachers and fellow students. You are doing your schoolwork and getting good grades as well as participating in school activities and doing well.

**Month 6, Week 4, Day 1**

Assume the state of meditation by first practicing a relaxation exercise. Inhale for four seconds. Hold the breath for four seconds. Exhale for four seconds. Hold the exhalation for four seconds. Repeat the process for as many times as possible.

Count from 100 backwards that is 100, 99, 88, etc, until you reach 1. Now count the normal way from 1 to 100. Concentrate on your counting and see the figures in your mind's eye as you count.

Now reflect on Faith by Martin Luther King:

Faith is taking the first step even when you don't see the whole staircase.

Now share your day with the rest of the family. This is the individual disclosure session. What happened to you, your friends and teachers during the day? What special role did you play in school? What contribution did you make in school? Did you get hurt at work or in school? If you did how did it happen and who was responsible? What have you done to address the issue? What did others do to address the issue? How do you feel?

Next take inventory of your activities today. Where did you go? What did you do? Who did you meet? What did you contribute? How did you affect your environment? How did the environment affect you? Is there any thing you did that you could have done differently? How could you have done it next time?

Next visualize the next day of your life in the family, at work or in school. What do you want to see happen? For the family you might want harmony, understanding and unity. For work you might want to accomplish your work goals and get along with your boss and co-workers. For school you might see that you are getting along with your teachers and fellow students. You are doing your schoolwork and getting good grades as well as participating in school activities and doing well.

**Month 6, Week 4, Day 2**

Assume the state of meditation by first practicing a relaxation exercise. Inhale for four seconds. Hold the breath for four seconds. Exhale for four seconds. Hold the exhalation for four seconds. Repeat the process for as many times as possible.

Count from 100 backwards that is 100, 99, 88, etc, until you reach 1. Now count the normal way from 1 to 100. Concentrate on your counting and see the figures in your mind's eye as you count.

Next reflect on Service, Generosity and Compassion by **the Buddha**: Teach this triple truth to all: A generous heart, kind speech, and a life of service and compassion are the things that renew humanity.

Now share your day with the rest of the family. This is the individual disclosure session. What happened to you, your friends and teachers during the day? What special role did you play in school? What contribution did you make in school? Did you get hurt at work or in school? If you did how did it happen and who was responsible? What have you done to address the issue? What did others do to address the issue? How do you feel?

Next take inventory of your activities today. Where did you go? What did you do? Who did you meet? What did you contribute? How did you affect your environment? How did the environment affect you? Is there any thing you did that you could have done differently? How could you have done it next time?

Next visualize the next day of your life in the family, at work or in school. What do you want to see happen? For the family you might want harmony, understanding and unity. For work you might want to accomplish your work goals and get along with your boss and co-workers. For school you might see that you are getting along with your teachers and fellow students. You are doing your

schoolwork and getting good grades as well as participating in school activities and doing well.

### Month 6, Week 4, Day 3

Assume the state of meditation by first practicing a relaxation exercise. Inhale for four seconds. Hold the breath for four seconds. Exhale for four seconds. Hold the exhalation for four seconds. Repeat the process for as many times as possible.

Count from 100 backwards that is 100, 99, 88, etc, until you reach 1. Now count the normal way from 1 to 100. Concentrate on your counting and see the figures in your mind's eye as you count.

Meditate on the following passage: Thoughts alone cause the round of births (samsara); let a man strive to purify his thoughts. What a man thinks, that he is: this is an old secret. By the serenity of his thoughts a man blots out all actions, whether good or bad. Dwelling within his Self with serene thoughts, he obtains imperishable happiness. If the thoughts of a man were so fixed on Brahman as they are on the things of this world, who would not then be freed from bondage? The mind, it is said, is of two kinds, pure and impure: impure from the contact with lust, pure when free from lust. When a man, having freed his mind from sloth, distraction, and vacillation, becomes as it were delivered from his mind, that is the highest point. Maitri Upanishad 6.34.3-7. How does the passage relate to your life? Discuss with the rest of the family.

Now share your day with the rest of the family. This is the individual disclosure session. What happened to you, your friends and teachers during the day? What special role did you play in school? What contribution did you make in school? Did you get hurt at work or in school? If you did how did it happen and who

was responsible? What have you done to address the issue? What did others do to address the issue? How do you feel?

Next take inventory of your activities today. Where did you go? What did you do? Who did you meet? What did you contribute? How did you affect your environment? How did the environment affect you? Is there any thing you did that you could have done differently? How could you have done it next time?

Next visualize the next day of your life in the family, at work or in school. What do you want to see happen? For the family you might want harmony, understanding and unity. For work you might want to accomplish your work goals and get along with your boss and co-workers. For school you might see that you are getting along with your teachers and fellow students. You are doing your schoolwork and getting good grades as well as participating in school activities and doing well.

**Month 6, Week 4, Day 4**

Assume the state of meditation by first practicing a relaxation exercise. Inhale for four seconds. Hold the breath for four seconds. Exhale for four seconds. Hold the exhalation for four seconds. Repeat the process for as many times as possible.

Count from 100 backwards that is 100, 99, 88, etc, until you reach 1. Now count the normal way from 1 to 100. Concentrate on your counting and see the figures in your mind's eye as you count.

Meditate on the following passage: Be humble, be harmless,
Have no pretension,
Be upright, forbearing;
Serve your teacher in true obedience,
Keeping the mind and body in cleanness,
Tranquil, steadfast, master of ego,
Standing apart from the things of the senses,

# SOURCES

**Books**

Hitchcock, Mark: 2012 The Bible and the end of the world. Harvest House Publishers, Eugene, Oregon

Kyle, Richard. A History of the End Times. Baker Books, Grand Rapids, Michigan.

Lau, D.C. Tao Te Ching. Penguin Books Ltd. Harmondsworth, Middlesex, England.

Olivelle, Patrick. Upanishads. Oxford University Press.

Mascaro, Juan. The Upanishads. Penguin Books, London, England.

Mascaro, Juan. The Dhammapada, Penguin Books, London, England.

Mascaro, Juan. The Bhagavad Gita, Penguin Books, Victoria, Australia

Miller, Barbara Stoler. The Bhagavad-Gita. Bantam Books, New York, New York.

Peterson, Ronald. Everyone is right. DEVORSS Publications, California

Prabhavananda, Swami & Manchester, Frederick. The Upanishads, Vedanta Press Hollywood, California.

Thompson, Norma H. (editor). Religious Pluralism and Religious Education. Religious Education Press. Birmingham, Alabama.

Wilson, Andrew. World Scripture. Paragon House, New York, New York.

Universal Holy Book, Soteme, LLC. Portland, Oregon.

**Websites**

http://www.usda.gov
http://www.drweil.com/drw/ecs/pyramid/press-foodpyramid.html
http://www.wisdomcommons.org

www.ingramcontent.com/pod-product-compliance
Lightning Source LLC
LaVergne TN
LVHW051540070426
835507LV00021B/2345